How Did You Get Here?

How Did You Get Here?

Students with Disabilities and Their Journeys to Harvard

THOMAS HEHIR
LAURA A. SCHIFTER
Conclusion by Wendy S. Harbour

HARVARD EDUCATION PRESS
CAMBRIDGE, MASSACHUSETTS

Library of Congress Control Number 2014952434
Paperback ISBN 978-1-61250-781-1
Library Edition 978-1-61250-782-8

Published by Harvard Education Press,
an imprint of the Harvard Education Publishing Group

Harvard Education Press
8 Story Street
Cambridge, MA 02138

Cover Design: Ciano Design
Cover Photo: Michael Rodman/Harvard Graduate School of Education
The typefaces used in this book are Adobe Garamond, Texta, and Scala.

For the students
who were willing
to share their stories

Contents

Foreword

Howard Gardner, among many others, has noted the enormous power of stories as tools for social change. While data is often useful for justifying and informing social change, great leaders motivate and guide that change not by providing information, but by telling stories that resonate, inform, activate, and inspire.

This book has wonderful stories. But what makes this an important book is not that these stories are good, or even inspiring. What makes this an important book is that these stories are *powerful*—they have the power to change us, and our culture. To my mind, a story is powerful only when it provokes me to revisit the stories I tell about my past, and having revisited those stories, to revise the stories I tell about my future. This book does both. Let me revisit a story from my own past in light of the themes gathered here.

I can still remember the first time I saw Harold Krents. I was an awestruck freshman at Harvard College, walking anxiously across the Yard toward my very first class. I wasn't paying much attention to anyone along the way, but one student passed me who was too remarkable to escape my notice: he was blind. That student was Harold Krents (or just "Krents," as everyone would later call him).

I was dumbfounded.

Silhouetted behind Krents was Harvard's Widener Library, the largest university library in the world, the centerpiece of Harvard's power and prestige. Widener intimidated me, as it was meant to, with its huge marble pillars, long and wide steps, and 9 million books. I had never been inside. As I passed Krents, with Widener in the background, I imagined all those books and couldn't picture how Krents was going to read any of them. I was confused and perturbed: "How did *he* get here?"

Like many freshmen at Harvard, I was worried about how *I* got here. I had come from a farming community in Maine where my rural high school offered no preparation for college-level work. Few students from my class went on to college, and only a handful in the entire history of my high school had gone out of state. No one had ever even applied to an Ivy League school. Many students with my background, the dean later told us, felt that we were imposters, glitches in the cumbersome admissions process, and that we had gotten to Harvard only by mistake.

But Krents seemed like a bigger mistake. He couldn't even walk to class unaided (he tightly clasped the arm of one of his roommates), and of those 9 million books, not one of them could he read independently. I still cringe as I remember my reaction on that first day: here, finally, was one student who was less likely to succeed at Harvard than I was. I was relieved, even jubilant.

But I was wrong. Our paths diverged at Harvard. I flunked my first exam outright, and my first three papers were "ungraded" because they were "not up to the level" of earning a grade at all, even a low one. I improved slowly over the four years but was never a distinguished student and graduated without much notice (except my parents', of course). Krents, on the other hand, was a star. He graduated with honors and went on immediately to Harvard Law School, and then to Oxford University. Soon he was a White House Fellow, among many, many other honors. I was jealous, of course, and still perplexed.

After reading this book, I found myself compelled to look back at my years with Krents (I never actually knew him, by the way, but everyone knew who he was), enlightened by the themes and vivid stories that are now rewiring my memory. In fact, I felt so much need to revisit the story of Krents that I found myself reading parts of his autobiography (more on that in a moment) and his obituary. There is too much to revisit here, but let me highlight several themes.

1. Krents was *extraordinary*. His path was extraordinary even to the outside, "real" world. Within two years of his graduation there was a Broadway play based on his early life called *Butterflies Are Free*, followed by a Hollywood film starring Goldie Hawn as his love interest, no less. An autobiography (still in print) came soon after. But

one of the powerful themes of this book is that our culture advances when what was once extraordinary becomes ordinary. All of the students in this book are impressive, to be sure, but what is also extraordinary is how much more ordinary their journeys are. That is the surest sign that our culture, and the environment in which these students are educated, is growing up.

2. Krents was *unique.* Another important theme in this book is that everyone's journey is unique. Individuals with disabilities, even individuals with the same disabilities, are strikingly differentiated. No two of these individuals got to Harvard in exactly the same way. Krents's autobiography reaffirms this point; his journey shared some elements with each of the students in this book, but had many differences as well. By bringing many stories together, however, this book is able to highlight some common patterns that are well worth noting. In that light, consider Krents's obituary in the *New York Times.* It summarized how he got to Harvard thusly: "his understanding parents, their encouragement of his fierce independence and the number of activities in which he was able to take part." That will sound familiar to any reader of this book.

3. Krents was the *problem.* The stories in this book are very hopeful in their revisionist view of disability. During Krents's undergraduate years, he was clearly *the problem.* Widener and its books were imposing, unbroken, and unchanging. Krents was disabled, broken, and forced to adapt. There was no concept of universal design and, as a result, only a very few of the students in this book could have used its resources (the library was not even remotely accessible). Knowing that, most of the students profiled here would not have applied to Harvard. In this contemporary collection, however, the stories reveal a changing landscape of expectations and abilities. Almost all of Harvard's books are available electronically, and everyone reads its journals online. Because of these changes, its resources are more democratic, more universal—available to any one, any time of the day. Widener itself now seems hopelessly disabled, a relic; it is the problem. All of the students in this collection have better access to knowledge than they would have had in its heyday. And Harvard is a better university for it. Students with disabilities, as usual, have led the way.

There is much that still needs to change, both at Harvard and in our culture. The stories gathered here, and the commentaries provided, will be important to guide those changes. But I wanted to tell Krents's story to open this book because I wanted to emphasize that the stories that we need now, and that are provided here in this book, are *different* stories. The future must be one in which there are fewer extraordinary stories about the heroism of individual students who overcame huge obstacles to do ordinary things. What we need now are stories about "ordinary" students who do extraordinary things. But there must be a greatly more inclusive vision of who is ordinary, and who can do extraordinary things. We will need fewer unique stories like *Butterflies Are Free*, and many, many more "ordinary" stories about butterflies that are free. This book is the right start.

—David H. Rose
Cofounder and Chief Education Officer, CAST, and
Lecturer at the Harvard Graduate School of Education

Introduction

Thomas Hehir

Professor Hehir, I would like a meeting with you to discuss my dyslexia and the accommodations I will need to take your class.

I HAD JUST TAKEN a teaching position at Harvard after years of working in the field of special education, most recently as the Director of the Office for Special Education Programs for the U.S. Department of Education. I was looking forward to preparing future teachers and school leaders to welcome students with disabilities into their classes and schools and giving them the foundation that they would need to implement good inclusive practice. After thirty years as a teacher, administrator, and policy maker, I found the prospect of sharing what I had learned during my career with the next generation of educators particularly appealing. I was, as Sara Lawrence-Lightfoot describes, entering into my "third chapter," a generative phase in which many feel compelled to share their experiences.[1]

Inspired by the exposés of institutions in the late sixties and early seventies by Robert F. Kennedy and Burton Blatt, I decided to pursue a career expanding educational opportunities for children with disabilities. I have never regretted that decision, as I have had a rewarding career and have been part of a larger movement that has changed the world for the better for children with disabilities. Although there is much that still needs to be done to ensure full, equal educational opportunity for all children with disabilities, progress is undeniable.[2]

1

A universal experience for teachers and school administrators is the joy that we feel when we know we have been successful. The student who finally understands quadratic equations, the school's reduction in dropout rates, the student who goes on to a successful career, the letter from a student crediting you with teaching her to write, and the parent who tearfully thanks you for creating an accepting environment for her child—these are all experiences that make school careers so rewarding.

The converse is also true. The sleepless nights over a class that has not gelled, the conflict between students that you handled poorly, the promising student who drops out, or the program you have implemented that is not working are also part and parcel of a long career in education.

Like most long-term educators, I have experienced both the highs and the lows. As a teacher, I helped high school students crack the phonemic code and I saw students transition successfully from an institution to a high school. As an administrator, I helped develop programs to get kids off the street and supported the development of inclusive schools. As a policy maker, I promoted the concepts of access to the curriculum and nonexclusion policies for students involved in disciplinary action. I am proud of these accomplishments.

On the other hand, I question past efforts I have been involved in to expand special education that may have overplaced students, particularly African American students, in separate classes. Further, there are times when I question whether my actions as a teacher or administrator may have reinforced ableism inadvertently.[3] Thus I embarked on my university teaching career hoping to impart to my students the wisdom I gleaned from my career and with the benefit of hindsight.

As is so often the case with teaching, it is the unanticipated that creates both challenges and opportunities. When I came to Harvard, I did not anticipate that so many students would have disabilities. Of course I expected an occasional student with a disability. I knew, for instance, that Harvard had enrolled a few blind students for decades, and I expected that I would have students with the inevitable age-related disabilities. What I did not anticipate was that I would have significant numbers of students who had disabilities when they were in elementary and secondary schools, including disabilities like dyslexia or deafness that had a direct impact on their ability to learn in typical schools. I had attended Harvard Graduate

School of Education in the late eighties as a doctoral student and do not recall anyone with an obvious disability from childhood in my classes or program. Thinking back, I should have anticipated this change.

Observational research studies have been documenting a steady increase in the numbers of young people with disabilities enrolled in post-secondary education.[4] As a policy maker, I had used this data to infer that the Individuals with Disabilities Education Act of 1990 (IDEA) and the Americans with Disabilities Act of 1990 (ADA) were having an impact. I had just not anticipated that teaching students with disabilities in large classes at Harvard would be a major part of my job. I thought my classes would be *about* students with disabilities, not classes in which students with disabilities would have a major presence, with some classes exceeding 20 percent.

Why were there so many students with disabilities in my classes? First, Harvard has consciously attempted to include disability as part of its efforts to diversify its classes. Many admissions officers view applicants favorably who have disclosed disabilities and have done very well in school and on admissions tests. I've had admissions officers take one of my classes for the express purpose of improving their ability to identify talented diverse applicants. Yet many of the students I have had in class continued to feel uncomfortable about disclosing their disabilities and did not do so in their admissions applications.

Another factor that may have been driving up my enrollment was an emerging phenomenon among some disabled students of viewing disability as part of their identity.[5] I have been impressed with so many of my students for whom disability is an integrated part of their identity, a community they are connected to, a source of strength in their lives. They regard their disability in much the same way students from other diverse background do. Some even eschew "person first" language. One student proclaimed in class, "I am a deaf woman, not a person who is deaf. I am proud of my deafness, thank you!" Many of these students may have enrolled in my classes because they were the only courses with *disability* in the title.

Finally, though it is not the subject of this book, parents and siblings of individuals with disabilities whom I've taught have significantly enriched my classes. Given that I teach graduate courses, I have students of all ages. Many of my students have the personal experience of disability through family members. Students who have had the roles of both teachers and parents have added invaluable insights to discussions about individualized education program (IEP) meetings. Those who have grown up with disabled siblings understand the concept of natural supports at a deep level. I recall one student in my class who has a deaf sister. He freely communicated in American Sign Language (ASL) to another student in my class who was deaf. His ASL was so good that the deaf student had assumed for most of the semester that he was deaf as well. In short, sometimes my class feels like a disability klatch.

The challenges I faced teaching a class about disability to so many students who had personal experience with it—either through their own disability or that of a family member—were significant. First and foremost, I had to create an environment where students felt comfortable being "out" about their disability and willing to share their experiences. Also, I had to, as one of my students with cerebral palsy said, "walk my roll." I not only had to emphasize the importance of students getting appropriate accommodations, I also had to demonstrate their use in real time. In both these areas my response has been, I believe, sincere but imperfect. I have devoted a chapter in this book to how my teaching has been influenced—both the joys and the continuing struggles—by having students with diverse disabilities in my classroom.

The opportunity that teaching many students with diverse disabilities presented to me, as an educator working in the field of disability for my entire career, was also significant and thus is the subject of this book. As I began to get to know my students, I was intrigued by a simple question: how did they get here? How does a child who cannot learn to read in first grade get to Harvard? How does a child who cannot hear speech learn to write a top-quality essay in English, a language so different from her native ASL? How does a boy of five with significant and multiple disabilities, including an inability to speak, avoid being placed in a special class and thrive in a mainstream environment to achieve valedictory honors in high school? How does the boy who can't read in fifth grade and becomes a significant behavior problem in class turn his life around in high school and ultimately receive a doctorate from a Tier 1 university? How does a young girl endure chemotherapy and successive surgeries as her vision deteriorates and maintain high performance in school? How does the young woman who made a serious suicide attempt in early adolescence develop the strategies to deal with extreme anxiety, learning disabilities, and the pressures of a demanding doctoral program?

As I got to know my students I wanted to hear their stories. After all, I considered this my life's work—expanding educational opportunities to children with disabilities. And I had examples right before my eyes of students with different types of disabilities who had achieved obvious educational success. They had gotten into Harvard and most were thriving!

I began this inquiry in an informal manner, simply asking the question, "How did you get here?" I expected to hear triumphant stories of effective IEPs, heroic teachers, and strong parents advocating along the way. And these elements *were* in many of their stories. Indeed, when I asked the question initially the most frequent response was two words: "My mom!"

However, as I began to get to know these students at a deeper level—particularly my doctoral students, with whom I have a multi-year relationship that involves their assisting in teaching my courses and my supervising their research—I realized that each student had a rather complex story.

METHOD

I decided to conduct in-depth interviews with thirteen students I had in class who had a broad array of disabilities. I collaborated on this project with two of my doctoral students, Laura Schifter and Wendy Harbour. Laura conducted many of the interviews with me, we analyzed the data together, and she has authored several chapters in this book. Laura has dyslexia. Wendy helped conceive the initial idea for the book and has written a conclusion on the implications of this work for higher education. Wendy is Deaf.

Each of these thirteen students was chosen using the following criteria. First, the student had to have a disability that was evident by grade three. Second, I chose students with different disabilities. Third, though we granted them anonymity and are using pseudonyms, some may be identifiable through their stories. For instance, there are relatively few deaf students who have gone to Harvard. All actually wanted their real names used in the book, but some asked that aspects of their stories not be revealed out of sensitivity to the feelings of their parents or service providers. We have therefore allowed each interviewee to vet the quotes attributed to him or her. This process was particularly important for the deaf students, as interpreters voiced for them and made some errors. Also, this process yielded additional information from some of the participants. For instance, one checked with her parents about whether they had threatened a due process hearing. This additional information enriched several stories. In addition to these thirteen students, I have included one insert written by a more recent student, Nick, who wanted to contribute his voice to the book.

It is important to also mention that this book has been influenced by conversations I have had with many of these students' parents. Though we did not do formal interviews of parents, in the course of getting to know these students I met their parents and the subject of their children's schooling came up. In several cases I verified with parents information that students were unsure of, particularly for events that took place when the students were young. I should also disclose that I have a continuing relationship with a number of these students since they have left Harvard. I've attended weddings and christenings, and am "friends" with many of the students and some of the parents on Facebook. Finally, though this book focuses on the experiences of sixteen students, I have incorporated my experiences with scores of other students, particularly in chapter 8 where I reflect on teaching.

The sixteen students (including Nick, Laura, and Wendy) comprise three who are deaf, one who is deaf and blind, three who are blind, one who has significant physical and communication disabilities due to cerebral palsy, another with milder physical disabilities due to cerebral palsy, one with physical disabilities due to a form of muscular dystrophy, one with significant anxiety and learning disabilities, and five with dyslexia.

As you read this book you will see that the path to Harvard was not a simple or predictable one for these students. I was struck by how tenuous their experiences had been in the K–12 sector and how easily things could have gone wrong had a particular person not intervened or a certain program or technology not been available. I was also impressed and saddened by the extraordinary lengths many of the parents had to go through to access quality education for their children. Many students also spoke about the positive influence of certain teachers and service providers without whom they doubted they would have been successful. Some also told stories of educators with little competence and apparently little desire to meet their needs. These stories were thus not, as I had hoped, a simple confirmation that IDEA and ADA are working. They are complex stories of individuals in the context of schools that appear to still need improvement in meeting the needs of all children.

Though each of these students is extraordinary in many ways, none conform to the stereotype of what Joseph Shapiro refers to as the "super crip," the disabled person who beats the odds through perseverance and superhuman abilities.[6] None made it on his or her own. All would say they needed others to provide the interventions, accommodations, encouragement, and advocacy that enabled them to ultimately be highly successful in school.

BOOK ORGANIZATION

Each of these stories is unique and stands alone. A couple of the students recall their experience in schools as relatively happy and uneventful. Others detail years of struggle in which they and their parents have had to take extraordinary steps to access high-quality, demanding education. For a few the struggle continued at Harvard, where accommodations may not have been as readily available as they would have liked. Others found it to be the first environment in which disability accommodations were easily accessed and where they felt "safe" to be "out" about their disability.

Though each story stands alone, Laura and I found recurrent themes that emerged from our interviews. Even though these stories are of students who attended Harvard, these themes relate more broadly to the experience of students with disabilities from birth through adulthood. We have organized the book around these themes:

- Chapter 1, which I have written, is titled "My Mother." By far the most prominent theme in these interviews involved the role the students' parents played in their success. From their early opposition to negative medical prognostications, to their advocacy with school personnel, to inculcating a sense of worth and empowerment among their children, parents are credited by most of our interviewees as the most influential factor in their success as students. Of particular focus here is the role parents played in countering the low expectations that many professionals had for their children.

- In chapter 2, "I Had Teachers Who Believed in Me," Laura describes the stories of educators and service providers who saw the potential these students possessed and provided opportunities for them to succeed. Most interviewees encountered individual teachers and service providers, such as speech therapists, who had a powerful influence on their development and education. Unfortunately, this is in contrast to many others who either underestimated the students' potential, or who sought to limit or even excluded them from educational opportunities. It is striking how strong the influence of a relatively few educators has been on the lives of these students.

- In chapter 3, "I Was Always Asking My Teachers for More," I focus on an unanticipated theme that emerged in our interviews: the intellectual drive of most of these students. We were impressed by how often students spoke about how they wanted more intellectually from schools, irrespective of their disabilities. One gets the impression that from an early age these students were intellectuals in the making and were driven by a deep desire to learn. Sometimes this intellectualism was nurtured by educators and other times not. But the intellectual drive of virtually every one of these students appears to be central to their success.

- With maybe one exception, school was very difficult for these students. In chapter 4, "I Found Things to Do Outside the Classroom," Laura explores the role of extracurricular activities in the development of these students. Most of our interviewees found an area, from sports to music, where they excelled and consider it to be central to their success.

- In chapter 5, "I Was Always Forced to Find a Way," Laura focuses on how these students developed strategies and an understanding of their disabilities to become successful. Even though this was a process for several students, all eventually did. This deep understanding of how their disability impacts their learning and the strategies they needed to be successful is impressive. From pain management to anxiety control to handling reading loads, these students know what they need and can easily articulate their strategies. And most have become impressive self-advocates.

- In chapter 6, "I Could Not Have Gotten Here Without Audio Text," I focus on the role that technology has played in most of these students' education and in life outside the classroom. Although it is closely related to the previous chapter on strategies, there were so many references to technology in the interviews that we felt the subject merited a separate chapter. Also, for several of these students newer technologies have enhanced their lives beyond the classroom, providing vehicles for communication and access that did not exist a decade ago. Further, technology is an evolving and dynamic aspect of their school, work, and social lives.

- In chapter 7, "My Disability Shapes Who I Am," Laura explores the theme of disability identity and the positive impact disability has had on the development of most of these students. She reflects on her own experience with disability and its influence on her as a student, teacher, researcher, and policy maker. Laura also describes how the themes identified in these interviews surface in her own educational history.

- I reflect on my experience of teaching and doing research for this book in chapter 8, "I Thought I Knew Something About Disability." The experience of teaching diverse students with disabilities in large university classes as well as conducting the research for this book has had a significant impact on both my teaching and my views of policy and practice, particularly as it relates to the K–12 system.

- In the book's conclusion, "How Can More of You Get Here," Wendy Harbour, who was involved in conceptualizing this book when she was a doctoral student and teaching fellow with Tom, reflects on the implications of this book for higher education.

MY COAUTHORS

Laura Schifter completed her doctorate in Education Policy, Leadership, and Instructional Practice from Harvard Graduate School of Education in 2014. She is an out dyslexic who taught elementary school in San Francisco after graduating from Amherst College. She received her master's in Mind, Brain, and Education from Harvard Graduate School of Education in 2007. She has worked in the House and Senate education committees as well as the Obama White House. She currently works as a research consultant and teaches a class on special education policy at Harvard.

Wendy Harbour received her doctorate from Harvard in 2009. She is currently the Lawrence B. Taishoff Professor for Inclusive Education at Syracuse University and heads the Taishoff Center for Inclusive Higher Education. She is also a visiting lecturer at Harvard Graduate School of Education. She first came to my attention as an incoming Deaf student when she came to my office in a panic over the failure of the school to provide her with interpreters because, "my speech is so good."

THE STUDENTS

To help protect the identity of individuals featured in this book, we have used pseudonyms for the students we interviewed.

Jennifer

Jennifer was diagnosed dyslexic in second grade after she failed to learn to read. Her parents disputed the school district's contention that she was "slow," and eventually she graduated from a public high school as valedictorian. Jennifer received her first master's in clinical social work. She decided to continue her education and enrolled in a master's program at Harvard Graduate School of Education in 2009 after having taught in Africa. She currently is working for a nonprofit focused on sustainable initiatives, education programs, and community development in Africa.

Justin

Justin received his master's at Harvard Graduate School of Education in 2006. He has dyslexia and attended independent schools prior to college. Unlike many in this book, Justin's school experience, after a rough start, was largely positive. He was an exceptionally diligent student, with great strategies around his dyslexia and an infectious, outgoing personality that students gravitated to. Currently a school principal, Justin credits his early academic struggles with making him a better principal and incorporates many of the strategies he learned into the design of his high performing school.

Lisa

Lisa is Deaf, having lost her hearing at age three due to interventions to treat Severe Combined Immunodeficiency (SCID), which also resulted in her being short in stature. She attended both mainstream schools and schools for the deaf. A native signer, Lisa does not voice. She was a frequent contributor to class discussions, and her impressive writing ability intrigued me given her deafness and the fact that English was her "second language." She came to Harvard in 2007 and now teaches at a school for the deaf.

R.J.

R.J. has a neuromuscular disorder that was diagnosed early in life; his mother has the same disorder. He attended both public and Catholic schools prior to going to college. He taught in an inner-city school before matriculating at Harvard Graduate School of Education for his master's degree in 2008. As with Justin and Daniel, R.J.'s positive, outgoing personality drew many to him. He is currently a doctoral student at the University of Pennsylvania. In his dissertation, he is researching how urban school principals take into consideration their students' physical and mental health in their practice as school leaders.

Eric

Eric has dyslexia and attended public schools. He has taught early childhood in a large inner-city school district and came to Harvard Graduate School of Education for his master's in 2005. He returned to Harvard for a doctorate and graduated in 2013. Eric's ability to "reframe" issues and get to the core of problems is exceptional, making him a sought-after research and teaching assistant at Harvard. He now works for a large research firm focusing on issues of early childhood education.

Nicole

Nicole attended Harvard Graduate School of Education for both a master's and doctorate; she received her doctorate in 2009. She works as an educational consultant. She was diagnosed with dyslexia after a suicide attempt in high school. She impressed me with her exceptional diligence and her desire to achieve.

Amy

Amy is blind, having lost most of her sight through unsuccessful cataract surgery when she was an infant. She comes from a mixed Polish-Colombian background, and she is proud of her ability to speak Celtic. A strong self-advocate, she added a great deal to my class on inclusive education. She graduated from Harvard College in 2011.

Erin

Erin was born deaf and has been losing her vision due to Usher syndrome. Growing up in a low-income household in the Deep South, Erin attended a pilot project for the deaf in a high school at age three, transitioned to a special education class, and then was fully mainstreamed into an all-hearing school for K–12. She also has a brother with Usher syndrome. When I first met her she described herself as *quadralingual*: "I speak English, ASL, French, and LSF." She received her master's from Harvard Graduate School of Education in 2008 and is now working as a human rights activist advancing international treaties for people with disabilities in the developing world. She was awarded a prestigious fellowship in 2014.

Daniel

Daniel enrolled as a freshman at Harvard College in 2008 after graduating valedictorian from a large, urban high school. He has had spastic cerebral palsy since birth that resulted in significant physical disabilities and speech issues. Daniel faced substantial challenges around personal care and accommodations at Harvard College and took numerous courses at the Graduate School of Education, where he felt more at home and received the accommodations he needed. He was such a "fixture" at the Education School that he received his undergraduate diploma during the graduate school ceremony. Gregarious and outgoing, Daniel became friends with many students, faculty, and staff during his four years at Harvard. An expert at relationships, he returned for a weeklong visit last summer to a full dance card of dinners and coffee dates from so many who miss him. He received his master's from the London School of Economics and is currently a doctoral candidate at Stanford.

Brian

Brian attended inner-city public schools and was diagnosed with a learning disability in reading comprehension in elementary school. Growing up in a low-income family, he credits influential teachers with his ultimate educational success: graduating from high school and then attending and graduating from a large state university. He received his master's from Harvard Graduate School of Education in 2012 and now works for a national youth development nonprofit helping low-income teens develop the cognitive and social skills to successfully matriculate into and graduate from college.

Monica

Monica has a significant vision impairment that is the result of childhood cancer. One of her eyes has been removed, while the other has very restricted vision. She received her master's in 2012 from Harvard Graduate School of Education, where she attended on a scholarship from the National Federation of the Blind. After receiving her degree, Monica worked as a policy fellow for a U.S. senator. She currently works as a policy advocate for an education-focused national service organization.

Alex

Alex is deaf and attended a state school for the deaf until fourth grade, when he got a cochlear implant. He then attended a mainstream, urban, independent middle school and eventually enrolled in a prestigious preparatory school with the help of financial aid. He graduated from Harvard College in 2008 and is preparing to apply to law school while working as a legal assistant. Alex has a deaf brother as well.

Michael

Michael has cerebral palsy that affects his mobility. He attended private schools and as a child was hospitalized numerous times, which interrupted his education. Active in student affairs, Michael helped cofound a student disability group. He received his master's from Harvard Graduate School of Education in 2010 and is currently a special educator seeking a career in the theatre.

Nick: In His Own Words

Nick lost his vision in the early grades due to the backup of cerebral fluid—a pseudotumor—that "crushed my optic nerve." Nick has taught in Japan and received his master's in 2014. He currently is working as a program associate with Creative Associates International in Washington, DC.

—■■■—

We have written this book primarily for students who have disabilities, their parents, and their teachers. We believe first and foremost that this book will help dispel the ableist myth that students with disabilities cannot achieve at the highest intellectual levels. From our perspective many students with disabilities have been harmed from pernicious low expectations. These stories attest to the importance of high expectations; the power of effective interventions, accommodations, and supports; and the need we all share to achieve and be accepted. However, this is not to say that the measure of success for students with disabilities is admission to an elite university. Wendy's conclusion includes her experience in higher education with students with intellectual disability, underscoring the importance of inclusion for all young adults. What we seek is a world in which children with disabilities are accepted for who they are; a world in which their gifts are nurtured; a world in which they can take their rightful place among their peers, whichever path they take.

CHAPTER ONE

"My Mother"

Thomas Hehir

JENNIFER CAME TO PURSUE her master's at Harvard Graduate School of Education in International Education. Having previously worked in Africa teaching students with disabilities and preparing teachers in special education, she had a deep desire to expand educational opportunities to students with disabilities in the developing world. Tall, cheerful, and optimistic, Jennifer struck me as a natural leader. She was "out" about her dyslexia and made great contributions in class. Like most of the successful dyslexics I have had in class, she was clear about the accommodations she would need to be successful in my class. She referred to them as "no big deal." She was also instrumental in starting a highly successful cross-university student group focusing on disability and international education. Now a graduate, she works for an educational nonprofit and continues to support the group she helped found.

Jennifer's story, like so many others, exemplifies the important role parents played in the success of their children. In Jennifer's case and in that of about two-thirds of the students profiled, parents effectively countervailed the low expectations schools had for their sons and daughters and successfully advocated for the interventions and accommodations their children would need to access challenging curricula.

Jennifer's mom was a Head Start director, and her dad a local minister; both parents had advanced degrees. Jennifer reported that her mom did not notice anything atypical in her development as a preschooler and actually commented favorably on her "executive functioning" skills.

It was not until Jennifer was learning to read that things started turning for her.

Authors: So, why don't you start with your earliest memories of education and when you were identified as having a disability?

Jennifer: It was about second grade when the reversal [happened]. I was
reading with my mouth. I would read [demonstrates with mouth]
and I remember my teacher not wanting me to do that. When it
was silent reading, I should have no mouth movement . . . When we
went to bed every night we would read stories with my mom. And
[one night] I was sitting in my mom's lap and said, "Wow! How do
you do that?" And she said, "Do what?" I said, "How do you keep
the words on the page? Mine just move around." And that's when
she was clued into this. So then she requested an evaluation and . . .

Authors: Now, do you remember this or does your mother tell you this?

Jennifer: I remember . . . I remember school being hard.

Authors: You remember school being hard?

Jennifer: I remember my teacher not wanting me to move my mouth. I
remember when I would write things, it would look different than
my classmates . . .

Authors: So this happened in second grade?

Jennifer: We were in a suburban community at the time. I don't know
the full details of that evaluation. I know that it didn't go well.

Authors: Was it a special ed evaluation?

Jennifer: It was a special ed evaluation. It didn't go well. After they sat
down with my parents and had a heart-to-heart and said, "She's not
going to amount to what you've amounted to. You just need to come
to terms with the fact that she is not like your other daughter. She's
slow. You just need to come to terms with it." My parents got pissed
and asked for a full evaluation at [major city] Children's Hospital,
which is when I went to . . . Children's Hospital for the first time.

Authors: So that was still in second grade?

Jennifer: Yup, all second grade.

The evaluation at Children's was done as an independent evaluation
paid for by the district in the context of a threatened due process hearing

on the part of Jennifer's parents. The evaluation confirmed that Jennifer had dyslexia and that she was not delayed cognitively, a very different result from the district's assessment. She recalled that the district did not object to the independent evaluation, acknowledging that her parents had to do "what they thought was right." A fundamental disagreement ensued over the nature of Jennifer's disability. Jennifer's parents had told her the district thought an ultimate goal for her would be to work in a convenience store.

Authors: So you had a dyslexia diagnosis in the second grade?

Jennifer: Yes.

Authors: And it came from Children's Hospital?

Jennifer: It came from Children's Hospital. Now, I don't know exactly what the full diagnosis was from [the school district], but it was much more severe than dyslexia. They were talking close to MR [mental retardation].

Authors: They were talking about a cognitive disability?

Jennifer: Cognitive disability. That I do remember.

Authors: And this is why your parents . . .

Jennifer: Right. They said, you're crazy.

Authors: And that's why their assumption that you would never . . .

Jennifer: Correct. This part's from my mom. I obviously wasn't in that meeting. They said you need to think about a convenience store career path. So, [the school was] pretty intentionally trying to lower their expectations.

Authors: So when your parents got the Children's Hospital evaluation, was there some sense of relief or was there a better approach to it? Do you know?

Jennifer: Yes. I think they realized that I was just going to need a lot more academic assistance than my sister did. I mean, from that moment on . . . Children's Hospital was active with getting me books on tape. So, from second grade on, I had the old-school books on tape from [Recording for the Blind and Dyslexic].

Jennifer was supported in a resource room program in elementary school. Though she felt she was not sufficiently challenged, she felt this placement protected her from a common practice in general education class-rooms of round-robin reading. "I'm paranoid of reading out loud. I grew up during the round-robin years. And so that would have just sent me over the edge." Her parents also provided her with a play therapist. Speaking of her parents' early role in her education, she said, "I think they were more 'here's what you can do' and then my parents were really proactive. They didn't want me to be defined by my disability. And actually, I saw a therapist for a couple years just to talk through it . . . it was a play therapist."

Her parents became involved in a very different way at another cru-cial point in Jennifer's education—the beginning of high school. Her dad had taken a higher position in his church; the family now lived in a rural area in a border state.

Authors: You went to an IB (International Baccalaureate program) school now?

Jennifer: My freshman year I asked my parents if I could be in charge of my IEP, and they said that was fine as long as they were still allowed to come. I said that was fine. I kind of took over and freshman year had all honors classes but wanted to take advantage of the advanced classes that the high school offered . . . but I didn't know how to do that. I felt like my friends were in all of the advanced classes and I wanted to be with them. Not that the honors classes were shabby by any means . . . At the end of my freshman year I said that I no lon-ger wanted to be in special ed. So, I called an IEP meeting, and I pulled myself out of special ed.

Authors: Now, in terms of your K–12 education, talk a little bit more about the role of your parents.

Jennifer: Oh, hands down, the biggest role was that they essentially gave me everything I have, in the sense that they gave me the oppor-tunity to advocate for myself, to learn about my disabilities, to be educated enough to read up on what it meant to have a disability, and then to understand the importance of audio books.

Authors: So, did they tell you right away after you were diagnosed? Did they talk to you about it?

Jennifer: Oh yeah, absolutely.

Authors: And what about their interactions with the schools?

Jennifer: Always positive. If there were any negatives, they kept that from me. They wanted me to have a good [experience] . . . they wanted me to think that school was a wonderful thing, to be accepted and flourish in it. And this is what defines who you are going to be when you grow up and you need to love school. If there were any negatives, they kept them from me.

Though she describes her parents' feelings about her dropping out of special education as "uncomfortable," they went along with Jennifer's wishes. Jennifer continued to receive accommodations in mainstream classes through a 504 plan and graduated at the top of her class as valedictorian.

Jennifer's parents became actively involved in her college decision process. Aware that her success in high school was due to the accommodations she received in the K–12 system, her parents were concerned whether all colleges would be supportive of Jennifer's needs. Jennifer researched schools with an eye for disability services. She became interested in a school a long distance from home.

Jennifer: So my dad and I went out to visit the college and met with the disability support program at the [university] . . . Amazing support. I mean, the program was just dynamic. If you were accepted to the University of [school name], then you had to be accepted to the disability support program. If I was to go, I would have a tutor, twenty-four-hour writing support, and technology rooms out the wazoo . . .

Authors: Did you have to pay extra for that college support program?

Jennifer: You had to pay extra. Absolutely. Which now I feel like anybody with a disability should have access to equally. But I didn't know that then. I didn't get that. I knew I needed the support and my parents could afford it. And I qualified for scholarships, merit-based scholarships. Mom and Dad didn't know what to do because by car it was so far away. And we finally got Mom out there. We took a family trip and they just loved it, just loved it. Supports you wouldn't believe. Starting my freshman year with every support you could imagine and by my senior year I'd weaned myself off and just had writing editors. Editors meaning line editing.

Authors: So you did well in college?
Jennifer: Yes, I graduated with honors—3.5 and above. I think the final
   grade point was 3.89.

The support Jennifer received from her parents was obviously crucial to her success. Had her parents accepted the district's initial diagnosis of cognitive disability, it is highly doubtful that Jennifer would have
been awarded advanced degrees. Her parents' decision to give her therapy so she would not feel bad about her disability may have helped form
the confident, optimistic, competent woman Jennifer is today. Her parents' reluctant agreement to let Jennifer drop special education services
in high school shows an admirable level of trust in their daughter's judgment and solidified her role as a self-advocate. Jennifer's parents fought
for her when she needed it and gave her the skills to fight for herself.

■ ■ ■

As one might expect, the role of parents is central in these interviews as
these students consider their academic achievements. All but one interviewee gave examples of how their parents intervened positively in their
education or provided them with opportunities that helped maximize
their development.

My first impression of Justin was how "matter of factly" he handled
his disability, focusing the discussion on my expectations and the strategies he had developed to be successful. He clearly wanted to do well in
my class and wanted to make sure that he could construct a road map
to success. Unlike some students who constantly ask for extra time for
assignments, Justin was more concerned with organizing his own time
up front to be successful. Justin's experience with his parents held some
similarities to Jennifer's. His mother also had a professional background
in early childhood. As Justin explained, she recognized both his intellectual ability as well as his dyslexia early on:

> I am pretty fortunate that I was diagnosed with dyslexia at a very
> young age. My mother was one of the founding parents of the [col-
> lege name] Infant Center in New York City where she was working
> at the time. I was enrolled in the first cohort, so to speak, of babies

(children six months to three years) at the center, where it became increasingly clear that I was different in certain ways from the other kids. I was a bit more aggressive and had no interest in learning numbers, letters, recognizing names that other kids my age seemed fascinated with. When I started formal nursery school my problems accelerated. I refused to do any pencil-and-paper tasks and was always getting into trouble with other kids. It was at that point—I was about four or five—that a decision was made to have me tested. That's how my learning disability was first identified. It was the late 70s, and . . . very little was known about what to do with a kid with learning disabilities that were not disfiguring or overt. The testing showed that I was bright but had a very uneven learning profile. Though the public schools in my neighborhood were good, my mom was fearful that because I was struggling to read and write, I would be ostracized and put with lower-functioning kids. She was a strong believer that content and information were just as important as learning how to read. Because of that, I was lucky to find a private elementary school in my neighborhood that specialized in gifted children. They were accustomed to kids with uneven skills—the music prodigy that couldn't read or the kid who read everything but couldn't do math. Having that testing information really helped because all my teachers were aware of my strengths and weaknesses. I was given the support I needed and never felt that I was dumb or anything like that.

Justin's story overall is a happy one. He spoke freely about his dyslexia in a matter-of-fact way and generally related very positive feelings about his education, one largely paid for by his parents. Growing up in a large city, Justin attended private schools. His parents paid for tutoring, and he started school with a positive attitude and a diagnosis that should have provided the help and supports he would need. Unlike the cases of the other dyslexics in this group, Justin's initial reading difficulties were expected.

Justin was held back in second grade with the hope that he would catch up. However, in third grade it became clear that he would have to find another academic placement.

By third grade, I was still very much behind in reading, and while the school was able to give me a great deal of support in the primary grades, the climate and expectations were radically different starting in fourth grade. It was at that point that my parents thought it best to seek out a school that specialized in kids with learning disabilities. That's how we found [school name], which basically was a school for kids like me. Classes were small and the curriculum was similar to that of any typical school but adapted for students with learning challenges. Right from the start, things started to click for me. I became a fluent reader and began to understand more about my unique learning style and how to advocate for myself. After graduation—the school ended at sixth grade—I actually ended up skipping a year when I transitioned back to a regular school. While at [school name], I attended various summer camps, in particular one at the [school name], a boarding school for kids with dyslexia. All the counselors were dyslexics, and the camp buildings were named after famous people who had dyslexia. It was really cool to see that you could be dyslexic and still function at a high level. One of the real strides I made at [camp name] was a major improvement in my handwriting. The skills that I gained at [school name] really stuck with me throughout my school career.

Justin went on to discuss the rest of his education as largely a positive experience.

As we discuss further in chapter 5, what is so impressive about Justin's interview is his understanding of the strategies he has used to be successful from middle school to Harvard and within his professional life as a school administrator. What is also clear in his interview is the role his parents played in ensuring that result. Justin acknowledged this: "My parents were actively involved with my education. They always made sure I was in a situation where people appreciated both my strengths and weaknesses and where I was never made to feel stupid. Once I mastered reading, things got a lot easier although I still had to work very hard. Even though I was able to achieve a certain level of competency, I still have learning issues that I have learned to compensate for. It's been tremendously helpful to have so many people in my life who believe in me."

Further on in the interview, Justin reflected on what is largely a happy story of educational success. When asked if anything would have made his experience easier or better, Justin responded, "I think in some ways I had probably the perfect combination of parents that cared and parents who fortunately had enough money to be able to get whatever kind of services I needed, which can be a problem for many kids in my situation. Particularly, when I was going to school, there were very few services in the public sector."

I had dinner with Justin's parents and asked them about their recollections. Clearly proud of her son's accomplishments, his mother related the sense of urgency she felt when Justin failed to learn to read in the early grades and her decision to send him to a special school. She said as a professional she knew that he was both a bright boy and a dyslexic boy, and that if something didn't change soon he would be in deep trouble. In talking to his parents I got the profound sense they knew exactly what their son needed and they, like Justin, felt fortunate to have the means to do what he needed.

Most of the interviewees recalled similar events when their parents aggressively intervened in their education to positive effect. Daniel, a student with significant physical disabilities, had parents who insisted on his inclusion from kindergarten on and protected him from a second-grade teacher who complained he "couldn't color in the lines" and therefore didn't "belong in her class." This is one of many such actions on their part. Monica's parents rejected a one-on-one aide the school district wanted to give Monica in first grade, as they thought that would promote dependency and isolate their daughter socially. Erin's mom refused to have her daughter sent to a residential school. These are but a few of the actions these parents took to advocate for their children, often in opposition to the service providers and school districts. And, in the eyes of their children, had their parents not assumed this role, they would not have been successful.

ACCEPTING MY DISABILITY

Justin's and Jennifer's parents not only advocated for their children and went to extraordinary lengths to make sure they were successful, as is evident from their children's stories, but also helped them develop a positive attitude toward their disability. Daniel's parents fostered a relationship with a professional woman with cerebral palsy.

Lisa, a Deaf student, was a top student in my class. Her contributions to class discussions were insightful and to the point. But what most impressed me about her was her writing ability. She lost her hearing at about age two, and had parents and grandparents who learned to sign and became part of the Deaf community. Her story is one of a family who clearly accepted her disability and recognized the importance of her growing up comfortably with her disability and becoming fully integrated into family life and within the deaf community.

Authors: Your parents are hearing?

Lisa: Yes.

Authors: And your parents learned to sign? When? Before you were born? After?

Lisa: No, well, actually I'll back up further. I was born hearing, and I became Deaf when I was about two or three because I was born without an immune system. So, I was very sick as a baby. And, of course, my parents were speaking to me when I was a baby, and I don't have any memory of that. I became Deaf because of the medication—the various medications. I had a bone marrow transplant. I became Deaf [pause] from the side effects from the medications. So, my parents were looking at what to do in that case, and they looked at the possibility of oral or, you know, spoken language as an option. They didn't think it made a lot of sense, so they decided to go the sign language route . . . And, in fact, my parents decided to learn sign language because of what they read in a book by Oliver Sachs. Sachs wrote about a family with a Deaf daughter . . . about how the family learned sign language. So my parents contacted that family. They took it from there, and they have become close family friends. I'm sure they would be very happy to pass that along.

Authors: Do you think that your parents learning to sign was crucial to your educational success?

Lisa: Yes.

Authors: How?

Lisa: Because I had direct communication with my parents. We could talk about anything, so it wasn't really about education per se but just the fact that we could communicate with each other. They saw what I was capable of and they were able to find the best educational places for me. And those educational settings all included sign language.

Authors: All of your educational settings included sign language? Through interpreters?

Lisa: You need to go through interpreters or, you know, residential schools for the Deaf. I hadn't gotten to that part yet. [pause with laughter] Always sign language in some respect. I never was in an oral school setting.

Authors: So, your parents took an active role in making decisions about you based on what they had read. Did they know Deaf people?

Lisa: Not right when I became Deaf. They had not met any Deaf people. Afterwards, they did meet Deaf people. They got involved in the Deaf community, and so if I tell my parents something about the Deaf community or about somebody, they often would know who I was talking about. They became involved on a cultural level, which was also nice. This was not just for the fact that they were able to communicate with me but also for the fact that they had an understanding of issues within the Deaf community, and so that is also very important. That was another piece of my education—a way in which they were also very supportive of me. Because I was a Deaf person and not just a person using sign language but a Deaf person. That was nice that they understood that.

Authors: How are your siblings? Do you have siblings?

Lisa: I do have two sisters. I'm the middle sister. My oldest sister was four when I was born, and she was the one who actually successfully gave me the bone marrow transplant. Originally we tried my dad two times, but my body rejected his. My sister was able to give me a transplant, and I have a younger sister who is three years younger than I am.

Authors: Do they sign?

Lisa: Yeah, the whole family signs.

It should be noted that both Erin's and Alex's parents also learned to sign, and both students have deaf siblings as well. All three deaf students reported close and sustaining relationships with the deaf community.

——— ■ ■ ■ ———

R.J. was born with a neuromuscular disorder. One thing that impressed me most about him as a student was the leadership role he assumed among the students. Popular, outgoing, and gregarious, R.J. was active in student government and always seemed to be surrounded by newly made friends as he pursued his one-year master's program at Harvard. He was also deeply intellectually curious, and organized lunches in the graduate dorm with classmates to which he invited me to discuss course readings. In short, R.J., like Jennifer, is a natural leader.

R.J. related what he had been told by his parents of early hospitalizations and surgeries. However, there was never a question in his parents' minds that he would be included.

> My parents had some choices obviously as I was growing up and going into school age. They put me into a Montessori school when I was young—first grade and kindergarten. I did really well there, and I thrived. I was very social and made friends very easily. So when we moved from [a large city] to [a suburban] County, they determined that I should be in the regular public school system. That was something that really became very important for me as I followed my own career in education and through my own career as a student that . . . you know . . . my parents recognized that my disability was not something—although it was very apparent that I had this disability—it wasn't something that was going to put me into a different school system. They thought that I should be able to do as well as everyone else. So I went through the public school system until eighth grade in [California] and did well. You know, I was probably an A or B student, but when I got into high school, I went to a private Catholic school. I think part of that was that [my parents] were a little concerned with the overcrowding at the high school level and the fact that with so many people and because my disability was a physical one, they wanted to give me a little extra

space. They also thought that this was a better academic opportunity for me. So, I went to a relatively new Catholic school at the time—and graduated from there with a lot of great references. I was involved in so many different things, and I still found a way to get involved with the football team and the basketball team doing different data analysis for them or doing film editing of the football games and stuff like that, which I really got involved with.

R.J. went on to relate how from an early age he needed to learn strategies to deal with his disability. Prominent among these is pain management and the more recent challenges of his dealing with Boston's ice and snow after having grown up in southern California. R.J., unlike most of the sample, benefited from having a parent with the same disability.

Authors: Did you get any help in figuring out strategies from anybody?
R.J.: My mom, definitely. I inherited this disease from her, and mine is definitely more severe than hers is.
Authors: Oh, so she has the same disease?
R.J.: Yeah, this is a genetic disease that was passed down to me. It is hereditary. When my mom was a kid, they had no name for it. They didn't know what it was. They didn't even think that she had a disease. It was just the fact that she couldn't run and things like that. Now that they have been tested in the past ten years and had muscle biopsies and things like that and gone back to figure it must have come from my grandmother all the way down to me . . . So, she's definitely been someone who has kind of given me options and suggestions on how to deal with certain things. Then also just the mother aspect of kind of being overly concerned, you know . . .
Authors: Do you remember when your parents first talked to you about your disability? When did you first become aware of it?
R.J.: Yes, I actually—one of the questions for the doctoral application for Harvard is an obstacle you've overcome—I wrote about that first conversation that I remember having with my dad, and my dad doesn't have any disability or anything like that. And I was probably in about sixth grade [and] I remember having this conversation when there was a school dance. I had Canadian crutches up until

I was about fourteen or fifteen, and then after that I just decided I didn't want to use them anymore. So, I'm used to getting around without them. In the sixth grade, we were all going to a sixth-grade dance, and it was the first time that I really remembered that it wasn't just an extension of myself anymore, it was something that very much made me different. Having that conversation with him about the fact that that's okay it's something that I'm going to have forever, and it's okay to be different. It doesn't mean that . . . different doesn't mean worse.

Most of the students are like R.J., Lisa, Erin, Justin, and Jennifer. They are comfortable talking about their disability, and have developed strategies that enabled them to be highly successful in schools. Disability is part of their identity, and they credit their parents with advocating for them and giving them a positive identity as a person with a disability.

DENIAL?

Eric has earned both a master's and doctorate from Harvard. As his former teacher, advisor, and research and teaching colleague, I would describe him as one of the most able students I have come to know. Outgoing and pleasant, Eric was popular among his peers and was sought after by faculty as both a teaching and research assistant. His skills are broad. He's a top-notch statistician, skilled teacher, and insightful writer. His early description of his education would hardly predict this. Growing up in the rural south, he struggled in elementary and middle school.

I think where I really had a tough time was in elementary and junior high school. I was retained in third grade. I had spent really from first grade up until high school as a major disappointment in school. So frequent fistfights, disorderly conduct in class . . . I had quite a mouth on me. Thinking back on it, I remember at the time just feeling like no matter what I did I was going to find my way into trouble. There was nothing conscious about it—like "Oh gosh, I'm really . . . I can't . . . if it comes my time to read, I'm just going to have to [act] up so I'm not going to have to read."

But looking back on it, I can see that that was a lot of what was happening. When I say that I was in trouble, it was every day . . . suspended from school. My mother tells these stories now of going home every day crying . . . In middle school, it was interesting. I went to a tracked public middle school (I had been in a private elementary school). I was retained in third grade because I couldn't read and particularly because I couldn't write in cursive. I still can't write in cursive, but that was important in third grade. In middle school, I left the private school and went to this tracked middle school and I had this experience every year where I would be bounced from class to class. In some years, I would start out in the advanced class. They even called them this at the time. They didn't even try to call it the "sparrows" and the "turtles." They would call it the "advanced class." Some years I would start out in the advanced class and then get put in the slower class. The other kids in the slow class were almost all boys . . . It was mostly behavior issues is how it was manifested. We were basically warehoused.

Eric went on to describe a more successful high school experience that will be discussed in chapter 4. However, Eric did not identify himself as a dyslexic until taking my course, in which we go into great detail about dyslexia. Eric recognized that not only could this realization explain his persistent difficulties in school but also that a disability diagnosis could help him get the accommodations he felt he needed in his reading-heavy courses at Harvard. He also thought accommodations would be useful to him in taking the GREs in preparation for his application to the doctoral program. He recalled discussing this with his mother, who shared with him the fact that he was diagnosed with dyslexia in third grade. Though his parents had a relatively definitive diagnosis and Eric was having great difficulty in school, they refused special education.

So, I was tested, and I still have actually the documents from, gosh, what would it have been, 1982–1983, in which I was tested and got the diagnosis of being dyslexic. Interestingly, after I got that diagnosis, they tested my brother, who is six years older, and found that my brother had largely the same profile . . . the difference being my brother is a pretty easygoing guy. He didn't really rock the boat and sort of cruised through school, whereas I was getting in fistfights all the time. So, I got the diagnosis but was never in special ed, and this was a concern of my parents—that I could not be in special ed. I could not be somebody with a disability. I think in part because they saw what that meant in our local public schools and in part there was a sort of stigma that was attached to that, that they couldn't accept. So they kept me in private school and then moved me to public school and went through the process every year of trying to yank me out of the slow class and find some better placement.

Looking back on his parents' decision not to place him in special education, Eric feels it was the right one. "Where I come from, special education is segregation and low expectations. It still is." He noted that his niece has dyslexia and attends a school in the same school district he attended. "It's just terrible. She is not getting what she needs."

■ ■ ■

The best words to describe Nicole are determined, diligent, and goal-driven. She has completed her doctorate against long odds. She is African American from a biracial family and describes her public school district as dysfunctional and low performing. Nicole has been treated for depression and anxiety disorders since she was a child. She also struggled mightily in school until high school, when after a suicide attempt she was placed in a school for students with similar issues. There she was also diagnosed with learning disabilities related to processing. Nicole recalls the impact of failing to address her learning issues early on:

Nicole: At K–8 I was in public elementary and struggling. I tried to get into a private school but didn't have the grades. At the Catholic school, it was the same thing. I was in over my head. It was a lot of reading. It was the math that was difficult.

Authors: Did you ever get help in reading when you were in primary grades or intermediate grades?

Nicole: No.

Authors: You never got help—you just went through the system?

Nicole: 'Cause I could always decode. My problem is the speed, and you'll see that in the Harvard report.

Authors: So it's fluency?

Nicole: Yes. My reading rate was at the 1 percentile.

Authors: Did you struggle with decoding when you were in, say, kindergarten, first grade, second grade?

Nicole: I don't remember having trouble decoding.

Nicole went on to describe how her father supported her and, like R.J.'s mom, had the same disability himself. She also related how her father's "determination" enabled him to have a successful career in the government though to her knowledge he never read a book for pleasure. In describing her dad, she seemed to be describing herself.

Authors: So you were not evaluated for disability until?

Nicole: Fifteen. And at that point, I had already told my mother that I had been contemplating suicide. So, that was another reason I think that my mother—basically, it had come to a head. Because what happened was my father had to go to Oklahoma for training with the government, 'cause he used to work for the government, and it was just my mother and I that were home alone, and were butting heads. My father wasn't there anymore to act as the cushion, and, and he understood learning disabilities because he used to run away from school, and he had lots of problems.

Authors: So your dad probably had learning disabilities?

Nicole: Yes, yes, yes.

Authors: So he understood them?

Nicole: Yes.

Nicole believed her mother's resistance to special education, like that of Eric's parents, may have been influenced by her perception of special education in her district: "Yes. And I went from home schooling straight to the most segregated environment (a residential school). But that was really the only choice I had left with them, 'cause I had just refused [to go to school]. And they had said, you know, you can be in our special ed department, and they showed me their special ed department and it was—special ed was just a catchall. It was for kids with mental retardation."

Nicole emphasized the importance that her therapist's diagnosis played in her life.

> She [her therapist] was able to diagnose that there was the depression. She was able to diagnose that there was the anxiety disorder. And she was able to diagnose that there was an obsessive-compulsive disorder. So all these things finally had names to them, and she was able to explain to my mother that I wasn't doing these things on purpose. And it kind of explained to my mother, you know, why I was doing the things I was doing. And she helped me to look at situations [as] more of, how do I get around it? And that was also from the school—the school was always, like, "there's more than one way to skin a cat." I remember them saying that. "There's more than one way to skin a cat."

Though Nicole wishes she had had a definitive diagnosis earlier and had not had to go through years of frustration and failure, she does credit her parents with doing the best they could. She emphasized the importance that diagnosis played in her relationship with her mother. Nicole said her mother took "a one eighty" and became her best advocate and supporter. She lovingly described the support her mother provided her through what was a challenging prospect to almost all students: writing a dissertation.

———■■■———

It is easy to render Eric's and Nicole's stories as ones of denial on the part of their parents. I do not. Looking closely at these interviews and having had the benefit of meeting both Eric's parents and Nicole's mom, it is clear to me that these people did the best they could within their contexts. More important, their children think they did. Disability diagnosis can be a double-edged sword in some school districts. On one hand, it carries with it the understanding of why children may be struggling in school and the promise of needed interventions, accommodations, and supports. On the other, the reaction of schools to disability labels may reflect pervasive ableism and stigma and result in children being placed in inappropriate programs with low expectations and diminished opportunities. Unfortunately, an earlier diagnosis for both Nicole and Eric would have probably meant placement in a segregated class and the low expectations often associated with these programs. Their parents understandably resisted. Though these decisions are Hobson-esque in nature, it is unlikely that these students would ever have made it to Harvard had their parents not resisted placement in segregated special education classes.

Jennifer and Justin lived in a different context, one in which early diagnosis was important and helped ensure they received the interventions and accommodations they needed to be successful. These stories together emphasize the importance of confronting ableism in education and resisting unnecessary segregation and low expectations. This book, by chronicling both good and bad educational experiences of highly successful students, hopefully contains lessons for educators and parents on the importance of making wise decisions about children and the imperative to make schools more accommodating for all of them.

PARENTS AS SERVICE PROVIDERS

Several of these students' parents went beyond the role of advocate, and actually became service providers for their children. Frustrated with the failure of schools to provide what their children needed, four of these students' parents took jobs in the schools their children attended.

After refusing to have Eric placed in special education, his mother took a job in his elementary school.

Eric: I think my mom got it . . . I think she saw it firsthand. She actually found ways to help. One of the things that she did when I was in third grade was she took a job at the school—a job as an assistant teacher at the school. She had professional preparation in other things, which she had left to raise the kids. I was the last of three. But she decided to go back to work, and go back to work in the school. Not in my classroom but in the school. I think it was to keep an eye on me. Not just keep an eye on me because I am going to get in trouble, but to be able to better inform the way she could help me. She is the first person who got me started using the computer. We had one of those Apple IIEs in our house, and she taught me how to type.

Authors: What school was it?

Eric: I had switched schools in third grade. She started in that school, and she stayed there until I went to middle school. So, she would do little things. She was the one who identified all these different . . . The music—she pushed the music. Plus, my father was kind of ready to let that go, so . . .

Authors: Do you think that your mother was critical to your success in school?

Eric: Absolutely.

Authors: As a dyslexic?

Eric: Absolutely. The learning how to type thing early on. I think she did a very good job of listening to me about why I was having trouble with things. And mothers tend to see the best in kids, and I think she was always looking for answers about, why does he behave like such a terror? What's the deal here?

Authors: Do you think she understood dyslexia?

Eric: No, I don't think so. And she's been interesting since I've come to graduate school. I sent her a lot of my books, so she read the Shapiro book and she'll talk to me about it. So I think to some degree, she does. But I think what she saw was that school was not working for me, and she really felt that it should.

■ ■ ■

Amy took my disability course as an undergraduate. I would describe her as a student with a pleasant edge. She has a well-honed sense of justice far beyond her years. She is a boundary crosser who eschews stereotypes and questions assumptions. She described herself as "the blind Latina girl who speaks Irish and Japanese." As with Lisa and Monica, Amy's disability became more significant due to childhood surgeries.

She said that in her Montessori preschool her low vision was not much of a problem. However, in elementary schools, as her vision deteriorated, she described a situation of great difficulty that became worse over time.

I think they tried briefly and in second grade, because I had transferred in, I was not in the same class as the other students. So I had my own little corner, but it was kind of, like, the machine was in the corner and my back was to the rest of the classroom, so there was no physical barrier between me and the class. This started out in third grade and, from what I recall, it eventually got to the point where only if we were doing reading and writing assignments would I move to that part of the room and work with the para [paraprofessional], who actually was a very lovely person. She became a personal friend—her daughter also rode dressage the same as I did—so it became more of a resource area for me. I think the other student spent a lot more time back there than I did, but I had a regular desk set with everybody, and just went there when I needed to. But it was a constant fistfight. The school constantly was trying to put me in the least demanding environment for them. The environment where they would have to do the least amount of work in order to, quote, pass me.

Amy's mom became so frustrated with how her daughter was being treated that she took a job in the school and eventually became a special education teacher for the visually impaired. She now has a faculty position in a university preparing teachers. Amy recalled:

Amy: After a while they stopped trying to put me in a separate classroom, but I remember as late as eighth grade . . . I remember [low expectations] very, very distinctly, and being absolutely disgusted. Once I got to high school, I mean, starting, I think, in sixth grade, my mother started working in the school to make materials accessible, 'cause people were just not doing it.

Authors: Specifically for you?

Amy: Specifically for me. They kept trying to lump more work on her but not give her more hours, and so she said, "You know, I'm sorry, but I'm here to do this. If you want me to do the other things I will, but you need to give me more time or I'm just going to do it in my spare time." Eventually, when the head of special education for our building—and I guess the only person with, with the license—left, retired, my mother decided to go to the [university name] and try and start working on her TVI [Teacher of Students with Visual Impairments] degree. She had a provisional license for a while, and so was the TVI in my high school for almost two years and was able to get a lot done to benefit all the students at that point.

Amy went on to say how her mother was such an influential teacher in her life.

And so she had worked with me a lot growing up—she was very, very involved—and subscribed a lot to the Montessori method. Doing, touching, motor skills—and had seen that I was very, very bright, and that I could handle all of this. And she knew that, that she was bright and that my father was bright, and there was no reason that there would be—I mean, yes, my eyes didn't work, but that was it. And so she couldn't conceive of how the school wanted to put me in intellectually easier courses. It just didn't make any sense to her. So she just didn't let them. Occasionally that meant bringing my dad in, because it being the midwest they were much more afraid of a 6'2" big guy than they were of a 5'3" Latin American woman . . . She would tell my dad when and where to show up, and he certainly had no difficulty getting angry . . . she fought against people, and eventually, once they left, she took their place and did their job better than they had—under the same circumstances, and sometimes worse circumstances. They had her as a half-time employee. Fourteen hours a week, I guess. No, $14,000. That's right, $14,000 . . . because she was half time. And she had almost thirty students who she was supposed to be handling.

Amy reflected positively on the role her mother has played in her education.

I guess the one thing that I would say, going back to my mother and how she's viewed things, is she really understood that in terms of blindness, learning by observation is just impossible. And so she went out of her way to make sure that I did many things. If I was interested in something, we didn't read about it, we didn't talk about it. We found a way for me to *do* it, or something as close to it as possible. So I did archery, I did marksmanship, I did sailing, I rode horses, I raised goats 'cause I wanted to be a veterinarian. I've hiked any number of terrains. When she knew I was going to be losing more of my sight, she said, "We need to see deserts." She hadn't seen deserts before. So we went there, we saw them, and we hiked them, and we interacted with them, and I touched everything . . . whereas in many instances, with a blind student the reflex is to have them sit things out. That's exactly what you shouldn't do. Learning by doing: they need to be in the middle of it, because that's the only way they're going to know what's going on. And she understood that, and I think that made a huge difference for me. I know many blind students are very well educated and very intellectual and don't have a clue what's going on in the world around them on the level that I do, because they've just never done it. They've never been allowed to do it, and they don't feel as secure in their world because it's always something that they've been taught to be afraid of. So for somebody who's dealing with a student or a child or whatever who's blind, I think that's something very important to keep in mind. Yes, make sure it's safe. Yes, make sure there are accommodations, but make sure they do it. And don't just go, you know, don't just walk through it. Don't just sit in a corner. Actually, hands-on, interact with it.

━ ■ ■ ■ ━

Erin was born deaf and eventually began losing her vision due to a progressive genetic disorder, Usher syndrome. Her brother has the same disability. Erin came to Harvard to get a master's degree and now works for a disability advocacy group and teaches salsa dancing to deaf adults on the side. She exudes southern charm and has a subtle, endearing sense of humor. Though she is losing her vision she still uses lip reading and ASL, and having studied abroad is *quadralingual*—English, French, ASL, and LSF (French Sign Language). Though her mother was advised to send Erin and her brother to a residential school for the deaf, she refused. Erin recounted:

I have a brother, and also at the time of my diagnosis, my brother was born and they found out that he was also deaf, and so they said to send my brother and me to the school for the deaf. But unfortunately that school was a hundred miles away. So my mother, being the wonderful woman that she is—a southern mama—declared that nobody was going to send her babies a hundred miles away from her. So she was looking into options for both of us in the local community and unfortunately there was nothing for the deaf at that time, but there was something that was about to be implemented. So she met up with a woman who was—I'm not sure what her title was, whether she was an audiologist or if she was a speech therapist or an educator—but she worked with me and a boy who was also deaf—suffered from meningitis when he was a child—and just, the two of us were supposed to start this brand-new hearing-impaired program that was going to be, at a high school, but obviously we weren't going to high school when we were two. It was the only place that they could find to do this. So that was basically starting the hearing-impaired program for the entire city, actually . . . [In kindergarten] we were kept isolated from the rest of the students. We were not allowed to have lunch together with the other students, or we had a different lunchtime. We had a different entrance to get into the building. Sometimes it might have been what they thought was for our own protection from the teasing and taunting of other children, but . . . So, all I remember from kindergarten was we didn't do much, we weren't part of much. It was just playtime and class. My mom also knew I was not happy at the school and wanted to go to the same school as my sister within our neighborhood. Often, the voice of the student is unheard in making academic decisions, yet I was lucky in this instance, that my mother heard me. My mom knew that I was not happy. She knew that I wanted to go to the same school as my sister, go to the same school as my friends that were in the neighborhood, and I think also, after the first half of kindergarten, she tried to get me enrolled in the same school as my sister . . . Mom pushed integration.

Erin went on to describe a relatively successful elementary school experience where she was supported primarily by a speech therapist, relied heavily on lip reading and her intellectual gifts, and was supported at home by her parents, who learned and used ASL to communicate with Erin.

Erin: Well, when I was diagnosed at two, we had two sides telling us different things. One side was telling us, refrain from using sign language with her because you will impede her language skills. She won't be able to communicate with her family. On the other side, they were saying, you can only use sign language. And my mom, once again, going back to common sense, thought, "Why can't she do both?" Because it seems that I needed a way to communicate with her. So she learned sign language. Our entire family learned sign language, and I learned sign language from school, and so that opportunity for us to learn sign language came. And I don't know, my mom took some sign language classes for adults. We all learned together. By the time of kindergarten, ASL was what I knew.

Authors: Now, did your dad learn sign language, too?

Erin: Yes. My dad, my mother, my brother, my sister, and my grandparents. My grandmother had the Sesame Street sign language book. So, they were involved in trying to communicate with me.

Erin related how her mother drilled her every night on vocabulary using lip reading and ASL, knowing there would be no interpreter in school, and how her family developed their own version of sign language: "We used sign language at home . . . We kind of had this joke that we used *TSL*, which is [family name] Sign Language. It was kind of a mixing of American Sign Language and signed English, and sometimes if we didn't know the sign we made up our own. So sometimes people outside of my family don't know what I'm signing. So I tell them I'm using TSL."

As Erin discussed both her brother's education and her own, it was clear that her mother, like Amy's mother, had become the expert in disability that their school district lacked.

And I think that is just a contribution to, well, how I got to Harvard. You know, having a family that believed in maybe different options and not necessarily agreeing to a "one size fits all" type of format. Because you might have thought that what works for me would work perfectly well for my brother, but my mom knew that he and I were different. She knew that we had different skills and we had different interests. She recognized us both as individuals, so that worked out very well for the both of us. So he didn't go to any of the same schools as I did.

Unlike Erin, her brother had significant problems in the specialized school due to bullying, and his vision had deteriorated at an earlier age. At first their mom became a substitute in the school so that she could also support him. Eventually she decided to place him in a private religious school where she became his interpreter. This ultimately proved successful for him.

———■■■———

I first met Daniel, who has significant physical and communication disabilities due to cerebral palsy, via email. He had been admitted to Harvard; had just read my book, *New Directions in Special Education: Eliminating Ableism in Policy and Practice*; and told me he was impressed with my take on disability issues.[1] His school district's superintendent had given him the book. Though he attended a large, urban school district he seemed to be on a first-name basis with all the higher-ups. He asked if we could meet when he came to Cambridge. That began a relationship, which continues today, that involved his taking two of my courses and also working for me as both a teaching and research assistant, a rare role for an undergraduate.

Daniel was supported by his dad in high school. As Daniel enrolled in more challenging academic programs, the paraprofessionals who had served him proved inadequate due to their lack of knowledge of the subject matter. Daniel needs scribes, as he is very slow at the keyboard and voice recognition software does not work for him due to the nature of his speech. In high school, he also needed readers at times due to eye fatigue and tracking difficulties. (At Harvard he was introduced to

voice-to-text technology that greatly enhanced his access to print material.) He recalled an incident in middle school when he had to explain
to his aide the concept of a negative number. "She was supposed to be
helping me by scribing. I didn't have the energy to teach her the math."

His dad, who has an engineering background, ultimately was hired
as Daniel's paraprofessional and eventually became a math teacher in
his high school. At the time, Daniel's mother was serving on a parent advisory panel to the district. When his parents sought approval
for his father to become his paraprofessional, they were successful only
because of an administrator who was sympathetic to Daniel's prior experiences. I discussed this over dinner one night with his dad, who said,
"Hey, it worked out. We got health insurance for the family [his wife
runs her own business] and I got a teaching job." Now retired from
teaching, Daniel's dad followed him to graduate school at a prestigious
European university to serve as his personal care assistant for a yearlong
master's program. Daniel could not qualify for this assistance under the
host country's health program, and his U.S. benefits did not transfer
overseas. Daniel and his dad made this decision in order to defray the
huge cost Daniel would otherwise have incurred. The university allowed
Daniel's dad to live with him in a disability accessible suite. I visited
them in Europe and had a great time touring around. His dad told me
what a great year Daniel had had. "How many people get to live in London? I've had a ball!"

■ ■ ■

Though I have not spoken to all the parents of the students profiled in
this book, I have spoken to most and have become friendly with a couple of them over the years. All of these parents see positive aspects of
their involvement in their children's education and are justifiably proud
of their children's accomplishments. However, all whom I have spoken
to wish they had not had to intervene so forcefully in their children's
education. They speak frequently about "broken systems" that do not
provide for the needs of children and youth with disabilities and the
prejudice their sons and daughters confronted, and in some cases continue to experience. They frequently talk about how they fear for other
children who "don't have the resources we did." Their wish is that others

would not have to endure what they have had to. One said to me, "I continue to do this work [advocacy] so other parents and kids won't have to go through what we did."

PARENTS HELPED MINIMIZE THE NEGATIVE IMPACT OF DISABILITY AND MAXIMIZE OPPORTUNITIES FOR STUDENTS TO PARTICIPATE

All the parents of the students profiled in this book faced difficult decisions about how best to address the needs of their children. Among these decisions were whether to have their child identified, the types of special services their child should receive, how much integration their child should experience, and how much input their child should have in making these very decisions. There are no simple answers to these questions, as each family and each child is different and the answers varied at different times in the children's lives. The school context also heavily influenced parental decisions.

For some of the parents early identification was critical to their child's success, but for others identification may have led to inferior educational opportunities and thus they resisted. Most of these students were educated in inclusive environments, and they credit inclusion as an important part of their success. Yet several of these students were educated in special education settings for part of their education and speak positively about that experience. Most of these students desired at some point in their schooling to have input into the educational decisions, and parents generally listened and acted on their concerns.

Generally speaking, the way that students described their parents' role in their education appears to conform to a framework I have written about that derives from the narratives of adults with disabilities about their upbringing and education.[2] These narratives are rich and varied and span several decades. Noteworthy among them is the work of the late Adrienne Asch, who was a university professor and was blind.[3]

Asch analyzed various narratives of adults with disabilities about their experience as children and identified themes that emerged concerning the way in which their parents and educators responded to their disability, some viewed as more positive than others.[4] One common response was to overreact to disability by showing excessive concern and sheltering. Asch theorized that this response is underrepresented in narratives because individuals who experience this type of upbringing do not have the sense of personal empowerment to write narratives. None of the parents here appear to have *oversheltered* their children, though there were times when some students reacted to being *overserved*. In both instances where this came up, parents listened to their children and acted on their concerns.

Another reaction discussed by Asch was denial of disability. This was communicated to these children through parental silence or denial. One narrative related how a young woman with significant vision loss was not given any alternative to the use of her vision even though she experienced significant academic problems. Though none of these students experienced outright denial of their disability by their parents, there are incidents related by students like Nicole and Eric where earlier identification and service might have helped them avoid school problems. However, it also appeared that in these cases parents might have been reacting to negative implications of disability diagnosis in the school context. Also, it was evident in these cases that parents buffered the negative impact of their children's disabilities.

A third major theme that emerges from Asch's synthesis of adult narratives is the desire among parents to "fix" their child's disability. She cited the writing of Harilyn Russo to make this point.[5] Russo has cerebral palsy and is now a psychologist. She writes: "My mother was quite concerned with the awkwardness of my walk. Not only did it periodically cause me to fall but it made me stand out, appear conspicuously different—which she feared would subject me to endless teasing and rejection. To some extent it did. She made numerous attempts over the years of my childhood to have me go to physical therapy and to practice walking 'normally' at home. I vehemently refused her efforts. She could not understand why I would not walk straight." Russo goes on to write how that interaction negatively affected how she viewed herself as a person with a disability.

It is interesting to note that Daniel had a similar reaction to physical therapy with a different result. He recalled an IEP meeting in the fourth grade that he attended. He stated, "Enough with the PT!" He remembered how shocked the group was, including his parents, that a boy with a significant physical disability would not want PT. He said, "I was tired of being pulled out and missing things in class. Further, by that point I knew I would never walk, so what was the point!" I brought up the incident with his parents and asked them if they remembered it all these years later. Laughing, they replied, "Do we!" They recalled how shocked they were at Daniel's request, but thinking about it afterward they realized it had merit because they said they knew that the most important thing for Daniel's future was education.

Asch, recalling her own upbringing and education, described a pattern of positive response to disability that appears to be a dominant way in which these parents approached their children's disabilities; that is, she credited her parents with minimizing the impact of disability while ensuring that she had a full life:

> In thinking about the writing of disabled adults and reflecting on my own life, I give my parents high marks. They did not deny that I was blind, and did not ask me to pretend that everything about my life was fine. They rarely sheltered. They worked to help me behave and look the way others did without giving me a sense that to be blind—"different"—was shameful. They fought for me, to ensure that I lived as full and rich a life as I could. For them, and consequently for me, my blindness was a fact, not a tragedy. It affected them but did not dominate their lives. Nor did it dominate mine.

We believe that Asch's narrative and those of parents described here by the students provide useful guidance for helping parents and students make the difficult but inevitable decisions they will have to make about their child's disability.

Minimizing the negative impact of disability and maximizing the opportunities for children with disabilities to participate in schooling and the community is a framework that parents can use when addressing the education of their children who have disabilities. It assumes that most children with disabilities will be integrated into general education and be educated within their natural communities, with special education serving as a vehicle for access and as a service that addresses the specific needs that arise out of their disabilities. This approach was largely followed by the parents of the students profiled here.

Minimizing the negative impact of disability does not involve attempts to cure disability, but rather involves giving the child the skills and opportunities needed to live as full a life as possible with his or her disability. For a blind child, this could mean learning braille, orientation, and mobility skills, and having appropriate accommodations available that would enable her to access education as was the case for Amy. Special education, once Amy's mom became involved, thus provided Amy with the necessary means of access that would minimize the impact of her disability. Erin's mom instinctively knew that sending Erin and her brother a hundred miles away to a residential school would disrupt their lives in ways that were clearly unacceptable to her. She fought for and ultimately provided the specialized services they needed so they could live at home and attend their local school.

Schools have long adopted roles that go beyond academic learning. Sports teams, choruses, clubs, and field trips are all fixtures of American education that provide significant benefit to children. Children who participate in these activities develop friendships, learn important skills, and cultivate leisure interests that enrich their lives. Laura writes in chapter 4 about how important these activities were to her and most of the students we profile. Again, Asch's narrative testifies to the importance of full participation to her childhood experience: "For me participating meant joining chorus, the drama club, writing and debating groups. It meant not being excluded from after-school activities and class trips by teachers, club leaders, or the transportation system."

These parents generally sought out schools in which children are welcomed and included in all aspects of school life. For Lisa's parents, at times that was a mainstream school and at times a school for the deaf. Erin's mom made different decisions for her two deaf children. Justin's mom knew that a radical change had to occur in his life after he failed grade three. Nicole's placement in a residential special school after years of failure and bullying was a "godsend" for her.

Another theme that emerged in many of these interviews was how these parents not only consciously tried to minimize the negative impact of these students' disabilities but also actively sought to have their children not internalize a negative view of their disabilities and instead identify the positive aspects of their disabilities. Bill Henderson emphasizes the importance of this in his book *The Blind Advantage: How Going Blind Made Me a Better School Principal*.[6]

Though by design this book focuses on highly successful students, Laura and I have been struck by how tenuous that success was for many of these students. Though all of these students have obvious intellectual gifts, many attended schools that either did not recognize these gifts or failed to accommodate their disabilities, and in a few cases were hostile and unwelcoming environments. This chapter is about parents, and clearly parents always play a critical role in their children's success. However, in too many of these cases these parents have had to take extraordinary action to ensure their child's success. Some of these actions, such as placement in a private school, required significant resources, resources most parents do not have. Expecting parents to become service providers and experts in disability is clearly not appropriate.

We are also dismayed that decades after the passage of Section 504, IDEA, and ADA, so many schools seem to fail these students.[7] Though we have made major improvements in serving students with disabilities in this country, what impresses us is how far we need to go if students who are this talented, and their parents, had such difficulty accessing quality education. It is simply inappropriate that so much of these students' success was dependent on exceptional parent advocacy and support. Schools need to do much better.

Finally, I was struck by how deep and sustaining the relationships between parents and their children appear to be among this group. Having met many of their parents and attended various family functions, from weddings to wakes, the relationships between these parents and their children appear unusually close. It is clear from these interviews how appreciative these students are of what their parents have done. This may reflect how deeply these students have thought about their own disabilities and the experiences they have had with others with disabilities. One deaf student commented to me once, "Do you know how many of my deaf friends can't even communicate with their own family members because they don't sign? That's never been an issue for me and

I appreciate that." Daniel, who worked with me as a research assistant, went with me to a separate school for students with similar disabilities to his. At the end of the day he tearfully called his mother and thanked her for not having sent him to a segregated school. "If I had gone here, I would have never gotten to Harvard." What parent would not want that relationship with their adult children?

The relationship between teachers, therapists, administrators, and parents of students with disabilities is a complex one. This relationship has presented both challenges and opportunities for me as a professional. Conducting these interviews and meeting many of these parents enhanced my appreciation for what Sara Lawrence-Lightfoot refers to as the "Essential Conversation."[8]

When I teach about the importance of this relationship and how important it is for parents and service providers to be "on the same page," I frequently get pushback about parents whose desires for their children do not conform to what educators feel is best for them. One special education director once stated that he simply did "what the parents want" as a means to avoid due process hearings. I think this is a mistake that potentially can hurt children and families.

Parents of students with disabilities confront the same ableist world that educators and people with disabilities do. Making the best decisions about education is complex and does not lend itself to simple or formulistic approaches. These narratives demonstrate that neither parents nor educators have always been correct in their decisions. Many considerations go into these decisions, including the age of the child, the nature of the child's disability, the context of the child's school, and family capacity. Educators need to engage parents at a deep level in conversations about their child, their aspirations, their experiences with service providers, and the challenges they face. Parents should also enter this discussion with an open mind, recognizing—as many of these students did—that competent, dedicated teachers and other service providers can make all the difference in their children's lives. Though there may not always be agreement, centering this conversation on what will minimize the negative impacts of disability and celebrate the positive ones, while providing the child with full participation in school and life, can go a long way.

INTERVENTIONS AND EXPECTATIONS

Brian can best be described as pensive and reserved. In class, Tom remembers him as quiet, rarely contributing to class discussions. However, his weekly posts to class Web sites were insightful and integrated the readings at a high level. He once apologized for his apparent lack of participation, saying he felt intimidated by all the "bright people here." Tom assured him that there were multiple ways to participate in class and that his posts were more than sufficient. He at times "warm-called" Brian based on his online posts to get him involved in the class discussion.

From Tom's perspective Brian was a refreshing example of a student who had not learned the "Harvard code," which is characterized by students who are verbose, self-confident, and self-promoting. Brian's background was quite different from that of most students who end up in the Ivy League and may explain his reticence. Brian's story is unique in this book in that his experience reflects the challenges he faced being from a low-income family and having a learning disability, as well as the interaction between class and disability. Where other families of students profiled in this book may have been able to afford different schooling options or additional supports, this was not the case for Brian.

Brian described his family as "dysfunctional" and is the only student who did not cite his parents as a major factor in his success.

> My family, you know, I grew up in an interesting household. Dysfunctional in a way. I have an older sister and two brothers. My mother, primarily, and my stepfather . . . that was the unit of my family. I get along with my family, especially my siblings. But growing up, there was a stronger bond with my siblings. They understood me, they were protective, and we had a shared identity by way of our experiences at home. My family—my mother and stepfather—they had a rocky marriage the whole time. And we understood what was going on, but we couldn't really do anything about it. What could we really do? [It was] rocky in the sense of extramarital affairs, money issues in the home, and abuse.

Brian recalled experiencing difficulty in school as early as preschool.

I noticed it was difficult in preschool. You know how you learn the letters . . . it was emotionally traumatic and embarrassing. Not being able to remember that *B* makes a "bb" sound . . . And everyone else can make it, except for me. And no matter how many times [teaching assistant name] . . . went over the alphabet sounds, I just couldn't do it. And it got even worse when we started learning about phonics—you know that . . . sound of words and letters. That was even harder. And remembering the numbers and the order. I remember going home and trying my hardest to remember it, all the way home. And just remember, this is a kid who is like four, or something. So it had a lasting impression. I still feel it, you know, how desperately I wanted to learn. But not being able to do it.

Early on in school, the teachers let it slide that Brian was not keeping up with his peers. He said, "I was always so polite. So I just passed by." In third grade, however, he was diagnosed with a learning disability. Brian recalled his diagnosis as being a learning disability related to reading comprehension. Interestingly, the symptoms he just described are similar to students with dyslexia, where the difficulty is in the process of reading. However, Brian was never diagnosed with dyslexia.

After receiving his learning disability diagnosis, Brian was forced to repeat third grade, and removed from the mainstream classroom. In his special education classroom, Brian recalled his special education teacher: "[Teacher's name], she's the one who taught me pretty much the basic things like phonics." He had this teacher for two years in a row, and he remembers "desperately wanting to please her."

In reflecting on his experience in the special class, Brian feels it was a positive one.

Brian: It was a place that allowed me to experience for once a basic mastery over something. Even though it was a basic level, that's where my confidence started to grow. I no longer sat in the back and held my head down. Especially when math came around or reading out loud [when] it was my turn and, well, there were other people like me—well, not really like me. Other people were labeled as LDs [learning disabilities], so I think the fear of messing up in front of them just went away . . . So, that's where my confidence began to grow. But it was only contained in that one class.

Authors: So when you said, "like you, [but] not like you"?

Brian: There were children there who were really smart, but they just had behavioral issues like ADHD [attention deficit hyperactivity disorder], conduct [disorder]. And then there were some who were significantly behind—not mental retardation or anything like that—it's just they were slower than me, a lot slower. And I was one of the top students in the class.

Although Brian taught himself to read, he credits his special education teacher as teaching him "the technique . . . how you break it down." When asked who taught him to read, he responded, "I actually taught myself how to read. She taught me [laughter], she just taught me to give a term to what I had kind of learned on my own . . . For example, the vowel-consonant-vowel . . . the magic *E* . . . but I learned it on my own and she just put a name to it. I used to watch a lot of TV and the words *blue, blow*; I just noticed the *b-l*, so I put those two sounds together. So, I just did that on my own, but she gave a name to it."

When Brian was eleven, he started going to counseling. "I've been in counseling since I was eleven years old. I think that's what saved me primarily, was the counseling; to have a person who really understood me and that validated my experiences and my fears and gave me some encouragement. Because I don't think I received much encouragement at home."

After several years in separate classrooms, Brian moved to a new part of the city, and for the first time had a teacher who challenged that placement.

I started a new school and the teacher . . . [teacher name] said to me, "I don't understand why you're placed [here]." She was a special ed teacher, full time. She told me that, yes, there are some subjects that I need extra help with, but there's no reason why I cannot be in the mainstream classes. She was the first person—now that

I look back on it—I think she was talking about inclusive educa-tion. I remember now that she was really into integrating the spe-cial ed students with the general ed students . . . when I graduated [middle school] she recommended full general education classes. *But*, I had to take one study hall class, which primarily was just a check-in to see how well I was doing.

Brian recalled going to a low performing high school:

It's funny 'cause my high school was probably the lowest perform-ing one. Like people consider that—whenever I walk in, I meet someone and they ask me which high school did I go to? And I say I went to [high school name]. And they're like [gasp], *"Really?! How is that possible?"* They're just baffled because the school is known to be low performing. It had a day care center. Teenage pregnancy was something that was really big there. We had metal detectors coming in. It was like a prison—that's what it felt like. We actually had a police station in our school.

Despite his attending a low performing school, high school is when things turned around academically for Brian.

Authors: So in high school did you do well?
Brian: Very well.
Authors: Why? What do you think changed?
Brian: I had teachers who believed in me. For example, to this day the three teachers who had the most profound effect are [teachers' names]. They were the best teachers I've ever had.

In reflecting on his high school, Brian noted: "I had a wonderful community of teachers, and if it wasn't for them I don't know where the hell I'd be right now. They really did save me."

■ ■ ■

As we noted in the previous chapter, in middle school Nicole began seeing a psychiatrist with whom she worked for fifteen years. It was beneficial working with this psychiatrist for several key reasons. In particular, Nicole described the impact her psychiatrist's diagnosis had in her relationship with her mother: "All these things finally had names to them, and she [the psychiatrist] was able to explain to my mother that I wasn't doing these things on purpose." When Nicole was having trouble in school, her psychiatrist also acted to help find a better option for her. "My psychiatrist said, 'You know, there's a school for kids who have a fear of schools, and I think it would be really good if you went there. I think you should be interviewed. Let's get the child study team involved.'"

Nicole ultimately applied and attended this special school. She described the teachers at her special school: "The teachers were just patient and understanding—I could make mistakes and I wasn't, you know, thought [of as], 'Well, she's just an inferior student.' It was more, the attitude was, 'Okay, how do we help her move up?' And they thought I was smart—boy, did they have high expectations of me, and they thought I was smart. And they kept saying that, and I started to believe it. And then I ended up with A's and B's. I had one B and then straight A's. I was salutatorian of the school, when I graduated. I had a graduating class of seventeen, but still, I got the award for most changed."

■ ■ ■

Monica experienced vision loss and recalled a teacher informing her parents that she may need accommodations. "I was in fourth grade when the process began. That year, for the first time, I was the last student in my class to finish a standardized test. I suspect I took a lot longer than all the other students, because my teacher really noticed the difference. That caused my teacher to go to my parents and say, 'Maybe you should think about a 504 plan for accommodations, because Monica's vision is beginning to become an issue.'"

■ ■ ■

As you may recall from chapter 1, Amy was sectioned off in her second-grade classroom with another blind student. Amy noted, "What was traumatic was the way I was treated, and the labeling, and the being put in a separate corner of the room with a para [paraprofessional], with the other blind student who, not his fault, but he had many, many,

many other disabilities aside from blindness." In third grade, the school wanted to keep Amy sectioned off. "They were still trying to cordon me off in a separate corner of the room in third grade. Thankfully, my teacher immediately called my mom and said, 'This is going on. I don't think this is what you want.'" After the call from the teacher, Amy's mother could act to get Amy removed from that placement.

■ ■ ■

Teachers and professionals serve important roles in that they can intervene on behalf of students when there are concerns. For both Monica and Nicole, professionals intervened at critical points to help them get additional support. For Monica, her teacher recognized that she needed accommodations. For Daniel, Brian, and Amy, teachers intervened to get them into the mainstream classroom.

For both Brian and Nicole, school was difficult, and they were struggling to succeed. They were lucky to have professionals intervene on their behalf. For Brian, a special education teacher recognized that he should be included in the general education classroom. For Nicole, her psychiatrist helped her name her disability, and intervened to get her into a school that was better equipped to support her. For both of them, after this intervention their academic trajectory shifted. They were able to find success in large part because they encountered teachers who held them to high standards, believed in them, and most importantly, let them know it. As we discussed in chapter 1, Jennifer moved out of special education. When she decided she no longer needed to be in special education, it was in fact her special education teacher who agreed. "I had a great special education teacher who said, 'Yeah, she doesn't need me.'"

Alex recalled that his preschool teacher supported him and his family. "I remember my teacher [teacher's name]; she was very close with my mother. She educated my mother about the benefits of sign language and how it would enable me to learn language as a deaf child. And she always supported my family and supported me . . . What I remember about her is she was a very cheery person, very eager to try to challenge me. And by giving me problems and things to do in the preschool . . . I recall that she played a role in pushing me ahead of other kids because I showed the motivation."

When he was six years old, Alex started speech therapy before getting his cochlear implant and met with his therapist once a week. He described his experience:

> I loved it. It was a great experience for me—unlike what some other deaf students would say about their experiences in speech therapy. My speech therapist is probably one of the reasons why I was intellectually motivated, and part of the reason for where I am today. The reason I say that is he made speech therapy, a typically scarring and painful experience for deaf schoolchildren, fun. He achieved this by making his lessons and exercises interesting. He's from Australia and he travels a lot for his work. He would incorporate his travels into our weekly sessions, and teach me about the countries he had traveled to. He intellectually challenged me and fueled my voracious reading appetite with his book recommendations. So my sessions were not just about speech therapy and learning the spoken English language, they were about general knowledge acquisition, as my therapist recognized my intellectual drive and nourished it. He went above and beyond the call of duty and provided me more than what was expected of him.

Many students had teachers or other professionals who, in addition to having high expectations, challenged them. Challenging the students helped to keep them engaged, and in Alex's words, "motivated," in school. Describing a teacher that helped her, Erin said, "She always tried to give me a little bit more than the other children, to challenge me, and that was helpful."

PROVIDING ACCESS

Erin's first speech therapist helped her learn how to lip-read in elementary school.

Erin recalled: "They had a speech therapist in that school and it turned out that she just happened to have some experience with hearing-impaired students. So this is another case of the timing was right—I just happened to be in the right place at the right time. I had a speech therapist who had an unusual background where she learned lip reading, so she taught me how to lip-read and she was so amazing and so wonderful that she agreed, on her lunch break, she'd meet with my brother on his lunch break."

To communicate, Erin relied heavily on lip reading, and she appreciated teachers who were willing to promote access. Erin recalled elementary school teachers who helped her:

> In kindergarten, I had a great teacher . . . the kindergarten teacher was very involved—was a very helpful, willing-to-learn teacher—and one thing [she did] had to do with [my] being put at the front of the class so I could see the teacher. Sometimes I had a buddy assigned to me, so if I didn't understand what the teacher was saying, I was given permission to talk in class to this particular buddy to catch up on what I didn't understand. Many times if I didn't understand, she would actually repeat that to me. First grade, I did have a nice teacher. She just treated me normal as every other student, invited me up in the front row. In second grade I also had a good teacher. So I would say mostly that they were accommodating and they would accommodate the requests that we asked of them.

However, not all of her teachers were willing to promote access for Erin.

> In third grade, I had a much older teacher and she was old-school. I don't think she had any experience with any student that had a disability. She believed that that should be in a separate place, and she was not accommodating to the requests that we asked. She had placed me by the air conditioner, which we said not to put me by because [with] these aids—these hearing aids I wear—I can hear noises, but I can't understand what they are. That is much easier to look up. So I didn't find the source of the noises. I thought she was talking to somebody throughout the book, that kind of thing. So it was [hard] to try and figure out how to combine the sound to the shape of her lips. So [teacher's name], she put me by the air conditioning because she decided she wanted me out of her way . . . I can't remember if I had a buddy. There's no one that pops

in my mind in my memory . . . But she never went out of her way to help, and I was miserable in that class because I could tell that she was looking down on me. That she wouldn't really let me participate . . . I told my mom how upset I was and [she] had several teacher conferences with [teacher's name] and [teacher's name] would complain I was a mean child, that I would not pay attention, I would not focus, so the fault was all on me.

In junior high, Erin started working with a new speech therapist. Even though this speech therapist "didn't have as much experience with lip reading," Erin acknowledged, "so much of what I was able to achieve was relying or happened because of her." Erin said this speech therapist "was actually trying to help me with speaking up in class, with becoming more comfortable with public speaking. And I guess she did a real good job." In reflecting on her experiences with both therapists, Erin noted, "[First speech therapist name] really laid down the foundation, for lip reading, for all communication. [Second speech therapist name], in junior high, was more responsible for taking that to the next level and implementing it in real life."

———■■■———

In middle school, R.J. had a physical therapist who challenged him to become more mobile.

I remember that I had one [physical therapist] for middle school that was really, really helpful. Literally she would put me on the ground and say, "Can you get up?" She would say, "Here are some things you might want to consider"—some ways to do it and different ways to deal with it. One of the things that I distinctly remember her teaching me was that it is okay to ask for help. But if you get to a position where there is no out . . . where [you think] "I don't know how I'm going to do this," if there is someone standing next to you, you can ask them "Hey, can I use your arm?" Something like that, which for—you know, growing up very independent and being encouraged to be very independent—was something that was a pretty new idea to me.

Reflecting on his high school experience, R.J. also recalled a teacher going out of her way to make school accommodating: "I remember my first week on campus there was an English teacher—[teacher's name]—who was really kind of 'Whatever you need just let me know. It's going to be all right. I'm going to help you with this.' The school was pretty well equipped with elevators and things like that for students with disabilities, so, you know, that was something that was very comfortable for me—being able to have that person that was going to kind of take me under their wing essentially."

———■▪■———

Amy began working with an orientation and mobility (O & M) instructor in sixth grade. "My first O & M teacher was the stereotypical, middle-aged white woman who wants to help the blind people and so takes them to an empty parking lot and is like, 'Here, learn to use the cane.'" In high school, though, Amy started working with a new O & M teacher "who was wonderful" and "had a wonderful attitude." Amy emphasized, "she really taught me orientation."

In eleventh grade, Amy also started working with a vocational rehabilitation (VR) caseworker who happened to have a blind husband. "My junior year, though, I was put in touch with someone who would be my caseworker at voc rehab, which was great. I mean, it was very early, but it was perfect for me. When we started talking technology, her husband was blind and had a dog guide and he was in many ways my post–high school blindness mentor." In fact, Amy remarked, "Everything I know about technology and dogs and everywhere I've gotten in the blind world is because of what he gave me."

Amy continued working with both her caseworker and the caseworker's husband for several years, and in fact, when Amy had some accessibility concerns the couple advocated for her.

> I was in touch with them professionally very often and personally we'd hang out. We just enjoyed each other's company, and he put a lot of time into helping me get my feet under me and ready for college. You know, this kind of program and that laptop and,

"Oh, did you know this gadget?" I mean, he consulted as an adaptive technology expert, and so it was great. And when I ended up taking some college classes at the nearby [college name] and was having accessibility issues, he and his wife came in professional capacities to advise and, in some respect, set them straight, because they were saying, "Oh, we can't provide this. It's not reasonable. You know, this is an equivalent to accommodation." He basically, in no uncertain terms, told them why it was not, and how many laws they were breaking.

Amy added, "I was aware of the disability, but I wasn't really meta-aware of it until meeting [name], who was my VR worker's husband."

■ ■ ■

Teachers and other professionals play a critical role in shaping the classroom experience for their students. While students with disabilities are entitled to appropriate accommodations, the effectiveness of these accommodations depends on the willingness of the teacher to appropriately implement them. In Erin's experience, several of her elementary teachers willingly provided appropriate accommodations to help her access the course content. However, her third-grade teacher was unwilling to provide that access, and in fact prevented Erin from understanding what she was saying. For R.J., he felt more comfortable in high school because a teacher reached out to make the environment accommodating for him.

Additionally, professionals outside the classroom can help provide access for students. In most instances, these students had positive experiences with such professionals. They taught students valuable lessons. Amy learned orientation, she learned important accommodations, and she learned advocacy. From their speech therapists, Alex and Erin learned communication. From his physical therapist, R.J. learned that it is all right to ask for help. Whether teaching specific skills, helping students access technology, or developing students' self-advocacy, these professionals had a critical impact on the success of these students.

TEACHING STYLE AND ATTITUDE

Monica started sixth grade with a homeroom and math teacher "who was just this crazy character and a mathematical genius." She added that he "saw something in me. Even early in the year, before any of this [her cancer diagnosis and decreasing vision] had become an issue, he was going to the principal's office saying things about me like, 'This girl's got it. This girl's got something to look out for.'"

> He was definitely an institution at the school. For a lot of eleven-year-olds, transitioning to middle school can be scary, and this teacher was a little intimidating on top of that. But what I loved about his class was that he didn't just teach math like all my other math teachers had up until that point. His class was fun and exciting, and it wasn't so clearly straight out of a textbook. He had spent a lot of time thinking about what he was going to teach, and he often incorporated innovative projects and assignments. I had always enjoyed math, but his class took that natural appreciation to a new level for me. I excelled in his class, and I remember times when he would put me on the spot. He would say to the class, "We're going to give Monica a whole bunch of rapid-fire math problems, and it will be fun for us, because we're going to watch her mind work!" Seems like a ridiculous idea, and maybe not exactly fair to a sixth grader, but I loved what we were learning so much that having to solve things in my head, really quickly, added to the challenge, and was fun for me.

———— ■ ■ ■ ————

Knowing that writing English can prove difficult for many ASL users, we asked Lisa how she learned to write so well. She described a particularly effective English teacher she had in a Jesuit high school she attended part time while enrolled in a school for the Deaf.

> I had a wonderful writing teacher—very precise, very organized in the way he taught writing . . . I remember that the writing teacher every week would teach something, some element of writing.

Then, we would be writing a paper or short story, and the teacher would have us focus on the element as well as previous elements we had focused on. The teacher literally had various rubber stamps he would stamp on the paper indicating which areas we needed to work on. [These elements of writing] would get stamped on my paper and [in my mind]. He was very precise, and I learned a lot from his really honest and clear feedback.

— ∎ ∎ ∎ —

Michael was born prematurely with the umbilical cord strangling his leg. He was not diagnosed with cerebral palsy until he was about three, after a family friend raised concerns about his walking developmental milestones. Following his diagnosis and throughout his schooling, Michael had several orthopedic surgeries on his leg and eye surgeries to improve his tracking. He commented, "That's what I remember as a kid—going to the check-ups."

In reflecting on a positive teaching experience, Michael described his tenth-grade biology teacher:

He made you work so hard, and it was great. But you always felt that you got what you deserved. He would give a take-home, open-book test over a weekend, but the questions were so deep into critical thinking and so expansive. It was really, truly all about learning. There was no gotcha . . . It doesn't mean he was any easier of a teacher. He made you work really, really hard. But you always had the sense that, "I'm getting what I deserve here." He really cared. And everything was very clear, but you still had to work hard. And I liked biology because of that guy. You know, and I didn't get an A in his class, but it doesn't matter. He taught me how to think. The other classes were really about getting the right answer, but this guy was like, "Let's really critically think about ecosystems or evolutionary biology and natural selection. Let's think about what it means because it's all related." Anyway, he was a standout.

— ∎ ∎ ∎ —

In highlighting teachers who made a difference in their schooling trajectory, these students spoke about teaching style. As Monica, Lisa, and Michael described, these teachers were different from the teachers they typically encountered. They made the class "fun and exciting." The teaching style was clear and explicit. They motivated students to "work so hard" and focused on learning.

Michael, in talking about his up and down experiences in math classes, also pointed to the importance of teaching style and how it could have a negative impact on education. "It's all about context. Now, my struggles with math specifically had to do with teachers in seventh grade and in eighth and again in eleventh grade. When I was taking different math from different teachers, like, geometry was a piece of cake. The one math class was constantly keeping me off of any honor roll . . . such a pain. No trouble in geometry. No trouble with [teacher name] and finite math. Basically, what emerged was I had a problem with specific teaching styles of specific people." Michael described two instances in particular. "They unfortunately represent the dark side of not understanding kids with tracking difficulties or learning problems. And I have to tell . . . one story . . . One teacher's manner of handing the math tests back was the following: he would sit at his desk, call a student's name, and the kid would come forward and pick up the test and return to his seat. Okay, and then he would mark the grade down. If you had a high grade on the test, he would hold the paper up here as he called your name. If you failed the test, it would be hanging off of the desk, and everyone saw that humiliation! Awful!" In describing another middle school math teacher, Michael recalled, "I remember that our notebooks in seventh grade had to be graded . . . like we handed them in and he looked at our notes. He gave me a C minus, and he would write mean things. He would write 'Too much misery!' So uncalled for to write that! That is unnecessary, you know, it doesn't do anything. It's hurtful."

R.J. recalled a computer teacher who did not handle his disability well. "I had a computer teacher who would just say things that were just kind of little digs at me, little things like 'Take your time, take your time, we'll wait for you.' Things like that. He's one of those types of teachers that would try to joke around and be friends with all the kids and that kind of thing. You know, even after saying something to him in private about, you know, 'I don't like the way that you do that.' That doesn't change. It doesn't change anything. Consequently I obviously hated that class and hated going there."

Eric's seventh-grade science teacher relied heavily on one teaching strategy that was not effective for Eric. "I remember seventh-grade science. Seventh-grade science was . . . his entire teaching repertoire, his one tool was 'We're going to start at that end of the table [then go around]. You're going to read a paragraph; you're going to read a paragraph; you're going to read a paragraph; you're going to read a paragraph; and you're going to read a paragraph. You're going to take the work sheet, and you're going to fill out the comprehension questions.' I was kicked out of that class for three days a week at least. He was awful. I was pretty awful in there too."

Michael, R.J., and Eric remember their negative experiences with teachers vividly. Michael remembers the "humiliation" he felt when teachers did "not understand kids with tracking difficulties or learning problems," and he was not successful in that class. R.J.'s teacher made "little digs," trying to joke around about his disability. As a result, R.J. hated the class. Eric's teacher was rigid in his teaching approach and did not recognize that some students learn differently. In each of these cases, the teachers' attitude and style created negative classroom cultures. Their inflexibility in addressing the needs of students with disabilities led to disengagement, and in Eric's case misbehavior.

■ ■ ■

Research consistently documents the importance of a student's teachers on that student's academic success.[1] These interviews paint that picture as well. The students describe how influential individual teachers or therapists were in the educational success they ultimately enjoyed. It is critical to note that beyond good teachers, many of these students had connections to high-quality professionals through wraparound services or additional supports. Counselors, speech therapists, physical therapists, and other specialists played essential roles in their academic success.

The interviewees vividly recalled these highly effective professionals and are deeply appreciative of the role they have played in their lives.

They speak of them in a reverential manner. They remember their names—the good teachers in their lives and the bad.

As I describe more in chapter 7, I decided to go into education because I knew the powerful impact teachers had on my own success, self-esteem, and schooling experiences. Too often, we devalue, underestimate, or underappreciate the long-term impact teachers can have on students. Some attribute this underappreciation of the teaching profession to the fact that historically it has been a profession for women.[2] Attending a highly competitive all-girls school, I sometimes felt frowned upon for saying I wanted to be a teacher. I remember people saying things like "But you go here; why wouldn't you want to be a doctor or a lawyer?" I think these comments came from a well-intentioned place of wanting to have girls break through the glass ceiling and push more women into these prestigious professions. But at the same time, for me, it emphasized the lesser value that society places on teachers. Hearing these stories, though, also reaffirmed for me why we need to place greater value on the profession of teaching and in particular good teaching.

In this field, people frequently debate about what makes a good teacher.[3] Can individuals become good teachers? Or is good teaching an intangible thing that some teachers have and others do not? In these stories, there are elements of both arguments present. It may be difficult to develop the charisma of Monica's math teacher or to foster the in-depth personal relationship with every student that Daniel shared with his teachers. However, there are many components here that any teacher can bring into his or her practice and that support the notion that teachers can become better.

Any teacher can make the decision to advocate for a student. Many of the teachers described in this chapter, upon seeing something that concerned them, made the decision to act on their students' behalf. Amy's teacher decided to call Amy's mother to inform her about a classroom setup change that was traumatic for Amy. That simple phone call made a difference to Amy for years to come.

Any teacher can also reflect on his or her teaching practices and curriculum and address potential barriers to access for their students.[4] In deciding to rely on round-robin reading to teach science, Eric's teacher created a barrier to the classroom content, and Eric responded by misbehaving. If the teacher had decided to address the barriers for diverse learners in his classroom, Eric may have been a much different student for him. Universal Design for Learning can be a powerful framework to help teachers address these barriers through providing multiple means of representation, expression, and engagement.

Finally, any teacher can make the choice to believe in his or her students and let them know it. As we previously stated, these students' success in education was often tenuous, and we wonder what would have happened had these professionals not been in their young lives. Brian's life could have gone in a different direction, but when asked what changed for him in high school, he noted, "I had teachers who believed in me." These notable educators reaffirm our faith in our profession and demonstrate once again the power and influence an individual can have. The image of the seventh-grade Daniel crying in gratitude at his therapist's funeral attests to a life well lived. This is noble work.

CHAPTER 3

"I Was Always Asking My Teachers for More"

Thomas Hehir

ALEX WAS BORN DEAF to hearing parents. His deafness was diagnosed in his first months of life, and his parents learned to sign. He attended a state school for the deaf as a day student until he was nine, when he got a cochlear implant and started attending a mainstream school that had a cooperative program with the school for the deaf. Though his lip reading skills are good and his speech is relatively easy to understand, Alex prefers to use an interpreter in class (but does not use that interpreter to voice for him). He attended one of my classes as an undergraduate at Harvard College.

The first word that comes to my mind to describe Alex is *preppy*, possibly reflecting the fact that he attended a prestigious New England prep school. Always impeccably dressed, Alex frequently wore bow ties. Like so many of the students profiled here, he is mature beyond his years, and he is now embarking on a career as a lawyer focusing on civil and disability rights issues. Alex's story reminds me of Justin's and R.J.'s in that it is largely a happy story of things going well for him in school. Unlike Justin, however, Alex did not come from a well-off home, and described his family as working class. He attended a private high school with financial aid. He would often ask me for additional readings in a course that students have rated as having a heavy workload. This is a well-worn path for him.

Alex's first memories of school are of his preschool at the school for the deaf.

In chapter 2 Alex talked about the teacher at his preschool and credited her with teaching his mother sign language and challenging him. However, as he advanced through the grades, Alex appeared to seek that challenge from other teachers. "Kindergarten was the same as preschool. And then first grade—I can't remember clearly—and then I skipped second grade. I remember third and fourth grades at [the deaf school]. And I felt frustrated in that classroom, because things were too easy for me and I was able to complete the next day's homework assignment while still in class. I asked for more work, but the teachers were busy with other students. So I just waited, or I did more of the same type of work."

As mentioned, at age nine Alex had a successful cochlear implant and started attending mainstream schools. He described this experience as mixed. Again, Alex's desire to be challenged intellectually comes through.

Authors: And how do you recall that experience at the mainstream school?

Alex: In fourth grade it was great. I was in this new environment. I was being exposed to hearing peers. I remember being supported. My classmates, they understood that I was different, that I used a different language, and that I was learning to speak. And I made some good friends that year. And that continued through fifth grade. And also my teachers were supportive and great—I couldn't say anything bad about them. And then for some reason sixth grade was a worse experience for me. I can't quite pinpoint what changed between fifth and sixth grade in the overall interactions between classmates and me, but it may have had something to do with our cultural differences, as my classmates had grown older and identified more strongly with their cultural background. I do remember feeling more left out, and it wasn't enjoyable for me to participate in the social aspects that year. However, the educational experience was great. I still loved classes, and my teachers served as a consistent source of friendship and support. But that was a tough year for me socially.

Authors: Seventh and eighth?

Alex: My social situation got a little better, but not quite as it had been when I began. I was able to bond with some of my classmates more during our final year at the school.

Authors: Did you feel challenged academically at this school?

Alex: Yes. More so than at [the school for the deaf]. That's the reason why I liked it there. If it wasn't for the academic rigor of this school, I wouldn't have been able to advance my education further in high school and make it to Harvard.

Authors: And you remember as a kid not feeling challenged at [the school for the deaf]?

Alex: Right!

Authors: You can recall that as a kid, thinking . . .?

Alex: Yes, I do remember asking for more work. I assume that meant I wanted to be challenged.

Authors: So [the mainstream school] was a challenging academic environment?

Alex: Yes.

Authors: Mixed social environment?

Alex: Mixed. I have to say that my social development, at least up until high school, was not typical. Because for one, my experience at [the school for the deaf] was an environment with all deaf kids. But I didn't feel a connection with them, because even though we communicated in the same language we were not interested in the same things. I found myself talking with the teachers more often than with the kids—this is something that I remember well, especially during middle school, when I was spending the majority of my time at [the mainstream school] and going to [the school for the deaf] only one or two times a week.

As we described in the previous chapter, Alex's desire for intellectual challenge was nurtured by an unusual source: a speech therapist. Remarking on his experience of speech therapy years later, Alex became visibly excited.

———■■■———

The theme of intellectualism is repeated in most of our interviews. In addition to supportive parents and critical service providers, these students appear to be driven at an early age to learn. A good deal of their success may be attributable to their intellectual drive.

In a conversation with Daniel, he told me he identified as "Jewish intellectual." Daniel was clearly an intellectual at an early age. As we detailed in chapter 2, Daniel had a preschool teacher who gave him a computer that enabled him to communicate, along with a gifted speech therapist who helped Daniel become a self-described "chatterbox." He is a frequent contributor to class discussions, though his speech is labored and benefits from a microphone. His grasp of course content is so thorough that he is the only undergraduate I have ever asked to be a teaching assistant.

His interview detailed his intellectualism at a young age. Though there were bumps, he did well in elementary school. His preschool teacher was correct: Daniel was clearly bright and intellectually motivated.

His sixth-grade creative writing class seemed to bring out this budding intellectualism quite well.

> I won several writing competitions throughout middle school and was sponsored at one that got my work into the Library of Congress . . . Then in ninth grade I started participating in the Teen Speaks program with the [big city newspaper], where they would pair you each year with a mentor who would check your monthly submissions to a Web site for teenagers and help you improve your writing. In sophomore year, I had [name], then the Executive Editor of the [newspaper], who absolutely loved my work. I wrote a lot of disability advocacy pieces and so forth. We lost touch for about two years, until—and this is why I bring it up—I'm doing my interview for Harvard and I get an email from the woman who's interviewing me. It's from the [newspaper], and so I decide to mention Teen Speaks and knowing [executive editor], and she says, "Oh yes, I love [him]. I miss him." . . . And so I wrote him for a recommendation letter and, sure enough, he gave me one, and [the teacher] knew from that moment, or so she says, that I would get into Harvard.

How many high school students have their work published in a major newspaper?

— ■ ■ ■ —

Amy talked about how she had to fight to get into advanced classes.

> My eighth-grade guidance counselor, when looking at my fresh-man year schedule—which, mind you, at this point I was a year ahead in math and had been in all the tracked classes in sixth and seventh grade. There was no tracking in eighth grade, so I was going into Geometry, I think, instead of Algebra I, because I'd already taken Algebra I. Geometry and none of the other courses were particularly accelerated, but they weren't not accelerated either. I remember her coming up to me with this very, you know, concerned, motherly tone of voice: "You know, this is a really ambi-tious schedule, especially for someone like you." And I remember thinking, "Someone like me. Someone who's pulling straight A's in your school without trying and is bored out of my mind. This is an ambitious schedule?" But of course I was twelve and thirteen and I wasn't going to say that.

— ■ ■ ■ —

As we described in the previous chapter, Brian had important teachers in his life who recognized his gifts. When he was moving from middle school to high school, however, he had a crisis that involved a suicide attempt. Through all of this, his intellectual drive was impressive.

> I had to get my stomach pumped or something because I took all the medication in the house. I was just really afraid of school, because I was doing so well academically in middle school and I didn't know what high school would bring—a new environment and a new teacher. Oh, I don't know. I didn't want to go to the school I was going to because—actually, I also, like, did a lot of journaling in middle school. I liked to do a lot of poetry. It was really, really an outlet for me. Even though the words were screwed up, I understood what it meant. But I applied—because in [city

name] you get to apply to the high schools you want to go to and either you are invited to audition or take a test to get in. I applied to the creative arts high school of in [city name]. And I remember submitting my part and getting in to the school for creative writing and my mom, she didn't want me to go, so she had me go a college prep school, so I had to go.

Though Brian struggled mightily to learn to read, write, and spell, writing became a central part of his life. "It was difficult, because I think throughout middle school and high school I had a goal and that was to go to college. That was the place where I was supposed to escape—the abuse at home, the learning disability, not fitting in—I was supposed to escape. That was my utopia." Though Brian continued to battle with depression, he graduated at the top of his high school class and went on to the state university on a scholarship. His college experience was difficult. "I went to college and it was not what I expected. It was difficult—of course it was difficult—and I did not have the tools to navigate. But also the culture shock of being a black kid in a predominantly white upper-middle-class school and, I felt like my voice didn't matter. I've always thought I was a shy person. But I'm not a shy person. I just overthink a lot of things; I think, 'Oh, I'm not speaking proper English,' or 'Oh, it's because of my environment,' or 'How do I say it?'"

After the interview I was taken aback by how little I had known about Brian. He certainly had been a very able student in my class. But unlike most of my students—who have been given so much by their parents and the educational opportunities they have been provided prior to Harvard—Brian, more than any of these interviewees, made it here through sheer drive. So much of that drive was intellectually based: teaching himself to read and eventually becoming a skilled poet and writer. Indeed, his writing and poetry went beyond academics and truly may have saved him. I deeply admire this young man.

■ ■ ■

Lisa's primary language is ASL and she does not voice. She identifies very strongly with the Deaf community and attended both Deaf and mainstream (hearing) schools. As I noted in chapter 2, in my interview with her I probed specifically about how she became such an excellent writer of English, even by Harvard standards. I was intrigued by how a Deaf person could develop such a high level of skill in standard English.

Lisa started school as a day student in a nearby residential school for the Deaf. She described her early schooling as pleasant but lacking challenge.

Authors: And so what happened after grade three?

Lisa: I . . . remember that in second and third grade I was frequently pulled out of the class to be taught different things from what my peers were learning, and I had some time alone. Perhaps I was just picking things up more quickly than my peers, and I kind of wished that I was with my peers rather than getting pulled out of the classroom. But my parents felt perhaps it wasn't challenging enough for me. I didn't really realize it at the time. Then they sent me to another school [a mainstream school] that is not a school for the Deaf, but they did have a Deaf program which is part of [a county program] . . . The program provided interpreters and note takers, and so it was a mainstream setting. There were four or five other Deaf students, and we were fully mainstreamed from the fourth grade through the sixth grade. But during those three years, I also went to [the school for the deaf] part of the day. I didn't want to leave my friends, and I think that my parents also played a big role in that decision because they knew that culture and that community were important for me. So, I spent half the day in each place. I remember in fourth grade I left at noon. Fifth grade it was a little later, and I spent a little less time. And so, by sixth grade, maybe I only had an hour at the school for the Deaf. So, every year, I spent less time at [school for Deaf]. When I was at [school for Deaf], I would take art and gym, but core or content classes were taken at the other school.

Authors: What are your thoughts about being in a mainstream school as opposed to being in a school for the Deaf at the elementary age? Do you have any judgments about that?

Lisa: Well, my experience was very positive. Because as an elementary school student, it was a novelty. You know, people wanted to learn sign language. If I didn't have the interpreter there, there were like fifty other kids that were dying to interpret for me. So, in the mainstream setting, a lot of them were picking up sign language, and I had a great time. But, in middle school, I had a very different opinion or perspective.

Authors: What about in terms of academic challenges in elementary school? Was the mainstream setting more challenging academically than the school for the Deaf?

Lisa: Oh, yes.

Authors: So, you would affirm your parents' judgment?

Lisa: Yes.

Lisa went on to a mainstream middle school that housed a small program for the Deaf. In ninth grade she had to have surgery, so she spent a year being educated at home by an interpreter who came two hours a day, and she kept up with all the classes she would have attended in school. She also spoke about the importance of summer camps in cultivating her interest in playwriting.

Authors: What about the summer camps? Were they important for your education?

Lisa: Oh, yes, definitely yes. Because I felt like that was where I really grew, where I was among Deaf people. I looked forward to summer so much. I went to [camp name], which is a camp, and I went to [another camp name]. I went to hearing camps too with an interpreter. I took painting classes and theater and playwriting. I always had interpreters for those types of activities.

Authors So you went to both Deaf camps and, for lack of a better word, hearing camps?

Lisa: Yup, or hearing programs during the year.

Authors: Now, it seems with your education at this point, you've gone between deaf schools and hearing schools . . . Deaf camps and hearing camps . . . do you have any thoughts about that? Would you have been better off just going to Deaf schools and Deaf camps? Just hearing schools and hearing camps? My point is . . . do you think this back and forth had a positive relationship to your education or a negative one?

Lisa: I think it's positive because I was able to meet more people. I had more opportunities. I was really interested in theater and there isn't a lot of opportunity as far as Deaf theater programs go, but I was able to do it . . . I was able to have more options because I was willing to attend the hearing camps or the hearing program and still get language access. Yet I still had the Deaf environments where I could feel more at ease and not need to use an interpreter. That is what I would prefer. But I think if I only had it one way, if I was only in a hearing environment using an interpreter, I think that would have had a detrimental effect on my education and on my self-identity.

Authors: So, it was good to have both?

Lisa: Yes.

Lisa went on to high school at a highly selective residential school for the Deaf.

Lisa: I really enjoyed being there. It was a lot of fun. I stayed there six weeks at a time. I took various classes there. I also was taking classes at the all-boys Catholic high school—because they had English classes. I actually had to go at it with my parents to, you know, make sure that I was getting a quality education. While this was supposed to have been prearranged before I started the school year, when I arrived at the Deaf school for the first day of school, they said that I was not yet set up to go to the Jesuit high school for that English class. It was about two weeks before everything was in order and I could begin taking that class. I also took Honors English at Gallaudet University the following year.

Authors: What school was this?

Lisa: It is [well-known Jesuit high school].

Authors: Were there other girls there?

Lisa: No.

Authors: Do you know how the school for the Deaf arranged for you to be able to take the other classes at the Jesuit high school?

Lisa: Yes. They arranged that. They arranged it before I entered the school. For some reason, I had heard about that opportunity, and I was eager to do it. I already had the impression that [school for the

deaf] was not going to be able to meet the quality education that I
had just left. So I wanted that.

Authors: So that was primarily in English. What other types of classes
did you take?

Lisa: Well, I was taking social studies and all of the regular classes. But
before I went there, you know, they didn't have a history at [school
for Deaf] of offering all these classes.

Authors: Now, one of the things that I noticed about you as a student
was that you are an exceptionally good writer. And writing is one of
the things that many Deaf students struggle with the most because
of the nature of second language—whether they are oral or whether
they are ASL speakers. Can you talk about the experiences that
shaped and nurtured this ability?

Lisa: Well, that was definitely the question that I pondered because now
I am studying deaf education and how to get people to become proficient in reading and writing. I do think that the communication
with parents . . . the language models . . . having stories being told
to me and having two languages—all of that, I think, plays in. I was
also read to . . . I think I learned how to read and write by reading
and writing. I don't think it was any direct teaching that brought me
to this place. Many Deaf people have a hard time reading and writing because people are trying to teach them how to read and write
rather than just exposing them and just letting them read and try to
figure things out for themselves. And also, I took writing courses.
My parents really emphasized that as a way for me to improve my
writing. You know, sort of drilled into me.

Authors: Did you enjoy reading as a kid?

Lisa: Yes, I loved it.

Authors: You did a lot of it?

Lisa: Yes.

Authors: And that would be reading in English?

Lisa: Yes.

Authors: Any other language?

Lisa: I learned Spanish in middle school. I became pretty good at it.

Authors: Can you read Spanish?

Lisa: Kind of. I mean, yes. I'd love to be more fluent.

In addition to crediting her English high school teacher with helping her learn to write, Lisa said her desire to write was evident at an early age.

Lisa: I remember growing up writing and showing my dad what I had written and having my dad critique me, and I was always eager for that. My dad never sugarcoated it. He wasn't like, "Good job." He gave me real feedback on my writing, and I loved it. I could see my own mistakes, and I could see the patterns and the tendencies that I was leaning toward. Getting that feedback allowed me to improve and to have knowledge of what my strengths and weaknesses were. That came later. This was after I was already comfortable with writing. And so, I think that's important. If a kid gets too much criticism when they are very young and they are not yet comfortable with the idea of writing, then the writing process in that way can become very uncomfortable for them.

Authors: Anything else you want to talk about from high school?

Lisa: High school [at school for the Deaf], well, I felt like I was in camp. Maybe I shouldn't be quoted as saying that. The education wasn't great. I felt like I often wanted more. I wanted a challenge. But I did really have a wonderful time. I was very involved in my school; I did sports, I did theater. I did a lot of different things that I wouldn't have done if I had stayed at [her town's high school].

Authors: Now, you mentioned before both the school for the Deaf you attended as a child and the residential high school. You said that the expectations were low academically. Am I right?

Lisa: Yes and no. I am sure it is not intentional on the part of the teachers. I mean, a lot of my friends were similar to me. I was not the only one in my situation. At [the first school], I was young and I was eager. I didn't have that from my peers, but I did have that at [the high school for the Deaf]. Many of us were on the same page. We were proficient readers and writers. We all wanted more.

Authors: You wanted more from the school?

Lisa: Yes.

— ■ ■ ■ —

The first word that comes to mind to describe Monica is *political*. After graduating from a prestigious undergraduate school, she worked for the school's president prior to coming to Harvard. She did her master's in education policy. It is not surprising that she is now working in Washington and has become a paid policy wonk. Monica is also someone we in Boston would say has a "wicked good sense of humor." Monica was diagnosed with cancer of the retina in both eyes at six months, when her mother noticed she was not making eye contact as was her cousin, who was four months younger. Monica's cancer was cured after rounds of radiation, but that treatment ultimately resulted in cancer of the bone at age twelve. The surgery performed to address the bone cancer resulted in her losing her right eye. She has some, limited, vision in her remaining eye and identifies herself as blind. She attended Harvard supported on a highly competitive scholarship from the National Federation of the Blind. As her teacher in three courses, I was deeply impressed with Monica's desire to excel. This predilection was developed early.

Monica described an early intervention program as being particularly important to her development.

> I went to the [program for the blind] when I was, gosh, I don't even know how old I was when it started, but less than a year old, I'm sure. They did all kinds of stuff with me. I actually explained this in a job interview once when I was trying to explain the importance of E.I. [early intervention] for children with disabilities. One of the things I remember clearly is they would have me roll around on those big exercise balls. The goal was to get me comfortable, not too cautious or fearful, in the space around me. I think this was critical in my own development, and in making me who I am today. I am comfortable in my own body and in my surroundings, and people often don't understand the extent of my visual impairment, because I am so mobile without the assistance of a white cane or service animal.

Monica went on to attend the same preschool that her brothers attended, which was run by their church. She attended mainstream public schools throughout K–12 in a large urban district. Her desire to excel in school was evident early on, even though accessing text through vision was a constant struggle.

> I was friends with a group of really bright kids in my first-grade class and, in all other respects, I think I was counted among them, except that I really struggled when learning to read. These friends had all attended kindergarten at the public school and—at least to me at the time—seemed to be strong readers by the beginning of first grade. I had gone to kindergarten at the school connected to my church and, in my six-year-old mind, managed to chalk up the difficulty I had with reading to the lack of some magical reading experience that my friends had all had with their public school kindergarten teachers. I had convinced myself that they had this year of what seemed like real school, while my kindergarten class of nine students at that nursery school down the street seemed somehow inferior and resulted in my not being able to learn to read as quickly. It seems absurd now, but I was genuinely jealous of what I imagined their kindergarten experience to be, even though I really did enjoy my kindergarten.
>
> The challenges I had with reading were really frustrating for me. I actually remember when, in first grade, we were divided into reading groups. All of my closest friends were in the advanced reading group, and I was not. This was so frustrating for me that I became determined to change the situation. My friends and I would take any free moment we had—during lunch, during recess, during free time—and we would sit and they would help me read the books that they were reading in their reading group. We thought this would help me get up to speed, and maybe the teacher would let me be in their group if I could learn to read the books that they read.
>
> I know my teacher spoke with my parents about how I was struggling to learn to read, and that I was progressing slower than she expected or slower than she would have liked. I think the explanation that was reached was that this was probably some developmental delay that was associated with my visual impairment. I think the adults around me decided that, since it probably would have taken me a little bit longer to figure out the world around me

as an infant and as a toddler, then that type of delay would also exist when working with letters and words for the first time. With my disability, I'm sure deciphering simple objects for the first time and learning how to receive and interpret limited visual information took a lot of work, and I had to develop those skills with the minimal sensory input that was available to me. So I think everyone thought that developing the mechanisms I might use to identify letters and words might take a little bit longer too. I don't know that anyone believed I couldn't learn to read; I think they just decided to give me some more time. I don't think I was given any additional help or support beyond what was taking place in the typical first-grade classroom around learning to read.

It is of note that, according to Monica (as we discussed in chapter 1), the "help" offered was an aide, not other accommodations and supports directly related to accessing text. Monica agrees with her parents' decision to reject that form of help.

Monica went on to describe her struggles with print while always seeking the most demanding academic challenges. Eventually she got access to large-print books and audiobooks under a 504 plan and ultimately an IEP, particularly as her vision became significantly worse following her surgery at age twelve. As we discuss more in chapter 5, Monica was able to "disguise" her disability because she "was able to excel in other areas that distracted from or directly mitigated that challenge."

She described being part of what appeared to be a pull-out program for the "more advanced students" and panicking over the increased reading load. "For the first time, it was physically difficult for me to get through the material that I was expected to have read for this special once-a-week program. I wanted to be a good student, and I wanted to go in having read what I was supposed to read, but it was completely overwhelming and upsetting for me. That was the first time that I clearly remember my vision becoming an obstacle that could jeopardize my performance in school." Shortly after that, she started getting large-print books through her dad's advocacy.

Monica's academic persistence was evident when she was treated again for cancer at age twelve. She was attending an academically advanced public middle school at the time through a district choice program, which she described as "one of the best middle schools in the city."

Monica: So I was diagnosed with osteosarcoma in my right sinus, and that would have been in March of 2000. I started a chemotherapy protocol, and a couple of months into that I had a fourteen-hour surgery to remove the tumor. Because the tumor was in my sinus, in the bone structure that supported my eye, my eye—which was otherwise healthy or as healthy as it had ever been—had to be removed as well. And then I had several months of chemotherapy after that. It was basically a yearlong process, and I stayed enrolled in my school the entire time.

Authors: You did?

Monica: Yeah.

Authors: Did you finish sixth grade with everyone else?

Monica: Yeah.

Authors: Through all of this?

Monica: Yeah, it was an interesting thing. I mean, there was a lot of conversation about what would happen. What do we do when we're clearly going through this very substantial treatment protocol? How do we deal with school? I so badly wanted to stay involved and connected. I didn't care what was going on in the rest of my life. On the few days a month that I was out of the hospital and feeling well enough to go to school, I wanted to be in school. I wanted to be with my friends and stimulated in a way that wasn't available to me at the hospital.

Monica went on to describe how her math teacher, profiled in the previous chapter, recognized her ability. Monica's joy in figuring out complicated math problems was obvious. It was clear throughout her interview that doing well in school and rising to academic challenges is central to her personality.

— ■ ■ ■ —

With the exception of R.J., these students had deficiencies in areas that schools value: reading, writing, spelling, speaking, and discipline. Yet, they ultimately excelled. I am struck by how, for most of these students, schools' recognition of their intellectual gifts required such effort from the students and their parents. The assumption often held by too many educators was that their disability almost precluded their being gifted.

Eric recalled dinner conversations when he was only nine that reinforced his mother's belief that his troubles in school were not due to intelligence. "I mean, particularly at the dinner table at my house . . . even as the youngest I was often the one who was sort of, like, pushing the conversation or talking about what was on the news or arguing with my brother and my sister. I remember in the 1984 election, right, nine years old, having these endless debates about how great Walter Mondale was. You know, my brother and my sister, they didn't care. They were older than me, and they didn't care. So, they saw that disconnect—*why is this kid struggling?*—but they didn't really understand it." Eric went on to discuss how in high school academics finally "clicked." He attributed his success primarily to the format of instruction, which seemed to minimize the impact of his dyslexia.

> In my junior year in high school, they gave these awards for each class. So there was an eleventh-grade award for English, and an eleventh-grade award for mathematics, and physics, and so on. Somehow that year, I won every single award except for Spanish, and the kid who won it was a native speaker. I'm not sure what that was about that year. It was just sort of like everything clicked. I remember in Physics we didn't do a lot of reading, but it was sort of big conceptual stuff. It was the equivalent in law school of booking a class, right? They give you this . . . you come down and you get this thing in front; everybody claps. Up until then, I had really struggled academically . . . And I think it may have been because the format of those classes that year was if you have an idea, let's talk about it. We were doing American literature, and we had to read these books. You didn't really have to read the book, right? I mean, you listen to what some other people say, and you're like, "Oh, here's the big idea. Wow, isn't this interesting! Doesn't this relate to, you know, President Bush or Clinton?" But I think it was just luck.

As Laura describes in the next chapter, Eric's earlier experiences in elementary and middle school provided few opportunities for his talents to be exhibited. Thankfully, Eric's high school education enabled him to shed this "badass" identity and replace it with that of a talented musician and nascent intellectual.

These students' intellectual drive was central to their success. However, in looking at their interviews I was impressed by the fact that this alone was insufficient. Had Amy not had her mother's advocacy and support, or Daniel not had his insightful preschool teacher, or Brian his influential teachers, or Alex his speech therapist, or Monica her math teacher, these students' intellectual gifts may have been for naught. How many students with disabilities have gone through school with their intellectual gifts ignored?

INCLUSION AND INTELLECTUAL CHALLENGE

Another issue that emerged in some of these interviews was the relationship between the desire for intellectual challenge and inclusion. Clearly all of them, for at least part of their education, had been exposed to the intellectually challenging environments they sought. Their intellectualism did not exist in a vacuum. Lisa, Justin, Alex, and Nicole all spent part of their education in special schools, and Jennifer and Brian spent part of their time in special classes. The picture that emerges here is complex.

Justin's short stay in a special school enabled him to learn the strategies he used outside the classroom and to catch up in school. Nicole described her experience going to a special high school as overwhelmingly positive and central to her success after years of failure in the mainstream. For her and her parents, the "more restrictive" special school was far superior to the special class offered by the district. Clearly these narratives do not support the notion that all students with disabilities should be educated in the mainstream all the time.

However, both Lisa's and Alex's narratives mention low expectations in special school environments. Though both accounts support the importance of schools for the deaf, they also speak to low expectations in these environments. Both Lisa's and Alex's intellectualism were nurtured in mainstream environments.

Brian and Jennifer both received resource room support at various times in their educational careers. Both saw some benefit from these placements. For Brian, the resource room exposed him to talented teachers who understood his disabilities and ultimately helped him learn to read and write. The resource room protected Jennifer from having to read out loud in the mainstream class. However, both Brian and Jennifer felt they "didn't belong there." Like Lisa and Alex, Jennifer spoke to the low expectations she experienced in the resource room.

Authors: So, do you recall how you felt about getting pulled out and put in the special class? You were in the special classes for most of the day for a while, right?

Jennifer: Yes. I was actually really okay with it. I had really nice [emphasis with air quotes] special ed teachers that didn't challenge me but were really, really nice. And so I enjoyed my time. I don't think I realized until high school that I wasn't getting the education I needed. And that was becoming clearer in the other subjects that I wasn't.

A frequent theme in all of the other interviews except R.J.'s was the dilemma of whether to place these students in special education environments or in the mainstream. Some parents, like Daniel's, Amy's, Monica's, and Eric's, actively resisted what they considered limiting special education placements. In hindsight these seem to be wise decisions. However, what strikes me is that these decisions were not without cost. Eric's acting out was a reaction to his dyslexia, and his mother's extraordinary involvement in his school probably protected him from becoming an educational casualty until he ultimately found a school that nurtured his talents. Daniel's continual struggle for the accommodations he needed to access challenging curricula and develop social relationships was one his parents joined with impressive dedication. Amy's and Monica's struggle to get text access should not occur in this age of braille, talking books, e-books, and digitized text. Yet their struggles continue.

What is frankly disturbing in all these interviews is the inflexibility these students encountered at many of their schools. It seems that many schools approach disabilities in the standard ways: with resource rooms, special classes, and special schools that appear ill-equipped to address intellectually gifted children who are also disabled. The widespread ableist assumption that disability and low intellectual capacity go hand in hand is reinforced throughout these narratives. It appears that our education system often reflects this in both general education's inflexibility and special education's low expectations.

This creates a dilemma for parents and students that appears to have played out differently for each of these students. For many the choices were unsatisfactory as they sought to make the difficult decisions that allowed these students to prosper both intellectually and socially. There were frequent tradeoffs. Daniel's dad's role as his paraprofessional limited Daniel's social interaction. Alex's feeling of isolation in his mainstream urban public school would have been unlikely in a school for the deaf. Jennifer's recognition that the protective environment of her special class was intellectually stifling fortunately came in time for her to prosper in high school.

The debate that so often rages around inclusion rings a bit hollow here. The binary choice so often foisted upon parents between an integrated environment or a segregated one is frequently no choice at all. These students and their parents dealt with the real dilemmas inherent in a mainstream system that fails to accommodate students with disabilities and a special education system too often mired in low expectations. Educators need to approach these decisions recognizing that those involving inclusion represent real tradeoffs.

Recently, I attended an IEP meeting for a family member who had been referred to special education in kindergarten. He had been a low-birth-weight twin who had received early intervention services for motoric issues. When I read his evaluation materials I assured his parents that there was good news: the psychologist assessed his intelligence as superior. At the IEP meeting after the psychologist read her report, his teacher replied, "But he can't use scissors. And scissors are important in kindergarten!" I thought of these students we interviewed for this book, particularly Daniel, and replied, "Really? No, they aren't!" I related Daniel's story to her, and I hope she changed her view. We have much work to do. I will speak more about this issue in my concluding chapter.

Finally, these narratives speak to the importance of self-determination. According to Field and Hoffman, self-determination is the "ability to identify and achieve goals based on a foundation of knowing and valuing oneself."[1] Field elaborates further: "This definition is consistent with the themes throughout various definitions of self-determination. Throughout all of the definitions of self-determination that have been offered, there is an emphasis on knowing oneself, making choices, taking control, believing in oneself, and taking action to reach one's goals." It is clear that all of these students, some earlier than others, took an active role in the critical decisions involving their education. Laura will speak more to the issue of self-determination and identity in chapter 7.

The intellectualism these students exhibited often fueled their desire for self-determination. These students were all intellectually driven at a young age and sought opportunities to nurture their interests. Fortunately, parents and some teachers provided access to the educational opportunities that nurtured this drive. The principles espoused by Field and Hoffman of knowing oneself, believing in oneself, and taking control are all evident in these narratives. Though many of these students had less-than-perfect situations, in most cases there were adults who listened and empowered them.

A final note is in order here. The theme of intellectualism emerged after several rounds of coding our data and revealed our own biases in conceptualizing disability issues. When we first developed our codes we assumed certain common disability issues would emerge, such as inclusion, the role of accommodation and modification, and the impact of interventions. To some extent we were using an "IEP" frame of mind, assuming that what was done for or to children by service providers and parents had impact. As the first two chapters demonstrate, it clearly did. However, we underestimated the degree to which the internal drive and curiosity of these students, even at young ages, influenced their outcomes. As former teachers we may have been focused too much on what adults do for children while failing to recognize the importance of fostering children's engagement and agency in their own education. One of the downsides of many educational practices in special education is that they run the risk of fostering dependency by focusing inordinately on services and supports. Maybe our own coding strategy reflected this subtle ableist bias. These narratives provide a strong antidote to the belief that what adults do to and for students is determinative in and of itself. Educators and parents need to foster this drive and love of learning in all children.

CHAPTER 4

"I Found Things to Do Outside the Classroom"

Laura A. Schifter

ERIC VIVIDLY REMEMBERS having a "tough time" in elementary and middle school. "I had spent the years from first grade up until high school as a major disappointment in school." In those elementary years, schools highly value reading, writing, and behaving. Being dyslexic, Eric had difficulty with those highly valued skills. Unable to read and write cursive, he had to repeat third grade. He was placed in fourth grade for a brief period, but was then moved back to third. Eric recalled, "The fourth-grade teacher was like, 'I can't do anything with this student. He doesn't know how to read. He doesn't know how to write'—all these things that she perceived as being what you need to be prepared for fourth grade. So, I was in there for two weeks and then got moved back. There was a lot of explanation about why I was getting moved back to third grade—you know, why this was going to be 'good' for me."

As we discussed in chapter 1, Eric responded to his academic struggles by acting out. "Thinking back on it, I remember at the time just feeling like no matter what I did I was going to find my way into trouble." Eric frequently got into fistfights and disrupted class. He cursed at teachers, got out of his seat, and refused to read aloud. Suspensions became a norm. Since he could not succeed at anything in school, he decided he would succeed at being a "badass." Given that his parents were well respected in the community, Eric recalled school personnel being confused—how could a child from a good family get into so much trouble? Eric said that some years he started school in an advanced class, only to be moved later to the "slow" class where he and other boys with behavior issues were "warehoused": "Academically, I was not engaged in much at all, and really spent most of my time trying to find my way out of the dean's office . . . A big transition for me was getting involved in music."

Toward the end of elementary school, Eric began going to a center outside of school for additional support. At this center, he had occupational therapy and physical therapy. Eric said of his time at the center, "There were some good things that came out of this." In particular, the professionals at this center recommended that Eric learn how to play an instrument. "That became the thing I did and was my way to have something to myself outside of being a student."

In middle school, Eric became aware of a magnet high school focused on the performing arts and wanted to apply. "They said you spend half your day—three out of six classes—playing music. I'm like, 'Ah, thank you.' . . . It's something that I enjoy, something that I am good at." Eric's parents, in an attempt to motivate him to do better in school, said that he would not get in unless he improved his grades. Luckily, the application required a musical performance, spelling did not count, and he was accepted.

Upon reflection, however, Eric wishes the academics were more rigorous in high school. He noted, "They didn't ask much out of us. Particularly . . . if you were in the performing arts program . . . We're in the performing arts thing, but I spent half my day playing music. Nobody really challenged you much academically so long as you kind of kept up with what you were doing in the arts and you kept your nose clean." Despite the lack of rigor, Eric learned valuable lessons at this performing arts school. He learned he "could be good at music." He also connected with teachers and peers through something other than acting out. "I had many good music teachers and a lot of people whom I connected with in that way."

Music reshaped Eric's perspective on learning, and helped him engage with school in a positive way. "It was important that I saw some value in study and learning and practice. I thought I could get better and do things that other people valued. That was a very, very big part of my life."

■ ■ ■

The majority of the students we interviewed participated in extracurricular activities, and they considered these activities central to their success in school. For instance, in describing his high school experience, Alex stated affirmatively, "the brass ensemble—that was one of several aspects that made my high school career enjoyable." From athletics to the arts to the school newspaper to the Young Astronauts Club, extracurricular activities served three critical functions for these students. First, participation in these activities helped boost students' confidence and develop their strengths. Second, it made students feel that they were a part of a community in a way that did not emphasize their disability. Lastly, it provided students the opportunity to make, develop, and sustain friendships. Jennifer summarized the impact of extracurriculars, describing her involvement in sports as an equalizer where she did not feel different: "I always played sports . . . there were no accommodations needed on the sports field. I was fine. I did well. I was pretty typical and had friends."

Despite these overarching positive themes related to participation in extracurricular activities, the issue is more complex. For students with nonvisible disabilities, extracurricular activities appeared to provide them with an avenue to excel without necessarily needing to identify their disability. Participation offered them the opportunity to feel as though they were not disabled. For other students, successful participation was contingent upon access to appropriate accommodations and successful inclusion in the group.

In previous chapters we discussed the importance of minimizing the impact of disability and maximizing opportunities to participate. Extracurricular activities that successfully included these students were able to accomplish both.

CONFIDENCE BOOSTER: "IT GAVE ME CONFIDENCE. IT GAVE ME SELF-BELIEF."

Michael took Tom's classes while getting a master's at Harvard. Michael has a passionate connection to the arts, and spent several years after college working in theater. He then decided to pursue a degree in special education and taught for several years before coming to Harvard.

Michael was diagnosed with cerebral palsy at a young age, and throughout his schooling had multiple surgeries and physical therapy. He recalled, "Two major surgeries were performed when I was three years old specifically to correct my right foot from toeing in so as to prevent me from tripping over it . . . So there were two major surgeries done at [hospital name]. This is the introduction of my orthopedist, [name], who to this day, believe it or not, has been the same orthopedist."

Throughout his childhood, Michael had multiple doctors' appointments, and in a public elementary school, Michael received some special education services.

Michael: When I entered second or third grade in the public system, I was put in . . . I guess it was special ed, but I never saw any documentation and I don't think I was hugely formally—you know, in terms of paperwork—put into the program. I was pulled out briefly for no more than one period for work on my gross and fine motor skills with two other kids . . .

Authors: And did you think that was helpful—that service that you received? Was it OT or PT?

Michael: It was kind of more PT. . . I don't really know. My sense was that the school was doing it to experiment. It was 1980, first of all. They were doing it to get a feel for themselves about what service they wanted to provide. That was sort of brand-spanking-new in the public system.

Authors: So this was at a public school?

Michael: Yes. I would put puzzle pieces into pegboards, and they were looking at hand–eye coordination. Also, I should say . . . in addition to the orthopedic surgeries, I had an ophthalmologist and I had to do eye surgeries.

One summer in elementary school, Michael had surgery again to try to correct his right foot, and he remained in the hospital for two weeks recovering.

Authors: Now where was this?

Michael: The Children's Hospital [of major city]. So, I just remember that, because I think recovering when you've got friends and a group of people is far preferable to being alone in a room. There's no question in my mind . . .

Authors: How long were you in here?

Michael: In that hospital for two weeks. That is a memory, and I remember my father walking away from me because he had to go to work. And I remember coughing up blood, I was so upset that he was leaving—because it really, psychically, it meant leaving, like leaving me here. That was so hard for him; I know it was. It wasn't wrong that he did. He had to . . . He could only take a certain number of days off. I remember him walking away, and I [had] never coughed up blood before, totally all over my sneakers . . .

Authors: The hospital experience was obviously a big one in your life.

Michael: Huge.

After this surgery, Michael transferred to what he describes as "a ritzy private school" and remained there for eight years.

Authors: Do you know why [your parents] chose private school?

Michael: They thought it was better than public school. I think it was just that simple.

Authors: It wasn't anything to do with your disability?

Michael: No, that's interesting. I think—and they've never articulated this and I've never actually asked them directly—there might have been some protective idea. Like, you know, "We don't want to throw him in the big public school because he'll just be a target for bullying and all this. We're going to send him to a nice church school and keep it a smaller controlled environment." That might have been part of their thinking.

He described the school as one that highly valued athletics—a place where "you suffered if you were not an athlete."

Authors: Well, were you an athlete?

Michael: No, no. I was the scorekeeper for the basketball team. I tried
    to do . . . I was an actor. Let me just . . . you had asked if there was
    another person with disability. There was. I think his disability was
    CP. He wore leg braces, and socially what this amounted to was in
    athletics doing laps, and we were always the last ones. And it was
    like "race of the crips" every single time. You know, me and this guy,
    and that guy would always win. On the rare occasion I would win.
Authors: So the "race of the crips"?
Michael: That's what I would call it.

In particular, the lower school had a field day where students participated in multiple track and field events. Michael recounted feeling
different during these field days: "Specifically, to the experience of disability, I recall those races in fourth grade. I recall once a year there was
field day and I never won a race. I participated and everything, until I
remember one field day really getting down on myself about it."

Luckily, through participation in the school's choir and later in acting, Michael found a "key" to "getting through school." He was able
to connect with the director of the choir as mentor. Michael recalled,
"Now I got through lower and middle school not because of athletics, but because there was an old-school boys' choir there. And it was
directed by the person who taught [school name] choir. In other words,
[the school] went and hired this guy. He was a genius from Juilliard, and
he was a mentor to me and took me under his wing and identified that I
had a voice. So my thing was choir, choir, choir, choir."

Authors: And when did you start that?
Michael: Fourth grade. And I think his mentorship was . . . it was so key
    to me getting through [school name]. Especially the lower grades
    because the lower school choir was a big deal.
Authors: And you were good at it?
Michael: Yes.
Authors: And how did you think that affected the rest of your education?
Michael: It gave me confidence. It gave me self-belief.
Authors: Did you feel you needed that?

Michael: I needed to do something. It's hard for me to recollect that far back, but you know, at the end of classes and everyone's going off to athletics, I definitely needed to be going somewhere and the choir rehearsal was great.

Students with disabilities frequently lack confidence when they struggle with things that society highly values. In the case of Michael, he struggled physically when his school highly valued athletics. In the case of Eric, he struggled with reading, a highly valued third-grade skill. Michael and Eric felt inferior. Michael responded internally by getting down on himself, and Eric responded externally by misbehaving. Given this blow to their self-esteem, these students could have continued down their paths with internal frustration and inappropriate behavior. However, in both cases, finding music—through playing an instrument and participating in choir—shifted these students' thinking and, in fact, gave them self-esteem.

Michael and Eric, like many of the students we interviewed, reported that extracurricular activities gave them something they could do and do successfully. When talking about their participation in extracurricular activities, these students spoke with confidence. Justin described his involvement in athletics: "I played soccer in the fall. I wrestled in the winter, and I played lacrosse in the springtime . . . even as a young child I was always fairly athletic, so that was a place that I always shined. So I really enjoyed that." Jennifer described her participation in sports succinctly, noting, "I did well." Erin recalled participating and placing in a spelling bee: "I think that was a little bit extraordinary, that I beat all the other hearing people." She added that being involved in student activities in middle and high school "helped me become more confident."

A PART OF A COMMUNITY

Erin found that being deaf in elementary school was not as challenging socially as in later years; having the same students from year to year made things easier. However, the transitions to middle and high school were more challenging for her. She noted: "[In elementary school] one or two fellow classmates said that they wanted to learn finger spelling—I should point out that each year, it was very typical to have the same classmates every year, so they're already used to my deafness. They were already accustomed to what they needed to do to have me in class. Every year it wasn't a whole learning curve like it was for sixth grade through high school when we had new classes, new teachers, and a lot of new students from other districts coming into this particular school." To help address the challenges that arose from transitioning to middle school, Erin decided to become very involved in extracurricular activities. "So, [in] junior high through high school, I was very involved with student activities." In fact, she credits her speech therapist with pushing her to get involved. "[Speech therapist name] also encouraged me to be involved with student activities. This was something new for me, student activities." Erin described the benefits of this participation: "It helped me become more—really, really—mainstreamed. I think it's important that mainstream is just not an attempt through the classroom."

For Erin, participation in extracurricular activities gave her access to the community. It empowered her, making her feel more "mainstream." For Eric, extracurricular activities provided him with a community where people valued what he valued; there were many people he "connected with in that way" through music.

Michael found that through choir and later acting he was among people who did not care about his disability. After college, he found himself working in theater. He describes this period with "show people" as "the happiest time." When asked to further describe the business, he noted, "There's no business like show business and they don't give a f*** about disability."

FRIENDSHIPS

In addition to feeling a part of a community, the students saw extracurricular activities as an essential place to make and develop friendships. Jennifer remembered, "I was on the basketball team, the soccer teams, and I did all that stuff, so . . . friend-wise, it [dyslexia] wasn't an issue ever." For Jennifer and the other students with learning disabilities in this book, friendships were fairly easy to develop. Extracurricular activities provided opportunities to spend time with friends. For students with physical disabilities, extracurricular activities also seemed to provide a pathway for developing friendships.

R.J. has a physical impairment; however, he did not want his disability to prevent him from accessing the benefits of participating in school sports teams. "Just because I couldn't physically participate in these sports, I didn't want to not have that experience." Since he wanted the experience of athletics, he devised ways to participate that minimized the impact of his disability. "I was involved in so many different things, and I still found a way to get involved with the football team and the basketball team, doing different data analysis for them or doing film editing of the football games." This involvement in sports helped him develop his social strengths as well as additional friendships. "I've always been a very social person, and even from that kindergarten and first-grade kind of age . . . With those groups of friends [I] met through the football team, I was able to still have a piece of that even though I wasn't on the team. I was still able to socialize in that group. That was something that was definitely my own idea."

Throughout his schooling, Daniel faced challenges socially, yet by participating on the school newspaper he was able to develop meaningful friendships. "I became part of a social group. For a while it felt like the first time, because of being on the newspaper staff." In fact, he found these friendships helped him through tough experiences. "Again, everyone was two years older than I was, but I made two very dear lifelong friends on that newspaper staff. And that was very special, especially when my aide died and my therapist died within the same year. It really helped having that social group to go to for self-worth."

To develop friendships, it is important for students to feel as though they are fully a part of the activity. Alex managed baseball in both high school and college. In high school, he had an easier time developing friendships on the baseball team because the students were more understanding of his disability. "I could definitely tell the difference between my high school team and my college team, in terms of how they interacted with me. The high school team was more accepting. I was more a part of the team. In college I was less so." While the college coach was accepting and tried to integrate Alex into the team, he still felt isolated from his peers. "I found that they were less likely to talk to me or to invite me to do things after practice." He attributed these differences to the college students having different experiences with disability. "Now I think the reason for that may be the result of everyone coming to college from different high schools, and everyone having different experiences of people with disabilities, whereas in high school everybody knew who I was—I was the only deaf student there."

BARRIERS TO EXTRACURRICULAR ACTIVITIES

In general, students' experiences with extracurricular activities were positive, but they were also complicated. Some students faced barriers to extracurricular activities because of limited access to accommodations. For instance, Erin noted, "I became very involved with student activities and was a [college] ambassador. I think they [the school] wanted to encourage involvement, student involvement, but it was new and sometimes there weren't enough interpreters to be available when I needed them."

Two students had rather different experiences in how their choice of school related to their ability to participate in extracurricular activities. In one case, the student viewed the prospect of attending a specialized school as a barrier to participating in extracurricular activities, whereas in the other case the student saw the school as creating a gateway to participation.

Amy's family considered sending her to [school for the blind]; however, Amy worried that it would take too much away from her life. "I looked at the [school for the blind], and I would have to be a residential student. I was going to have to give up all my extracurriculars—4H, my animals. It was going to cut so much out of my life." In Amy's experience, she felt going to the [school for the blind] would limit her participation in the community.

Lisa, on the other hand, saw her choice of going to a school for the Deaf as opening up her ability to participate in extracurricular activities. "I did really have a wonderful time. I was very involved in my school; I did sports, I did theater. I did a lot of different things that I wouldn't have done if I had stayed at the mainstream high school." She described these activities as being "very important" to her education. In fact, she added, "I think that's why I am now very supportive of afterschool programming for students so that they can be with each other . . . so that they can learn from adults who talk to them like adults."

— ■ ■ ■ —

Modern neuroscience points to the powerful effect of engagement in learning.[1] Students' affect can often be the most critical determinant in whether a student is successful or not. Finding ways to better engage more students in school can help to keep them in school and help them succeed. Eric's characterization of music as a "big transition" and Michael's description of the choir as the "key . . . [to] getting through school" emphasize the powerful role extracurricular activities can play in keeping students engaged. To support students with disabilities, it is essential to find ways for them to engage with school and be success-ful. Participation in extracurricular activities can provide an avenue for engagement with school.

In addition to engagement, extracurricular activities can provide critical social and educational benefits.[2] Social activity through extra-curricular activities can help students develop self-determination skills, understand their own strengths and weaknesses, and build relation-ships. Prior research examining high school graduation for students with disabilities has found that students who participate in extracurricular activities are more likely to graduate high school, as are students with self-determination skills.[3]

It is important to note that because of Section 504 of the Rehabil-itation Act, students with disabilities have the right to participate in extracurricular activities with accommodations. Additionally, recogniz-ing the benefits of extracurricular activities, the Individuals with Dis-abilities Education Act requires that IEPs address the special education and related services a student may need to participate in extracurricular activities. Despite these protections, students can face barriers to partic-ipation. When I was working in the House of Representatives, my boss, Representative Miller, had requested that the Government Accountabil-ity Office (GAO) examine the participation in athletics of students with disabilities.[4] GAO found that while students with disabilities did partic-ipate in extracurricular athletics, they did so at a much lower rate than their nondisabled peers.[5]

In chapter 2, we discussed the impactful role professionals can play in the lives of students, and in considering extracurricular activities, we again see how professionals can help students' lives. Erin's speech therapist encouraged her to get involved in student activities when she had not previously been, and the professionals at the center Eric attended pushed him to learn how to play an instrument. While participating in choir, Michael discovered he "had a voice" thanks to his choir director. The GAO study also highlights the critical role teachers and school leaders have played in creating or eliminating barriers to participation to school athletics. It points to an example where a parent recalled that administrators recognized her daughter's strengths in athletics. As a result, they included in her IEP that she could participate even if her grades were below the cut-off point for participation.[6]

When students struggle in school, those in authority sometimes jump to take away their extracurricular activities. The ableist focus becomes about remediating the disability. Students with dyslexia can be forced into hours of reading interventions, or students with CP into hours of physical therapy, leaving little time for these students to engage and succeed in activities outside the classroom. While these interventions can provide crucial benefits, they should be balanced with opportunities for students to succeed in areas where their disability is not the focus, where they can engage with their peers, and where they can excel. Teachers and other professionals can help ensure that students with disabilities can access extracurricular activities by connecting them to the opportunities that are available and supporting their continued involvement. Encouraging participation can help students with disabilities maintain engagement in school, build confidence, and develop friendships.

CHAPTER 5

"I Was Always Forced to Find a Way"

Laura A. Schifter

As we described in chapter 1, Justin's mother—who ran a preschool program—became concerned early on about some areas of Justin's development and decided to have him evaluated. At five he was first diagnosed with a learning disability. Justin recalled that having an early diagnosis helped him. "Having that information really helped quite a bit because when I started elementary school, all my teachers were aware of that and I was given supports and I never sort of felt that I was dumb or anything like that . . . [I knew] I just needed some extra help there."

In elementary school, though, Justin avoided reading.

My way to avoid work would be to get up and walk around; that usually resulted in getting into trouble. Another thing I did was to pretend to read books I couldn't possibly read. This strategy had some benefits because I did get something from these books. One that sticks in [my] mind is *Ralph and the Motorcycle*. I liked the pictures and though I couldn't read all the words, I did understand the story. I certainly didn't fool my teachers who were always trying to interest me in books at my own level. I guess I felt more like everyone else reading more grown-up books.

In part because of difficulties reading, Justin repeated third grade, but for his second year in third grade he attended a special school that focused on educating students with learning disabilities.

Authors: So, you went to the school for kids with dyslexia in New York City in third grade?

Justin: Still in existence today.

Authors: Still in existence today. And that was a good thing for you? Bad thing?

Justin: It was a terrific thing for me because it really helped me develop the skills I needed to be successful and helped me feel that I could be successful. So they were very clear in terms of helping me with my handwriting. Very clear in helping me identify strategies for reading comprehension and for mathematics, and I was able to excel in a lot of those areas once I got my bearings. And that really boosted my confidence in my ability to get things done.

Authors: What were some of the things they did, if you recall?

Justin: Let's see, what were some of the things that they did? Well, we really worked a lot on handwriting. I had made progress the summer before at the [name] school camp, but the continued emphasis on handwriting helped to reinforce what I had previously learned. Another important thing I learned was how to take notes and not write complete sentences, which was very time-consuming. The first desktop computers had just come out. I believe that we had one of the first Macintosh computers that enabled me to spell-check my work. Spelling has always been, and still is, a big problem for most people with dyslexia. I think I made big strides in reading because for the first time at [special school name] I was taught phonetic rules as well as how to use syntax to ascertain meaning. My large vocabulary helped me there because I could often figure out what things meant by using contextual clues. They also taught me other comprehension strategies, such as rereading certain areas in a paragraph to pull out pertinent information.

During elementary school, Justin also attended a camp that specialized in helping students with learning disabilities. In reflecting on these experiences, he said, "One of the turning points was when I started to really get a grasp of what were the skill sets and my strengths that I really needed to capitalize on." He continued, "Those two experiences really helped me figure out my learning style and what I needed to do in order to sort of make sure that I either took the time that I needed, or that I was able to ask for the help that I needed. So those things kind of really stuck with me in terms of my school career."

After two years in the special school, Justin returned to a traditional school, and in fact, skipped a grade, ending up back in his original grade. At this point, Justin had become proficient at self-advocacy: "Once I left [special school name], I was pretty good about being able to advocate for myself." He added, "I would say that especially once I got to the [school name], I knew how to study better than most kids there and my grades were pretty competitive."

When asked to describe further how he studied better than most kids, he remarked:

Justin: I understood what I needed to be successful as a learner and I did have a pretty solid foundation. I knew how to extract important information from a text as well as how to effectively organize my writing. For example, in order to write a well-organized paper, I knew I needed to spend time developing my ideas and putting them into detailed outline form. I knew I also needed to go back to the text to identify specific details to support whatever I was writing. I was able to apply the same strategies to reading where I learned to highlight text and summarize as I went along.

Authors: How did you know this?

Justin: Like I said, these things were explicitly taught at [special school name] and at the special camps I attended. The more I used these skills, the more proficient I became and also the more successful. In the process, I acquired some pretty good work habits and was accustomed to sitting down and concentrating. As I moved up in high school, these strategies helped keep me on track and, in many ways, I felt better prepared than most kids at tackling and solving problems.

Authors: So you were explicitly taught strategies?

Justin: Yes.

Authors: And strategies that you found effective?

Justin: Yes, exactly. We were taught to reread passages and to underline key words or words we didn't understand and needed to look up. We were taught, depending on the genre of writing, to look for certain telltale clues. We learned how to scan and summarize by reading the first and last lines of a paragraph. I found all these skills enormously helpful in test-taking situations as well as for more complex reading and writing assignments.

When deciding where to go to college, Justin used his knowledge about his own strengths and weaknesses to find a suitable match. "I chose [college name] because it was a small liberal arts school where I knew that I would be able to have close contact with my professors and that I'd be able get the kind of attention and things that I might need."

While in college, Justin continued to rely on his strategies. "I had developed strong work habits in high school. By the time I graduated, they were pretty ingrained." He also planned his course load to focus on his interests and strengths. "In college I had a lot more flexibility in selecting courses that were enjoyable and where I knew I would be successful. I chose philosophy as a major, a long-term interest of mine, and looking back, I was pretty successful at managing my course work."

He chose not to disclose his dyslexia to professors in college, and instead used the natural supports that were available to all students. "I didn't necessarily explicitly go to my professors and say, 'Hey, I have dyslexia, and this is what I need.' Instead, I took advantage of my professors' office hours and got feedback before handing in papers. I was sure to get clarification on anything that confused me. Things like that enabled me to do as well as I did."

By the time Justin attended Harvard for graduate school, he had relied heavily on the strategies he had refined over the years. Justin explained how he managed the reading workload: "I've learned to accommodate pretty well by learning how to skim things effectively. Instead of reading one word at a time, I taught myself to read four or five. I definitely have to slow down when I need to really concentrate." He continued to seek out help from professors as well. "Just as in college, if I didn't understand something or needed help, I wasn't shy about asking questions. So in your class, Tom, I spent a fair amount of time picking your brain to see how things were going and I did the same with all my professors. That really helped me feel confident that I was on the right track." He added, "Another thing I've learned over the years—if I hear it, say it, and write it, I'll remember it. I think that's probably true for most learners."

Justin easily described how his disability impacts his learning.

> One of my biggest handicaps is processing speed. It takes me longer than most people to read and write things down. For example, I had a hard time learning how to read, but once I learned, I was pretty good it. Still, reading speed is a problem especially when I have a lot of reading to do in a short amount of time. Another area I have difficulty with is rote memory. I have trouble recalling nonconnected things, such as repeating a string of numbers backwards or remembering things in sequence. I compensate by taking copious notes at meetings.
>
> I'm a terrible speller. Most people with dyslexia are. I've improved, but spelling is still really difficult for me. I've learned to spell-check my work or get someone to check it for me especially if it's something of consequence. When I became a classroom teacher, I always kept my Franklin Speller handy to make sure I hadn't misspelled anything on the blackboard.
>
> When I read out loud, I have to use my word attack skills to make sure I'm pronouncing words correctly, particularly names and unusual places. Sometimes I look at a word that I know, but it comes out totally wrong. I'll go, "Duh, that was this word."

Justin is currently a principal, and recognizes that his dyslexia can impact his professional life.

> I've learned the hard way that I need to take the time to have someone read what I've written especially if it's important. I've gotten into trouble when late at night I need to get something out, but I don't have time to show it to anyone. More often than not, after I've sent it, I realize, or have pointed out to me, that I've made some foolish error. As a school principal that can be embarrassing. I also have to monitor how I use my time to make sure I get the

most important things done. I often get caught up in a project and realize too late that there are more important things I should have gotten done. I often come home from work with too many things still hanging over my head. I try to take tons of notes to help me remember and stay on track. An upside of that practice is that they supply useful data when I need to document something.

In reflecting on his success, Justin noted:

Having the support and the willingness of my parents, teachers, and other professionals to help me go the distance has been key. From the time I was really little, I received encouragement for the things I could do really well and was fortunate in being able to master strategies that enabled me to overcome areas of difficulty. On reflection I would say that two things—speaking up when I needed help and truly practicing the strategies I had been taught— have helped me the most in my school and professional life.

Having dyslexia and going through the very structured process of learning how to learn has made me a more aware and effective learner and has helped to define my character and my values. I know I have to work harder than most people and that I have to be more organized if I'm going to succeed. And I have succeeded by applying these principles.

Over the course of his life, Justin has successfully learned strategies and learned how he learned. In some instances, he naturally developed these strategies; in other instances, the strategies were explicitly taught; and in most instances, the strategies evolved as Justin encountered new challenges. These strategies helped Justin become more self-aware about his strengths and weaknesses and about the accommodations he needed to help him succeed. This metacognitive awareness helped him become an advocate for himself.

SELF-ACCOMMODATIONS: "I CAN FIGURE ALL THIS OUT."

Justin's experience of relying on strategies is consistent with most of the students we interviewed, and in particular the other students with learning disabilities. For many other students, though, strategies were not explicitly taught as much as they were developed.

Eric, although also dyslexic, had a much different experience than Justin in developing and using strategies. As you may recall, Eric was diagnosed young, but he was not aware of this diagnosis until he was much older. Even though he did not know about this diagnosis, he developed strategies to get through school. When asked about how he handled reading books in school, Eric commented:

> I tried. [laughter] I really tried, and I always felt like it was enough if I turned all the pages. You know, if I sat there and I turned all those pages, then I had kind of done my best. But in terms of strategies, sure, I think that I was coming up with strategies from the very time I started school. In middle school, I think the strategy was to be kind of a badass. If I'm not going to do well in school in the classroom, then I better be able to hold my own on the playground. Just to kind of get by as a kid. In high school, I learned that if you could be good at something, people will generally let you be. I learned that I could be good at music, and I wasn't getting hassled about grades and the teachers didn't really care and let me do the music thing. So, in that way, I think I continued to learn strategies. They were different throughout, and I think the strategies I use now are different than what I was using in high school.

In high school, Eric even developed a strategy for reading for pleasure: "I wanted to read for pleasure in high school because it was—with this certain group of folks I was hanging out with for a while—it was like the cool thing to do . . . The time everybody was reading *Catcher in the Rye* and *The Stranger*, I really wanted to do it, but I just couldn't get through the damn books. And so, again, I was going to get by . . . by asking the right questions."

In college, the reading became heavier, but Eric learned to rely on his strengths to help him get by.

Eric: I went to a fairly unique school in college in [state name] . . . a small liberal arts school, which is the honors college for the state of [name], in which students are permitted to design their own curriculum in collaboration with their faculty advisor—have a set of goals per semester . . . a lot of independent work . . . a lot of independent reading . . . There were parts of it that worked really well for me and parts of it that did not. So, the basic pattern was, you would put together a group of two or three students who were interested in military history, for example. You would create a bibliography that you would read together as a group and sit down with the professor and you would have an hour a week to talk about it with the professor. The reading was heavy. It was a book a week per class. I quickly realized I was in over my head. The only way I was able to survive was the main way we were evaluated and it was the way we talked about it. So we would sit down in a room very similar to this. The professor would say, "So, Mr. _____, tell me what so-and-so said." Now if I had to go and just do this by myself and read it, I was cooked. But what I figured out—

Authors: You were cooked? Why were you cooked?

Eric: Because I had a really difficult time going from the material in the text to that conversation. So, that was some sort of intermediary way of processing it. Often what would happen—this is what I would remember most from college—is I would be in the library after reading the book and I would get through maybe five pages, maybe six pages, and I would start to feel a little bit overwhelmed and I would fall asleep. I was always asleep in the library and it wasn't because I was staying up all night. I just couldn't get through the text, so what I figured out I needed to do was to talk to my classmates—these two or three people who I organized this course with—prior to the meeting with the professor. Once I got the basics of what happened, I'd say, "Okay," in the military history class, "Hannibal did X, Y, and Z, and the Romans responded by doing this." That sort of gave me the basics of it [so] I could thrive in the sort of academic environment by moving beyond that, and with the analysis and by connecting things together. In a traditional classroom, where I think I would have been evaluated more on my writing and regular writing—a lot of the stuff we do in graduate school—I don't know if I would have been as successful. I think the main way that I was evaluated and was able to move through college was on my ability to communicate orally. My writing was problematic, and there was always some writing component which I would get back just blood red with [corrections].

Authors: Did you say that your strength was in the analysis and the tying of the themes together? Is that what you said?

Eric: That's what kept me alive in college, and that's what I do. I think that's what I offered to my classmates as the reason why they would sit down and talk to me before we got together for our meetings with the professor. Otherwise, what am I offering? Because I would go in and . . . I would play it off a little bit. I'd say, "Oh, okay, guys, what do you see going on here with the French Revolution?" I became very adept at drawing out some of the core ideas and then spinning those core ideas.

Even though Eric did not explicitly know why he struggled with reading, he did understand what he did well—making connections—and he was able to leverage that strength to compensate for his weaknesses. In graduate school, he continued to rely on the strategy of talking with peers about the readings and then making connections across them.

Authors: Do you still rely on study groups here to talk through the readings, or is it primarily the text-to-speech that you use?

Eric: The first year of my doctoral program I used a lot of study groups, and what I've done since then is . . . I don't have a formal writing group like a lot of people do. I have two folks I work with, and we share all of our work. I read everything that they do. They read everything that I do. They know where I struggle enough that they are able to help me. For one class, for Professor [name]'s class, I realized that I needed—this was kind of a big lecture seminar class where he will call you out and everyone has got to be able to perform—I realized quickly that . . . this was very much like undergraduate where I needed to . . . I could not digest all of that really dense text all at once, but if I had some people to work through it with me and to ask them questions, then I think I could excel in the class. And I did. When it got time to stand up in class and say something, I was prepared to say something that went beyond the reading.

In a statistics class at Harvard, Eric recognized that the "detail-oriented stuff" was difficult for him. In order to compensate, he again relied on peer support.

> In that preliminary statistics class, I identified the person who was the best at the details. I took her to lunch . . . and talked her into being my partner. And we did very well. You know, you have partners in this course, and I think I was really good at kind of getting the big-picture questions and she helped with the details. And together, we got an A in that class. It was a hard class to get an A in. I realized that I need her to help me do it. So, I guess it was a lot of the things that I was doing as an undergraduate. You have to be very socially aware, right, figuring out, "Okay, they are good at that. I'm going to partner up. I'm going to partner up with her," and it actually turned out to be really good. We've remained partners on a lot of different things.

As a doctoral student, Eric also learned the importance of pacing himself to help manage his workload. He remarked, "I'm going to be taking classes; this is going to be my sixth semester. And I am still taking classes, but I kind of knew that. I knew that I was going to have to take two at a time, three at a time, in order to do it well."

Since Eric did not rely on standard accommodations but rather on self-accommodations, when applying to graduate school he took the standardized tests without accommodations. He acknowledged, though, "for some reason, I loved these standardized tests." He recalled frequently taking the classes to help him prepare: "I did well enough. I always took the class. Each time I took the class—the Kaplan. For the SAT, the LSAT, and the GRE, it really helped my scores. The tricks and the strategies." He understood where he might experience difficulty and addressed those issues:

> I did pretty well on the verbal section. I drilled a lot. I think this is one of the lessons of being a dyslexic . . . you kind of learn how to

work through some things. You know, like the papers. You know that it is going to take you longer, so you start a week ahead of time. I think with the GRE I knew that I was going to struggle on the GRE. Whereas most people, you know, [approach it as] "I'm going to take the GRE and in two weeks I am going to start studying," I started studying the spring before. As I said, I took the class. I went through book after book after book. I practiced and timed myself . . . I really made it my job to do well. I think if I had approached it like most people, I wouldn't have gotten near the scores I did.

No one explicitly taught Eric strategies. Eric developed self-accommodations and coping mechanisms for himself. It was not until he came to Harvard that he became consciously aware of his own disability.

It wasn't really until I took [Tom's] Students with Disabilities class that I started to really understand myself better as a learner and what's going to help me to access the material and to get around some of these shortcuts and different things that I was taking to survive as an undergraduate.

I think even in college I attributed [my challenges] at the time [to the belief] that I just wasn't smart . . . I just sort of carried that with me from grade school, from high school, that I didn't read well. And it meant that I wasn't very smart. I think now that I am in school—and consume much larger amounts of text than I ever did in college, but I do it in different ways—I think I recognize that I wasn't using kind of the tools that were available to me. So I didn't even know . . . One of the things that I started doing after I got out of school was kind of marking off, line by line, using a ruler or a piece of paper and isolating a line of text that I was reading. This is something that I kind of developed in my pleasure reading after college and that would have been tremendously helpful for me in college. I just didn't have that tool. I didn't have any of the text-to-voice, which is what I use for everything. Everything is text-to-voice. I stopped being able to get through sentence-by-sentence, word-by-word, after a few pages.

Even though Eric was able to develop strategies for learning to get through school, he wishes that he had been made aware of his disability earlier so he could have better understood how he learns and why he learns the way he does.

When asked what may have made his experience easier or better, Eric responded:

> I think that if somebody had explained to me why I was struggling in school . . . I mean really explained it to me. Because what I got was "you're slow," and I internalized that. That really set me on a trajectory. I look at the kids that I used to run with; they're in jail. They're really all in jail! I think that very easily could have been me. A big part of it was thinking, "Well, I'm a slow kid. These are the kids I run with. So this is where you wind up." Once I got here . . . in college, I thought I was working the system. The way I was smart is, I knew how to get around all this stuff and all these expectations. That was true in my kind of professional life. I figured out I'm not so much smart as I am clever. I can figure all this out. It wasn't until I got here that I understood, "Okay, so I learn a little differently. Apparently, here's why I struggle with these things." I think if somebody sat down and explained to me in third grade when I was being retained and kind of continued to explain that to me—"Well, Eric, here's why you're struggling with this, and here's how we can fix it"—I think my experience would have been different.

■ ■ ■

Brian relied heavily on strategies throughout his schooling. In fact, he taught himself to read relying primarily on the strategy of memorization. In elementary school he took bible study, and he had to prepare for it himself.

Brian: I just had to prepare for it myself. In order to do that, I had to be able to read it. And my mother never sat down with me to read it. She stressed how important it was for me to attend the bible study very prepared. So I sat down with the dictionary—the big fat dictionary—and read the book . . . You know, I'd just read it. I'd look up a word to understand and I'd sound it out myself. So that's where I actually learned how to read by myself. So actually looking at words and following on tape—and "Oh, that's what that word means and this is how you pronounce it."

Authors: Did you have a tape of them?

Brian: Yes. Well, some of them, like a children's book, they'll have a tape that goes with it. And I'd look it up and underline the words I did not know. And I'd play it over and over, and make sure I'd memorize the word. And if I saw it again I'd say, "Oh, I remember hearing that word from before." And that's how I learned to read.

As we discussed in chapter 3, Brian experienced difficulties transitioning to college. To adapt to college, Brian recognized the importance of evolving strategies. "I had to learn new strategies. I still had the skills I've always had, but I had to adapt them in a different way."

■ ■ ■

Nicole also realized when she faced challenges that she would need to figure out a new approach to address them. "I just was really stressed out and I just was banging my head up against the wall, because I felt like no matter what I did it wasn't good enough. And I realized I had to step back from the work and really look at it and figure out, you know, how to do this. What's the different way I can do this? What's the other way I can skin this cat?" As we noted in chapter 1, it was Nicole's school that helped her rethink how to approach a problem. When she got stressed, her therapist also taught her explicit strategies to help her calm down. "If I started twitching, he gave me strategies, you know, go and, like, wash a cup. And just focus on washing the cup, you know? Or focus on just breathing. You know, you're breathing in, you're breathing out."

NATURAL SUPPORTS

Early on in her life, Jennifer recognized the challenges she faced because of her learning disability and tried to tackle them head on, compensating for her weaknesses. She acknowledged, "Spelling has always been atrocious." She took an AP Humanities class in high school, and did not want the teacher to dismiss her work because of her spelling. She was up front with the teacher: "I remember having to sit down with the teacher, and I remember handing [the work] in to her and saying, 'You might need help with this. You need to call me up and let me know because I can come back if you get stuck on a word.' I remember saying that to her. 'If you get stuck on my English, let me know.' They were all great, and they all knew that it was the spelling, it wasn't because of the capabilities."

In college, recognizing her own weaknesses with language, Jennifer made an explicit decision to take ASL for her foreign language requirement. "My undergraduate foreign language was American Sign Language during the time when I thought I couldn't handle another language. English was always kind of hard for me, so why would I try Spanish or something else?"

Jennifer also acknowledged that writing is very challenging for her.

Authors: In other words, people just passed you by as far as learning the skill of writing?

Jennifer: Right, hands down.

Authors: Because of your dyslexia, you think?

Jennifer: Yes. It was assumed that I couldn't do it, [that] I was defective . . .

Authors: And you wish that assumption had not occurred?

Jennifer: Yes, and I had consistently gone into writer editing [services] and said, "I don't know how to do this." I really genuinely don't want to sound . . . [pause] . . . I never know how to say it: "I don't know how to do this." "I want to learn." "Please don't skip that." "You have to tell me what you are doing and why." It's never . . . it's not what they are trying to do. I mean, they are given a mission to align and look at stuff.

Jennifer worries that because of low expectations, she relied too much on supports and never had enough opportunity to develop the strategies for herself. She noted, "I overuse editing services because I am so self-conscious. I really expect it."

When working on a paper at Harvard, Jennifer found herself in a tough situation with a paper. "I wrote my first draft, and I knew it was choppy . . . I knew my thoughts weren't clear. I knew what I wanted to say, no problem, [so] I went back and talked to the teaching assistant during his office hours. We were on the same page. I was feeling confident. It came down to the writing component. [I] wrote it out. I thought, 'I don't think this is saying what I think it is saying. It's not what's here.'"

Jennifer was aware that what she wanted to say was not what was written in the paper. At first she relied on her ingrained strategy of going to the writing services. But the writing services gave her conflicting information from what she saw in the exemplar memo that was distributed to the class. So then she relied on another ingrained strategy—talking with her family.

> So, my poor husband is sitting at the dining room table with us [her and her parents], and I'm getting up saying, "This is not fun. But the editor said. I don't understand; I've always had great editors. I always trust my editors." And Dad said, "Do you want me to read it?" And I said, "No! I'm thirty. We need to move on. We should not be having parents editing papers. We're thirty. I'm sorry; we need to move on here." Got the paper back. Sat down with the teaching assistant, and talked it through. Again, no problem cognitively, talking it through. I totally understood. Went back, reworked it, re-edited it, and then I said, "All right, Dad, I surrender. You need to read this over." So I would read it out loud, and Dad would say, "Here's what I got from that." He would tell me what he understood, and I would say, "No, you didn't understand this right." Then he would say, "Then you didn't write it right." And that's not what an editor should do. That's not what they're trained to do. They're trained to look for *there, their, they're.* They're trained to look for everything. So I said, "All right. Now, [husband's name], you read it. Tell me what you read." So he would read it, and he would explain it. 'Oh yeah, that's way closer. That's way closer." So that was my process, and so then I did that on my final.

Jennifer had come to learn that she could not rely on one strategy alone to do well. Acknowledging her weaknesses, she sought out support and continued to work and rework her paper until it was successful. This story illustrates both her intellectual drive—common among the students we interviewed, as we discussed in chapter 3—as well as the dangers of oversupporting students who can and want to learn to perform independently.

Jennifer noted that being dyslexic is not a deficit because "if anything, it enhances what you can do." She added, "You have to learn what you can and can't do. There's no—you can't have an illusion about who you are if you are true to your disability. I'll never have a job where I need to depend on my editing skills, and to take one would be asinine. Like, why would I do that?" She appreciates how her disability has helped her learn more about herself, her strengths, and her weaknesses.

—■■■—

While the students with learning disabilities relied heavily on strategies for approaching their schoolwork, students with physical and sensory disabilities also relied on strategies to help them in academics and to navigate through society.

R.J. recalled facing challenges because of his disability and specifically his back pain. "I think [in] the majority of the instances I was always kind of forced to find a way. That kind of brought me to the point where I am now. When I went through college, I always found a way . . . I knew it had to get done and I didn't always know how it would get done, but I knew it would. I was kind of having to jump my own little hurdles, you know?" From planning out his path to go around town to planning how to handle his academic assignments, R.J. has had to think strategically to make things work.

> Through middle school and through high school, I distinctly remember . . . trying to plan out a path of how I am going to get from one point to another. If I can see a hundred yards in front of me that there is a curb with no wheelchair access, then was there a post or a bush or something that I can push off of to at least kind of get that positioning I needed? I mean, that was something as easy

as just walking around to knowing that, okay, well if I've got these three papers all due on the same day and I know that I can't be sitting that long—I just can't sit in a chair for four hours straight or something like that without having to lay down for a minute and rest my back. If I've got to do that, how am I going to plan this out to know that I'll have everything done when it needs to be? If that means that on the last night, I am up for three hours and down for an hour or up for an hour and down for three or whatever it is. So, that's always been something I had to take into consideration.

In college, R.J. had become so accustomed to finding his own way that he did not frequently utilize the disability service office.

Outside of registering for classes early—which allowed me to plan my path and what my day was going to look like in terms of walking from class to class and using the tram to be mobile around campus—academically, I didn't take advantage of too much that they had to offer. I felt that at that point I was already—I had done this for so long that it was something where I was really comfortable going out on my own and kind of finding ways . . . You know, if I had an issue with anything . . . my first instinct wasn't to get in touch with DSS to talk with them. My first instinct was, "Well, how I am going to handle this?"

"I WAS ABLE TO DISGUISE MY NEED FOR ASSISTANCE."

As we discuss further in subsequent chapters, Erin and Monica tried to use strategies to hide their vision impairments. Erin relied on self-accommodations to hide her vision loss. "It was better for me to walk closer towards the walls instead of in the middle of the hallway, because I wouldn't be able to see students on both sides. If I went on one side, then I'll be able to see the spectrum, so I was able to adapt my vision impairment growing up." As her impairment continued to progress, Erin's strategy became less effective. "As I got older, my vision got worse. The tunnel where I see kept getting smaller and smaller—people were starting to notice that things were off about me, and they didn't think it was because I was deaf."

Monica also relied on self-accommodations to try to hide her vision impairment. She recalled:

> I think I was able to disguise my need for assistance with access to text, because I was able to excel in other areas that distracted from or directly mitigated that challenge. I think I've always compensated in this way. This might sound awful, but a good example of this is how I am able to perform—or how it looks like I am able to perform—on written exams, especially in math. It may take me longer to read the text of the questions and that may be extremely difficult for me, but if I can identify what I need to do, solve the problem, or draft the response faster than the average student, the net-net of it all balances things out. So the challenges I faced with text didn't always present as clear, undeniable deficits that needed to be addressed, and I don't think these challenges were as clear or obvious to others as they may have been to me.

Upon reflection, she is perplexed by how she coped without anyone knowing or without systematic accommodations.

> I always kind of wonder, looking back on it, how I did it. Because now I wouldn't stand for some of the things I put up with or worked around when I was younger . . . But how did I get around and, in the early years of school, how did I do so without a real grasp of the fact that I even had a disability? Sure, I would sit in the front row on the rug in elementary school, but there must have been a whole system of coping mechanisms that I developed over time that I didn't even know I was using. Not knowing or fully realizing that I was different from everyone else, I didn't know any better. I was going to do what I needed to do in order to get things done. It's fascinating. It's a blessing and a curse, though. Having developed that system of coping mechanisms, whatever it was, I was able to do well enough in school to prevent anyone from asking if I needed extra help.

—■·■—

The reliance on strategies appears to largely have been beneficial to these students; however, in some instances it may have hampered their success. For Justin, his explicitly taught strategies provided a key for getting him through academically. Eric, Monica, and Erin, on the other hand, relied on strategies and self-accommodations to hide or compensate for their disabilities. Their success in self-accommodating potentially prevented them from accessing needed interventions and supports that may have proven more effective in helping their learning. For Jennifer, an overreliance on editing supports throughout her schooling prevented her from learning strategies to successfully write on her own.

One lesson in particular from my Mind, Brain, and Education master's program has been ingrained in my mind: the brain is constantly learning.[1] In the learning phase of any task, the neural pathways being used are more complex. A novice at a particular skill uses more areas of the brain, and over time, as that novice develops more expertise, the neural pathways become considerably more efficient and use less of the brain.[2] As it strives toward efficiency, the brain seeks to categorize, develop patterns, and make connections.[3]

In many cases, this process is advantageous, because after you have become an expert in something, you would not want the learned skill to require a lot of processing time. To describe the benefits of this process, one of my professors, David Rose, used the example of learning to recognize a lion. Our ancestors needed to grasp the concept that a lion is a lion whether you see it from the front, the side, or behind, and they needed to apply this skill quickly. They developed a strategy for recognizing and categorizing a lion as a lion. Whether it be looking at the fur, hearing the lion's roar, or applying some combination of factors, the strategy needed to be generalizable, efficient, and not dependent on context. Our ancestors who did not develop good or efficient strategies to rapidly generalize—for instance, always needing to see the lion's face in a particular lighting to recognize it—were likely the ones eaten by the lions.

Our brains are wired to develop and rely on strategies to accomplish tasks, and in continually using these strategies we become more efficient. In some instances the strategies can be adaptive and helpful, but in other cases, like always needing to see the lion's face, they can be harmful and maladaptive. Regardless of whether the strategies are good or bad for us, forming them is what we do, and we get better at using them.

For "typical" students, the embedded teaching and curriculum of the classroom may be sufficiently aligned with the strategies they need to become efficient at a given skill or task. However, students whose learning does not align with the specific teaching or curriculum must find different ways to achieve the particular learning objective.

For the students featured in this book, in many cases, their learning needs fell outside what was typically provided in the classroom. When they were not receiving the accommodations they needed, they took it upon themselves to, as R.J. put it, "find a way."

R.J., with a physical impairment, describes this difference concretely. When someone without his disability approaches a curb without wheelchair access, he or she may be able to simply rely on the strategy of stepping up over the curb, but R.J. needs to find a different way—locating a post or bush to assist him in getting over the curb.

In "finding a way," these students' strategies and self-accommodations evolved to become more efficient and more adaptive than maladaptive. For Erin and Monica, their initial strategies and coping mechanisms to hide their vision impairments ultimately hindered their learning. While they developed efficient strategies to hide their disabilities, to become more efficient learners they ultimately needed to seek out and use accommodations and supports.

Dyslexic students experience barriers in learning to read and need to find a different way. They can respond differently depending on the schooling environment. In unaccommodating environments, some dyslexic students might learn, "I can't do this. Reading is bad for me." In these environments, they might develop harmful strategies like Eric initially developed—early on, without an efficient strategy for reading, it was easier for him to act out than read. Some students may stop here and become very successful and efficient at getting into trouble, getting suspended, and potentially dropping out of school. Fortunately, this was not the case for Eric, and in college, he realized he needed the content from books and recognized his strength at making big-picture connections. So he self-accommodated by working with peers to discuss the readings and offering them the bigger connections. Now, his efficient path for reading (as we'll discuss more in the next chapter) requires text-to-speech technology. Unfortunately, Eric was unaware of this most efficient strategy for his own reading until he was in graduate school. Eric wanted someone to help him understand, noting that it would have been better "if somebody had explained to me why I was struggling in school . . . I mean really explained it to me." Contrast this with Justin, who initially also learned that reading was difficult, tried to avoid it, and got into trouble. But Justin's reading difficulties were caught early, and he was taught strategies to help him efficiently read. He then continually relied on these strategies and experienced success throughout his schooling. He said that the taught strategies "really helped me figure out my learning style and what I needed to do."

Recognizing these fundamental systems for learning, parents, teachers, and other professionals can explicitly teach strategies to help diverse learners become efficient "expert learners."[4] Whether the student is learning what the teacher intends is not a given, but he or she is learning something, categorizing it, developing patterns, and making connections. Rather than going through a trial-and-error process seeking efficiency on their own, students with disabilities can benefit from teachers scaffolding different strategies and self-awareness within school. Over time, for the students in this book, their disabilities forced them to develop a keen self-awareness about their own strengths and weaknesses as a survival tool. Educators can and should help students become the most efficient learners for themselves. It is critical to understand that to help students find their most efficient way, we must acknowledge and embrace that each path may be different.

IN HIS OWN WORDS

After I wrote this chapter on strategies, Tom had a student in class whose strategies were particularly well developed. Nick Hoekstra is blind, having lost his vision as a young child. We decided to include his essay in this chapter in his own words.

On Reading, Writing, and Walking Around
Nicholas Hoekstra

From a Universal Design for Learning (UDL) perspective, one of the most important processes involved in learning is metacognition: the act of thinking about the ways we ourselves learn. It is fitting, then, that Professor Hehir has asked me to contribute an essay regarding my own strategies as a blind student here on the eve of my graduation from the Harvard Graduate School of Education. Of course, these strategies are my own. There is no guarantee that any trick of mine would apply to the life and circumstances of another person. Beyond our strategies, however, beyond our successes and failures, are the attitudes with which we approach disability and our own place within the community. I want to keep this essay as truthful as possible and, at the same time, relatable to others. Therefore, I will begin with the foundation from which every successful strategy begins: our mindsets.

At the heart of every success, at the core of any person who has overcome diversity, is the mentality of someone who will not take no for an answer, a person who can decide what they want and figure out the means by which to achieve their goals. My mother has always referred to this as my "being stubborn as a mule." Coming from a Polish Midwesterner, this always felt a bit unfair to me. Bull-headedness is as much a part of our culture as long cold winters and dry senses of humor. Speaking from the viewpoint of someone with an obvious disability, however, I think it is important we have an absolute conviction that leading a normal life is natural. Studying abroad as an undergraduate or spending a couple years teaching English in a foreign country, while not commonplace, are not unusual activities for many college students. That is also the way we, as peoples with disabilities, have to view it. I reiterate: we have to believe in our own capability to lead as interesting a life in as special a place as we choose, never letting disability dictate the options before us. We will confront people who are incredulous when we decide to travel abroad or even travel across town. This is not a question of "if" but a matter of "when." That is why our convictions must be strong. Of course, once the decision has been made, it is up to us to figure out how we'll accomplish our goals.

The rest of this essay will focus on the three most important skills I have found, as a blind person, are essential for leading a successful life. These include learning to read braille, well-developed cane and mobility techniques, and a near-neurotic obsession with organization.

According to recent statistics regarding braille literacy, only around 10 percent of school-aged blind children are learning to read. This shockingly low number seems a crime, especially when one considers that visually impaired, braille-literate adults are employed at far higher rates than visually impaired, braille-illiterate adults. We justify this failing in education by turning to new technologies as acceptable alternatives for literacy. E-readers, such as Kindle and Blio, have opened up a seemingly endless library of books that were once inaccessible to the blind.[5] Audiobooks, too, have become vastly more available with the increasing popularity of the genre and of MP3 devices that are smaller and capable of holding ever-greater amounts of information. While I am an avid user of both a Windows computer and an Apple iPhone, I pose this question: should sighted children stop learning how to write because they have an iPad? Though I'm sure many children would happily agree to this, no educator in their right mind would ever support such a statement. So why does the topic change for blind children?

Braille is "our" language. Braille was the blind person's method for reading and writing well before the advent of computers and long before technology made text-to-speech possible. When the power goes out, braille will still dimple the pages of our books. Not only is it a part of our history, it is a fundamental part of our independence. This includes everything from creating cue cards for a presentation to passing notes back and forth in class. Every girlfriend I have had has learned braille; not because she needed to and not because I asked her, but because the ability to write a letter from your mind to mine is one of the most intimate forms of communication. Similarly, nothing can compare to the enjoyment gained from reading a book directly: when it is your imagination that puts voices to the character; when you can reread that interesting passage a second or third time to capture its meaning. Intimacy, imagination . . . these are features inherent to braille that an audiobook or e-reader with text-to-speech cannot readily offer.

This is so much more important for children who are developing their imaginations while learning how to read and write. Audiobooks are too much like TV for the blind; yes, the literature remains literature, but the subtlety in how words have been written and sentences constructed is lost. In a sense, the story enters the mind passively without active participation. From a purely educational standpoint, students fail to gain the reinforcement of seeing the ways words are spelled and the correct use of punctuation. I am honestly embarrassed by my own frequent errors in orthography; I know many of these mistakes stem from the fact I so rarely observe the way new words are written when listening to text read aloud.

While I no longer use braille for the majority of my academic pursuits—the turn-around time on production combined with the sheer size and weight of the thirty volumes needed to contain a textbook make it impractical—braille is still a very important part of my daily life. Open up the cupboards in my kitchen, for example, and you will find a wide array of herbs and spices in small jars. For the longest time, my friends assumed I would open each jar up individually and smell it while I was cooking. Though I would like to believe I could tell the difference between parsley, sage, rosemary, and thyme, I do not want a head cold to result in a Simon and Garfunkel interpretive cake. Instead, I have taped small braille labels to the side of each spice jar. If you open my closet, you will find a similar system in place for my clothing. Subtle knots of thread form a network of braille dots on the tags of many of my shirts and pants. Just a couple letters is all it takes to distinguish green "gn" from gray "gy" from blue "bl" or black "bk." Admittedly, until about a year ago all my clothing matched all the rest of my clothing, but strong-willed friends have imposed upon me a sense of fashion, and being able to reach in my closet and consciously choose my clothing helps me appear more professional. These strategies are about much more than convenience, they are about leading an active, professional adult life in real-world situations.

As much as braille has represented an independence of thought, my cane has represented an independence of movement. Not only a freedom to leave my house and travel to school or the store, but a freedom to leave my home country and travel around the world. This is perhaps the skill I have cherished most in my life. Having grown up in a suburb without sidewalks or a well-developed system of public transportation, I was acutely aware of my dependence on friends and family for rides. There is nothing worse than the feeling of being trapped in one's home or letting the availability of a ride dictate one's social life. This is why I believe mobility training is one of the most important skills a person with any disability can learn.

I can still remember the first time I tested my own mobility in an unfamiliar setting, without the safety net of a mobility instructor following me or friends I could call if I became lost. It was the day after I arrived to the University of Michigan in Ann Arbor. Prior to my move to Ann Arbor, I had sat down with my family and created a basic tactile map of the downtown area, replete with braille-labeled streets and felt-sticker buildings. I set as a goal the university's office of special services, studied my map to gauge an idea of how many blocks I would have to travel, and left my dorm with cane in hand.

It would be a lie if I claimed I wasn't nervous. I was terrified that first time exploring a new city on my own. The techniques my mobility instructors had taught me over the years had prepared me for this experience; however. I was taught to observe my surroundings—look for landmarks such as the materials buildings were made from; hedges, fences, and other unique or distinguishing features of a path; and the sounds and smells of the environment—and I was told to never rely on specially installed aids for the visually impaired such as beeping traffic signals or bumps on the sidewalk. These assistive features are nice, but what happens when you move to a new city where they haven't been installed? Even the act of reading a map is an important skill: researching your destination and gathering information about the route you will take are important mobility techniques students must "learn."

My mobility training focused on the correct use of my cane and on the use of my other senses for independent travel. These are hard skills I have taken with me to Chile, Spain, and Japan; not features of a particular environment but features of my ability to read an environment. This important contrast was made especially clear to me when I moved to Kitakyushu. In Japan, raised yellow lines trace their way down many city sidewalks and traffic lights often play cheerful renditions of

"Comin' Thro' the Rye" or "Auld Lang Syne." While these scaffolds for independent travel can be very useful aids, it is nearly impossible to outfit every city sidewalk with "Tenji-Blocks," as they are called. On the other hand, if every traffic light were to have a melody, the city would sound like a regular carnival. The traffic lights, at least, also imposed a particular curfew on the blind. Audible signals were shut down after 9:00 PM so as not to bother local residents. What would a visually impaired person do, then, if they found themselves on a new city street of an evening? Presumably, this just didn't happen.

This dependence upon such features was also clear in the Japanese attitude toward disability. When I arrived to my home in Kitakyushu, I was told by my employers that it would be better that I not leave my apartment alone. It was "too dangerous," they felt, despite the fact that neighborhood preschoolers were trusted to walk unaccompanied to school each morning. Again, I felt the near-claustrophobic dependence upon others for my own locomotion: a feeling that became especially poignant when I considered the fact I was missing the opportunity to experience a new culture. I ignored my employers' "advice," of course, and left my apartment whenever I chose. Thanks to my own refusal to give in, I discovered that Japan is one of the most convenient and accessible countries for the blind. It only served to demonstrate that it is often attitude that disables far more than individual difference in ability.[6]

The final strategy I have worked to develop over the years is what I like to refer to as "a near-neurotic sense of organization." Friends often express envy at my amazing memory. My "memory" is less a product of brainpower, however, and more a result of years of ingrained habits. Life as a person with a disability is, inevitably, more difficult in some specific ways. Denying this truth would be as fruitful as denying the disability itself. Yet developing strategies for organization can be one of the most effective ways to live a successful life. For example, I know it will take me longer to read a particular text for class. I cannot put things off as long as some of my sighted friends. So I begin my work early and plan ahead. Similarly, I find the task of grocery shopping to be very overwhelming. While I know I can go to the store on my own—this is something I did frequently when living in Spain—supermarkets in the U.S. are huge and daunting. Some stores will provide a staff member to accompany shoppers with disabilities if given advanced notice. Additionally, many stores offer the option to order groceries online. For my part, I prefer shopping with friends whenever possible. This means I have to plan my week according to my friends' schedules, but I have always found shopping with friends to offer added bonuses. As a blind shopper, the phrase "out of sight, out of mind" applies. There are so many products I am just unaware of. While shopping with different people at different times, however, I have experimented with new products, new brands, new fruits and vegetables.

Organization applies to more than just time, especially for the visually impaired. We do not have the luxury of being able to quickly scan through a stack of papers or spot an object we have placed out of the way on the shelf. Developing habits of organization in our environments can be hugely important in our professional as well as personal lives. I can speak from experience that a person with a disability who can demonstrate a neat and orderly organization in his work is far more impressive to a potential employer than is a person who must fumble or delay in a task. In preparation for each semester at the Harvard Graduate School, I created a series of folders where I could store notes and readings for individual classes. I adopted a similar habit for separating grade-level materials while I was teaching middle school English as well. These strategies for organizing my computer helped me bring up specific documents with just a few keystrokes: the first letter of the class, a few arrow presses to reach the correct week's folder, and then selecting the needed document.

At home, in closets and cupboards, even in my own pockets, I have habits of organization that have become so ingrained as to be second nature. My keys and ID are always in my right pocket while my cell phone is always on the left. T-shirts are typically on the right side of my closet while dress shirts are on the left, and the clothing I wore yesterday usually goes in a pile on the floor. I can quite literally get dressed and ready in the dark. Perhaps more importantly, I can have a few too many drinks with friends and still manage to put everything back in its appropriate place.

An attention to organization does not mean I am unable to deal with change. I have frequently lived with friends or roommates who did not follow my same system. I remember a teacher telling my parents soon after I lost my sight that it was important to always maintain objects in the same places. This is horrible advice. Personal organization is hugely important and a necessary skill, but asking other people to conform to one system of organization is unreasonable. My own ingrained habits help me deal with a world where things might change, but that change must be expected. My roommates have always moved things—sometimes on purpose, just to annoy me—but this is bound to happen. Raising a child in an environment that seeks to prevent such change is failing to prepare a child for life outside the home.

As we move forward into a future with powerful assistive technology, life for peoples with disabilities will only continue to improve. E-readers are opening up a new world of literature; smartphones with accessible GPS devices are opening up a new world of travel. Education will increasingly have to include training in the use of these technologies, but the basic skills must come first. Braille, mobility, even organization are fundamental for the independence of the visually impaired. Technology can only succeed when building upon these solid foundations. Similarly, these skills will be useless if we do not cultivate the right attitudes.

Whereas my mother viewed my determination to succeed in the light of a strong will, my Japanese judo instructor had a slightly different take on the matter. Nakajima Sensei is one of the world's leading advocates for inclusive martial arts. When I first told him I had lost my sight at the age of eight, he jumped out of his chair, slapped his hands down atop the desk, and shouted, "That's great!"

While I was temporarily shocked into silence, he continued, "Every person has some problem to face in their lives, but most people don't even know what that problem is. But you, you know what your problem is. You're blind! Now you've had all these years to get strong!"

I love to tell this story because it was pivotal in changing the way I think about disability. I had never let blindness prevent me from doing the things I had set my mind to. At the same time, I had never before viewed my disability as a strength in itself. As Nakajima Sensei so simply expressed, peoples with disabilities have obvious problems. These "problems," however, serve as a focus for our determination. We do not need to seek out reasons to fight or challenges to overcome. It is up to us, however, to learn those strategies that will best prepare us to go out into the world and succeed.

CHAPTER 6

"I Could Not Have Gotten Here Without Audio Text"

Thomas Hehir

The teacher in the early intervention program introduced me to my first computer, which ultimately transformed my life because it allowed me to express myself.

—DANIEL

As DISCUSSED in chapter 2, Daniel's early intervention teacher had a lasting impact on his life by introducing him to a computer, which enabled him to express himself even though his speech was extremely limited at the time. Most of the students profiled have benefited from technology, some profoundly so. Also, for many of these students innovations in technology continue to improve their ability to access high-level content at Harvard.

In addition to using a computer to express himself, Daniel eventually started using a computer to do most of his schoolwork long before that became common for his classmates. In middle school he informed his teacher that he would be using a laptop to produce his material, which was a novelty then for his teacher. It is important to note here that Daniel has become an articulate public speaker and is a sought-after presenter. Once, while Daniel was participating in a panel with MSNBC host Chris Matthews, Matthews enthused, "Talking to you is like talking to Henry Kissinger—you speak in paragraphs!" Daniel once shared with me that his verbal ability may have been enhanced by his disability. "Given my difficulties with speaking I choose my words very carefully."

For Daniel, using computers to produce written assignments, however, required him to have someone—often one of his parents—keyboard for him. His physical limitations do not allow him to use a keyboard efficiently, and voice-to-text technology has not evolved to the point where his labored speech can be recognized. At times this caused some teachers to question whether Daniel or his parents had produced the work. However, as one of his former teachers, I never had that suspicion, as his class participation was insightful and at times deeply nuanced. His understanding of course content was so deep that, as I've mentioned previously, he is the only undergraduate I have ever used as a teaching assistant.

An incident during Daniel's sophomore year demonstrated how profoundly his success was tied to technology. He asked me if I would join him in advocating for a scribe to help him complete written assignments. I was a bit taken aback, as I had assumed he had this support during his freshman year when he had taken my course, which had eight writing assignments—all of which he had submitted on time and on most of which he had earned a strong A. The disability office at Harvard College had denied him a scribe for "homework" based on an obscure U.S. Department of Education Office for Civil Rights ruling pertaining to K–12 education. I asked him how he had done his work for my class. He informed me that he dictated his papers over his cell phone to his mother and revised them using Google Docs. I was outraged that this student—whose speech, though articulate, is slow, labored, and subject to fatigue—was forced to this extreme. Daniel had written to President Faust about his situation, and she eventually intervened to provide him this necessary accommodation.

When I first met Daniel at the beginning of his stay at Harvard, I asked him if he used text-to-voice technology or screen readers. He said he did not, as he never had trouble learning to read. Another student I knew who, like Daniel, had cerebral palsy influenced my concern. This student had started using taped books in fourth grade, and ultimately progressed to screen readers primarily because he had tracking difficulties and suffered fatigue when reading. I asked Daniel if he experienced the same. He responded that he did. I asked him what he did when that occurred, and he said his parents would read the text to him. I told him that I thought that this was clearly an unworkable strategy here at Harvard, where he should expect triple the reading load of what he had in high school. At this point he started using screen readers, and he credits this technology with his being able to keep up with course work independently. His reading rate with screen readers far exceeds the rate most readers could auditorily perceive. He graduated in four years with honors.

Daniel's story is similar to several others who use technology as an important accommodation. Various technologies are critical to these students' success, but at times the institutions that serve them do not sufficiently embrace their potential.

Amy's interview was replete with references to the advantages of technologies and the struggles she experienced obtaining them. She is clearly a techie with a deep understanding of how technology can be used to enhance her life. You may recall Amy is a student who experienced deteriorating vision to the point where she had great difficulty accessing print at all. She currently uses an old technology to assist in mobility: a seeing-eye dog.

After illnesses and surgeries during her preschool years, Amy attended a Montessori school in which she was not "labeled" but received some accommodations around her vision. Amy was first provided with services as a visually impaired child when she attended public school. Her first experience with technology was a closed-circuit television in her second-grade classroom.

> This was a very, very traumatic time for me; it was the moment when I became aware that I had a disability. It was also just much more obvious in a room where everybody had to do the same thing at the same time. I had this enormous CCTV that I didn't really like much . . . It was in the classroom, and the two CCTVs and another table formed an *L*-shape that kind of locked us into a corner . . .
>
> There was a long table with the CCTVs, and then another table to form the bottom of the *L*, and there was just enough room for us to get in and out of it, but it completely cut us off from the rest of the classroom, physically. And what would happen is, on the

playground that boundary would remain, because that's what the students had learned—I wasn't one of them.

In Amy's case the early use of technology in her class turned out to be more of a barrier than an enabler. As we related in previous chapters, Amy's mom became her special education teacher, and a relationship with an adult with vision impairment through vocational rehabilitation became critical to Amy's success. Part of what this man did was help Amy figure out the technologies that enable her to access challenging curriculum. He directed Amy to "this kind of program and that laptop." He would ask her, "Oh, did you know this gadget?" She noted, "I mean, he consulted as an adaptive technology expert, and so it was great."

A simple question concerning her use of technology resulted in a sophisticated chronology of how technology had become central to her life. She went from disliking her CCTV to referring to her laptops in almost personal endearing terms.

Authors: And so [your friend] taught you a lot about technology and use of technology. That's one theme that's kind of coming across in our interview. I was wondering if you could give me a little bit of a rundown on when you started using technology to help you and how you use it today.

Amy: So, starting out, the kind of accommodations I used were usually, you know, larger lined paper or darker pens. Of course, at the Montessori there were all the manipulatives, so it was in some ways already accessible. Everything was different colors, different shapes, and different sizes. As things progressed, the school, as I said, got me a CCTV, which I hated. It gave me horrible headaches, 'cause of how I had to crane my neck. There was just no way to make it work. Also, when I was trying to read along with the class, it didn't scroll fast enough to keep up with the class without blurring, and I'd lose my place. It was just not practical. We eventually tried enlarged textbooks, but as I said, they were in black and white. They were on yellowish paper—kind of the color of this table—with what would have been black ink but was actually starting to look like tan or brown on that paper. So very low contrast and my geography book—"Look at the green section of the map." So what shade of grey are we talking about? You know? It was totally useless. They also came in three volumes and were incredibly bulky. We were trying to keep me in a normal kind of environment, so [a] normal kind of desk. And these were the full desks; they weren't the little elbow prop desks . . . So, sixth to seventh grade, the [State] School for the Blind invited me to go to Space Academy, in Huntsville, Alabama, and when I went to my ophthalmologist to have him sign the medical form and fill it out and then the waiver, he said, "You know, I signed another one of these for another Indiana student. You should meet." What? So he gave me the student's name and he and I started talking and his family was much more up on technology. He had a few cognitive impairments along with the blindness, but you wouldn't know it to meet him . . . it was basically his dad who did all the technology and scanned all the materials. They used a laptop. They used Win and Zoomtext, because it was more important for him to have mouse accessibility than menu accessibility. I think part of it may have been dyslexia, but I'm not entirely sure. So the fact that Win could space things out differently and put more contrast and just make it visually clearer was really important. They used that on a laptop, and then his father would slice up the textbooks and scan them and do all of that for him. So starting [in] seventh grade, I guess, I got my first laptop. It was paid for by the school. I think it was a very nice laptop, and, of course, had to be to run Zoomtext with speech and Openbook; they were the two programs I started with. Since Openbook was kind of the lower version—lower-vision version of Win—I started that in the seventh grade, and my mother, again, was doing the scanning on her own. I think the school also provided the scanner, just not the labor and I remember my seventh-grade geography teacher looking at me and going, "So everything's okay now, right?" I was like, "What?" She was like, "Everything's fixed?" I'm like, "Excuse me? No, it's—I'm not sighted, but now I have textbooks." Basically through sixth and seventh grade I had been going without textbooks. Materials were taught well enough in class and whatnot, at a slow enough pace in the mainstream classroom, that I was able to keep up, no problem.

But I didn't have textbooks. I was keeping up without real access to text due to intelligence. So it definitely made things different. I got a laptop in seventh grade and then it finally died—the poor little thing—I want to say my junior year of high school, or maybe my sophomore. That was . . . a great little laptop. That's when Toshibas were good . . . It was this Toshiba Tecra. It was about that thick. So, I don't know, you can eyeball that for the tape recorder. But, um, sleek, little, fast—I loved it. It had Windows 98 second edition, which I almost still to this day think is the best operating system out there . . . I didn't have Internet at home, so research was interesting. Of course, my school didn't really require me to research much. They didn't assign a whole lot of homework because they knew people wouldn't do it, even in the top classes. So at that point the school replaced it with an HP, which they had several in what they called mobile computer labs—basically a bunch of laptops that were carried around in a cart that also housed a wireless router, because it was wireless in the high school—

Authors: So that was what you got after the Toshiba?

Amy: After my Tecra died they gave me, basically, a souped-up version of that. I think they installed a little more RAM or whatnot. I don't remember the details at this point. It was terrible. It was an overpriced paperweight, poor thing. It was awful. My senior year—I want to say my senior spring—I got my college laptop from VR, which was a nice little thing. It was a Dell. Unfortunately, it died my freshman spring during finals period.

Amy's sophistication in the use of technology has served her well at Harvard.

Amy: [The Dell] went down in this fiery ball of disaster. The hard drive started clicking and then stopped recognizing as a hard drive. That was bad, but it was very nice to have it my senior spring. I just stopped using the HP altogether, and transitioned to the system that I'd gotten through VR, which was a laptop, a docking port, printer/scanner. It was a portable scanner, which back then was a big deal, and so that's what I used. At that point I transitioned from using exclusively Zoomtext and Openbook to using Zoomtext without speech and Windowize as my screen reader instead of a screen narrator. [My mentor] was one of the first people who mentioned that and, you know, really, really advocated—especially since I was losing sight—he said, you're going to need this and, you know, if you set it up this way, then as you lose sight you can just transition to technology that you already know how to use. You can start relying on Windowize more than Zoomtext, which is, in fact, what I'm doing. I still had my Openbook from high school. They, uh, didn't seem to notice when the disc went missing and nobody else used it. And I had Kurzweil 1000, which I still have. I don't tend to use either of those at this point, but I had all those.

Authors: So it's primarily Windowize that you use right now?

Amy: Yes, just Windowize.

Like Amy, Monica has difficulty accessing text due to vision impairment, but unlike Amy she can access it through enlargement of text. Even though Monica had clearly struggled with print in the early grades, it was not until fourth grade that her teachers recognized the need for accommodations and technology. "I was in fourth grade when the process began. That year, for the first time, I was the last student in my class to finish a standardized test."

Monica began to get enlarged print at this time. Then, as is the case now, though Monica could access text that had been enlarged, reading in this manner was slow and laborious. Her dad recognized the need for recorded text as well.

Though Monica began to get some recorded text and some large print, the use of these technologies was not systematic. What strikes me about Monica's interview was how much easier her education would have been if these technologies were used. As highlighted in chapter 3, so much of Monica's success appears to be due to her intellectual drive. What is also striking in her case and Amy's, but not Nick's, is that an old technology that has enabled blind people to access text for over a hundred years, braille, did not seem to be offered.

Monica: When I was in fifth grade, as the size of the print in books became smaller and we were starting to deal with a lot more content, I began to use large-print books and take out books from the library for the blind. It wasn't a systematic shift, though. My teachers didn't suddenly provide everything to me in larger print. It was much more haphazard than that.

Authors: In terms of you ultimately getting the 504 plan and your receiving books from—was it Recording for the Blind?

Monica: Well, I did get some Library of Congress recordings at that point, but there was also a great library that was just a couple of blocks from my house that had an entire large-print collection that was much larger than the typical large-print collection.

Authors: But would you ever, say, in fourth or fifth grade, get some materials that were not in large print?

Monica: Oh, yeah. All the time.

When asked whether she or her parents had a problem with the lack of accessible materials, Monica responded:

> At that time, as I was just beginning to recognize the impact of my disability on my education, I don't think so—not in so many words. I was ten years old, and so badly did not want my disability to be an issue. I don't think I would've come out and said to my parents or to my teacher, "I had a lot of trouble in class today, because I couldn't see the handout or what was written on the blackboard." That never would have come out of my mouth back then. I was embarrassed. I think I was mostly nervous that people would discover how little I was reading and think, in some way, that I wasn't working hard enough . . .
>
> And I always kind of wonder, looking back on it, how I did it. Because now I wouldn't stand for some of the things I put up with or worked around when I was younger . . .
>
> It's amazing the conversation you can have when you've actually read the book.

Reflecting on this experience, Monica laughed.

In my class Monica accesses my PowerPoint slides through a program called Collaborate, which displays them on her laptop in real time. The computer can enlarge the slides so she can read them. She also uses her laptop to enlarge course reading and all other class material, as they are all digitized on my class Web site. However, reading text is laborious for Monica, and she also uses screen readers. Once she told me that she has had to spend so much time reading for school that she rarely reads for pleasure. We have had ongoing discussions about whether she should use braille. She has considered this. I hope she does.

As we have described in previous chapters, Erin has Usher syndrome, a genetic condition that results in deafness from birth and gradual loss of vision due to retinitis pigmentosa. "My condition is called Usher syndrome, and it wasn't diagnosed until [my brother] and I were about ten years old, and [my brother] was, I think, seven. [My brother]'s vision [impairment] was more severe than mine, and it could have been also the reason why he had some difficulty in his younger years. We thought that, because—first of all, there's no cure or treatment for Usher syndrome, and there was no treatment for the visual side of things." Erin talked about how she concealed her vision limitations from others until she was twenty-five. "And we also struggled so much with trying to just have people accommodate our deafness, that we felt, what if we say—oh, I'm talking and, by the way, they can't see very well either. We thought that people wouldn't understand that."

Erin largely hid her vision impairment until she was an adult. She was able to do this due to the progressive nature of her condition. Her decision to be "closeted" may have been justified given her experience with discrimination. When Erin was an undergraduate at a large southern university, her advisor dissuaded her from seeking a career in medicine. In retrospect Erin believes that was probably inappropriate, as she thinks with technology she could have been successful. Prior to coming to Harvard, she worked as a research assistant in a large hospital.

> It was microbiology, and I wanted to be a pre-med, but after the first year, the pre-med advisor told me that a deaf person could never get a medical degree. So I'm upset, I'm hurt, and I do not want to say this is—I hope it's not the case that—but I think that

the South is a little bit behind in the technology and understanding how to incorporate students with disabilities at all levels. So I
think the ultimate feeling was, how would I be able to use a stetho-
scope? How would I be able to take a heart rate—all these different things that depend on hearing. Therefore, I shouldn't go if I
can't do that myself. It was actually my dream to be a pediatrician
my whole life, and to have that dream burst . . .

At Harvard, as Erin's vision loss became more acute, the search for
the correct accommodations and technology was somewhat experimen-
tal. As we discuss in chapter 5, Erin had developed effective strategies
around her deafness. However, those strategies relied on vision. Like
Monica, Erin could still use her vision to access text through enlargement and used the same strategies in class as Monica. At the time we
experimented with using speech-to-text during class sections and even
lectures to enable Erin to get access through her laptop by enlarging the
feed. Our efforts were met with mixed success.

Erin currently works for an international disability nonprofit in Boston, and I have remained in contact with her. She has become friends
with a deafblind student at Harvard Law School. This student has no
vision and minimal hearing in one ear. Though I have not had her in
class, I have gotten to know her as well. I recently had coffee with them.
There was no interpreter, and I had to use my very rudimentary signing
skills in augmenting my communication with Erin. However, the other
student had a keyboard with a braille display. There was no barrier to
our communicating. I was struck by how this technology enabled me to
communicate so effortlessly with the other student and how I wished
Erin had the same skill and technology.

In Erin's case as well as Monica's, their efforts to underplay and
even deny their blindness precluded opportunities for them to learn an
important old technology, braille, and new technologies that capitalize
on that ability.

■ ■ ■

For all of the students with dyslexia, technology was the means by
which they accessed challenging curricula. In Laura's case, recorded text

and ultimately text-to-speech technology were always a major part of her educational experience. (See Laura's reflection in chapter 7.) Brian and Justin used technology primarily in written production, not in accessing text.

Brian's story has similarities with Eric in that he never understood the nature of his disability until he took my course. Though Brian was served with an IEP throughout most of his K–12 education, no one had ever discussed the nature of his disability with him. Like Eric, Brian called his mother while taking my course, and she confirmed that he indeed had been diagnosed as dyslexic in elementary school. We discussed the nature of his disability in our interview.

Authors: When you read, do you read rapidly?
Brian: No. It's very slow. I'm the slowest reader in the world.
Authors: So you're the slowest reader in the world . . . How about a speller?
Brian: [Laughter] Oh, I'm terrible at spelling. I'm a terrible speller. And I was an English teacher. And, oh my God, I was terrible. My spelling and my handwriting is shit. [laughter] Well, not too bad. I really do practice my handwriting. I wonder if I'm just resistant. I'm just being resistant, maybe.

Brian recalled how technology assisted him in written production in high school. "I'd just spend a lot of time writing papers by hand. My handwriting is so bad . . . I'd get tripped up, I didn't know how to spell, it took time." He said he would spend so much of his time focusing on his handwriting or looking up words in the dictionary for spelling that he could not focus enough on the content of the writing.

It was a turning point when he was able to use a computer to complete his writing assignments. He did not have a computer at home and had to arrive at school early to use the computers there. Despite that inconvenience, Brian said being able to type on the computer and use spell check and the word processor helped things "flow easier" and "freed up my ideas."

Brian's success, like Monica's, seems to be primarily driven by his inordinate intellectual drive (see chapter 3). Neither had close-to-ideal accommodations or access to potentially helpful technology, which could have made school so much more accessible to them.

Justin, also dyslexic, came from a completely different background than Brian. Justin was supported by affluent, knowledgeable parents, and his account of his education is largely positive. For him technology played less of a role than his well-honed strategies. Yet technology was still important.

In discussing his experience in a special school after he had repeated third grade, Justin cited the importance of his having access to relatively new technology at the time, a PC with spell check. As we noted previously, Justin was an early tech user. "That was also at the very beginnings of the [personal] computer. I believe that we had one of the first Macintosh computers. So, we got to use spell check at that point." The use of this almost universally available technology continues to this day for Justin as a school principal.

Jennifer's interview reads like a chronology in the uses and advancement in technology-based accommodations. In middle school she began to access more mainstream curricula through technology. She recalled how she accessed core academic class content:

Jennifer: No round robin. You know, it was "read a chapter and answer the questions at the end"—pretty typical. Spelling has always been atrocious. So, I would write [my answer], but oftentimes I would have to dictate it to the teacher because the teacher wouldn't understand my writing.
Authors: And you were allowed to do that?
Jennifer: Yes.
Authors: So, in other words, you were allowed to use taped books in middle school?
Jennifer: Yes.

Her sophistication about technology is reflected in her assessment of the limitations of Recording for the Blind & Dyslexic taped texts as opposed to current screen-reading technology.

Authors: In your mainstream classes you used taped books?

Jennifer: Yes, I was [using them], but that was during the time where it was tapes and they read everything because it was for the blind. So, I could get through a couple of paragraphs and then there would be a chart. And the direction was to describe the chart and I would sit there for twenty minutes, so [I] ended up really having my parents read to me. Chart descriptions were good for the blind, not best for the dyslexic. So my parents read.

Authors: Were you given the texts to be read to you?

Jennifer: Yes, I was.

Authors: Did you do well in those mainstream courses?

Jennifer: Yup, straight A's.

Authors: Straight A's? With accommodations?

Jennifer: With accommodations.

Authors: With accommodations (she rose . . . her eyebrows went up. [laughter]).

Her high school use of technology was similar. In describing her accommodations, Jennifer remarked: "Extra time if I needed it. Extra time on tapes or extra time with tapes if I needed tapes. Again, technology wasn't to the point where I could really utilize it the way you can today."

Commenting on written production, Jennifer talked about how the technology she used had begun to become more universal.

Authors: When you did papers, did you do those on a computer?

Jennifer: Yes.

Authors: In high school?

Jennifer: Yup.

Authors: Was that typical for kids in your high school at this point?

Jennifer: To type papers?

Authors: Computer . . . word processing papers.

Jennifer: Yes, absolutely. They were all expected to use word processing.

Authors: They were all expected? So that was just the expectation. And when did you start using a word processor to produce written work?

Jennifer: Middle school. I was doing computer . . .

Authors: Did you feel as if that was an accommodation for your disability? Spell check and other software?

Jennifer: Yes. You got to go through and fix it all up and do that type of thing. So, I'm definitely a PC kid . . . So, I cannot spell.

Authors: You cannot spell at all?

Jennifer: Oh, it's so phonetic. So phonetic.

Authors: And so therefore, using the spell check is, in a sense, an accommodation?

Jennifer: Yup, absolutely.

Authors: And you were allowed to use a computer to take an exam in class where other kids might be doing it longhand, or allowed to use the spell check to do English assignments?

Jennifer: Yeah, I absolutely was. I'm trying to think how often I utilized that, though. I took an advanced humanities class, an AP Humanities class, and, you know, I still haven't taken the blue books due to the spelling; it wasn't because of the capabilities.

Jennifer's extensive use of technology expanded through college and graduate school. The disability support program in her college exposed her to speech-to-text technology that gave her further independence.

Jennifer: [The disability support program] got me hooked up with Dragon, so I used Dragon software. My roommate loved that because it seemed like I was talking to myself for hours. Yeah, just, I mean, they were great. But by the end, I mean, they had given me so much support and taught me so much that . . . I didn't need it so much.

Authors: Yeah, but you still use Dragon on your own then?

Jennifer: I still use Dragon on my own. I had a scanner, which is very in now. I mean, it was the beginning of scanning. So, I would scan text, put it on the screen, and then I used Dragon to read my screen, which was way advanced.

Authors: Dragon is your screen reader?

Jennifer: It was at that time. I would upload it, and I would upload it to Word, and then I used Dragon as my screen reader.

She went on to talk about how she used technology at graduate school. Her work study job in disability services expanded her technology expertise even further. "She [the disability service coordinator] gave me the opportunity to learn how to really use all of the technology and then even when I go home, I still know how to work the technology. I'm not afraid and not ashamed of my learning disability and so, when I'm in the library, I use my iPod to listen to a text. I think we're going to have a lot of people that wish they were dyslexic now because they are a little jealous of the iPod-ability."

Jennifer gave an important caution about expectations for dyslexics using screen readers.

Authors: Now when you use the screen reader, is it much faster than you speak?

Jennifer: No, it's not much faster. I would love to think it would be, but it's not. I know how fast Daniel [the same Daniel profiled in this book] listens to it because oftentimes I'll say, "Good God, that kid can read. He can just fly." So, I've asked, "Did you just understand that?" And he's said, "Uh huh." And I said, "It's not that fast for me." I'm not ashamed to say it. It's pretty much speaking and a little bit higher depending on how familiar I am with the text.

Research on dyslexia using FMRI (functional magnetic resonance imaging) technology has led researchers to conclude that dyslexia involves the language processing areas of the brain and that dyslexics process information from text much slower than nondyslexics.[1] This explains the fluency problems many of these students have even after learning how to word-attack. So it is unrealistic to expect that dyslexics will be able to read at a much higher rate even with screen readers. Jennifer and Daniel are using the same technology but for different purposes and with different results.

As we discussed in chapter 5, Eric had developed somewhat effective strategies around his dyslexia during high school. However, with the increased writing demands of higher education, those strategies proved limited. For Eric, technology became important. "My writing was problematic, and there was always some writing component which I would get back just blood red with (corrections)." He added:

Eric: I started out with a word processor. So I started college without a computer and didn't have one until I did my senior thesis in my senior year . . . I was using a word processor, but it didn't have the level of sophistication that you see in word processing programs. It was actually a word processor, rather than a PC with some word processing component. It would tell you that the word was misspelled, but it wouldn't tell you how to spell it. You would actually have to go and get the dictionary.

Authors: And was spelling a problem for you?

Eric: Yes, spelling was a terrible problem for me. So that was college.

Though he did well as an undergraduate, Eric still had lingering questions about his intellectual ability: "I think I was lucky to get into the master's program." He thinks it was his professional experiences that helped him get in. "I had done some interesting things professionally. I had started a school. A lot of people come here wanting to start a school, and I had kind of had that experience and was looking for the next thing. I'd been a teacher in a variety of different settings, and . . . I was working on early childhood [education], which was hot at the time. So I think there were a couple of things that lined up to get me in here." He added, "Then once I was here, I did a good job. And that's what helped me to get into the doctoral program."

As he has moved along in school, his strengths have become more useful:

I think as I have gotten older, the stuff that I am good at has become more valuable. Being able to make connections between ideas and to think a little bit at thirty thousand feet, they don't want to see that in high school. They certainly don't want to see it in junior high school. They want you to diagram that damn sentence. They want you to read the story and pull out those three comprehension questions. In some ways, I think they didn't like that I had ideas that I wanted to move beyond things. But as a professional, I think it helped me to move along very quickly . . . and I think it helped me here as a graduate student as well.

Eric developed a clearer understanding of himself as a dyslexic and what he needed to be successful in graduate school. "I learned after my master's here that I need to go up to the faculty at the beginning of the semester, introduce myself, explain that I am dyslexic, and explain what that means. Mostly it means that I am going to have digitized text and that if there is anything that you want us to read during class . . . if you could send that to me—even during class—I will have my computer, plug in my headphones, I can listen to it, and we will be all set." In graduate school, Eric quickly saw the benefits of technology as a means to minimize the impact of his disability. He noted, "[In college], I didn't have any of the text-to-voice, which is what I use for everything [now]. Everything is text-to-voice."

The work of a doctoral student goes beyond courses and often involves working as a research assistant. Eric had done a great deal of work in this area, as he has highly developed research skills. He sees technology as integral to his being able to do this work.

Authors: And the work that you do outside of here, like with the [research center], do you identify yourself there and get accommodations?

Eric: No, I don't. Luckily, most professional work around here tends to be electronic anyway, and so I'm able to get everything electronically and, kind of, the accommodations are built in. Actually, you know what, I take that back. I did request some software on my work computer. I went to the office manager and was clear about why I needed this software.

Authors: What software was this?

Eric: It was . . . well, there were two things that I needed. I needed a readable version of Adobe so that I could take PDF files and render it into text. I needed a text-to-voice for Windows. They bought it for me. They were like, "Sure, whatever you want." I told them that it would make me work faster. They were like, "If you'll be more efficient, go on." It was interesting I did not talk to the, kind of, head people or the chief intellectuals around there about it. I went around to the ops manager and said, "Hey, can you do this for me?"

Authors: You've mentioned technology a lot. As a dyslexic, what is the role of technology in your learning? Has it been computer-based technology?

Eric: It's hard to say because it is so much a part of the way that I've done my work, you know, over the last two or three years. I can say this: I can't imagine doing what I do—being a doctoral student and doing research and doing the level of or volume of writing that I do—without the technology. I mean, it's everything—every sort of idea that I interact with and every piece of work that I do. Certainly in the time between when I was an undergraduate and now, there's just this understanding of myself as a learner, but there's also the way that technology has advanced. The things that I use today just weren't available in the mid-90s. Had I been here when you were a student, I don't know.

Eric has collaborated with me on various program evaluation projects involving large data sets. In addition to his highly developed quantitative skills, Eric has developed some exceptionally creative ways to display data using interactive maps. He credits his dyslexia with helping him see the big picture and translating this for broad audiences of educators and parents. When we present our data, I am always impressed with how his slides so effectively communicate our findings. Referring to his methods compared to most statisticians, Eric asserted, "They [statisticians] are used to communicating with one another and love their graphs and charts. But most people need to have the data come alive for them and I think my methods work best for that." I agree. Eric, like many other dyslexics, is a big-picture thinker.

■ ■ ■

For Alex and Lisa, technology did not have a prominent place in their narratives. Both relied on interpreters to access spoken language, and they considered that the most important accommodation they received. It appears that technologies like captioning and electronic communication, once huge technological innovations for the deaf, are simply taken for granted by them—although, Lisa added, "most of the educational videos we viewed at school were not captioned, and that was very irritating to say the least." As someone in his sixties who remembers the world before these innovations, I find that so refreshing. There was, however, one exception in Alex's interview.

Authors: There is one question I didn't ask you, though: what role did technology play in your education?

Alex: My cochlear implant was a game changer for my education. Otherwise, I don't think technology played any significant role.

Authors: Because again, that is fine, but in this study technology was a pretty big factor—but the cochlear implant is technology, there's no question about that. Now if you didn't get a cochlear implant, do you think you would have ended up here?

Alex: That's a good question. I can't say. I couldn't say, really.

Authors: After you had the cochlear implant you still had interpreters, right, all the way through school?

Alex: All the way . . . Well, you have to remember I was nine when I got my cochlear implant. I didn't learn spoken English during the same "critical period of language acquisition" as other deaf kids who received their implant at a younger age, so I had to work substantially harder to master spoken English. [His younger brother received his after his first year.]

Authors: Yes. That's interesting. But sometimes some people with cochlear implants need interpreters and they don't get them. And they lose. They don't hear everything, or they don't understand everything they hear—that's probably a better way to put it.

Alex: Right.

Authors: You agree with that.

Alex: [Nods his head affirmatively.]

With few words Alex has communicated an important point about technology reinforced by others we interviewed. Technology does not exist in a vacuum, but rather is part of a broader array of supports and strategies that has enabled these students to be successful.

---■■■---

As these narratives demonstrate, technology has had a powerful impact on the education of these students. However, several of these students could have benefited from technologies that were denied them. For Eric, Monica, and Erin, the lack of access to appropriate accommodations and supports broadly, and technology specifically, was related to the failure to recognize the full impact of their disabilities when they were children. The contrast between Jennifer's and Justin's stories and between Brian's and Nicole's is striking and reflects a broader issue of access to accommodations and supports based on social class. I will elaborate further on these issues in chapter 8.

Though their social class may have influenced access to technology for these students, the increase in the availability of technology in schools and within families should lessen this discrepancy. I recently visited an urban school with strong inclusive practices, the Dr. William W. Henderson Inclusion Elementary School in Boston. Here technology greatly helps students, both with and without disabilities, access high-level content. I asked these mostly low-income students if they have access to a computer at home. One second grader corrected me, saying that yes, she had access to a "device." For her a computer is just one device she can use to access technology-based accommodations.

Yet I continue to be concerned over the failure of many schools to provide students with disabilities with the technology, both high and low, that can greatly assist them in school and ultimately in life. Too many blind children are not learning a very old technology, braille, and I continue to see students like Daniel who do not have communication devices that can open up the whole world for them.

Jennifer, Eric, and Laura (in the next chapter) recount how round-robin reading was difficult and painful for them. I recently observed an "inclusive" high school English class taught by a special education teacher and a general educator in an affluent suburb. The students in this class were students with disabilities and "regular education" students who struggled. Students read out loud in a circle, a very bad practice for dyslexics, and there was no evident use of technology. The expectation was that they would "get through" two books in the year. The students appeared disengaged and bored. This practice of pairing a general education teacher with a special education teacher and other kids who struggle appears to be quite common in some districts, and to me seems to be just another form of segregation based on low expectations—the opposite of good inclusive practice. Think about how technology could have helped these students access the wonderful world of books.

However, technology in and of itself is not a solution to the problems many students with disabilities face. Returning to our discussion of ableism, attitudinal change regarding the capability of students with disabilities seems in order here. Teachers, administrators, and parents need to begin with assumptions of capability and seek the means by which children can learn most efficiently while staying highly engaged in learning.

Beyond attitude change, many educators and parents need support in identifying which tools work best in the classroom and at home and how they can be used. My experience with Universal Design for Learning (UDL), through both implementing it in my own classroom as well as observing it in others, underscores to me the importance of supporting teachers in learning how to use these tools. Most teachers want to do right by their students, and many teachers who use these technologies report that they have made their job easier and more fulfilling.

Nick's words from the previous chapter bear repeating here:

As we move forward into a future with powerful assistive technology, life for peoples with disabilities will only continue to improve. E-readers are opening up a new world of literature; smartphones with accessible GPS devices are opening up a new world of travel. Education will increasingly have to include training in the use of these technologies, but the basic skills must come first. Braille, mobility, and even organization are fundamental for the independence of the visually impaired. Technology can only succeed when building upon these solid foundations. Similarly, these skills will be useless if we do not cultivate the right attitudes.

CHAPTER 7

"My Disability Shapes Who I Am"

Laura A. Schifter

After being diagnosed with dyslexia in first grade, I experienced the powerful effect teachers had not only on my academic success but also my self-confidence and happiness. When I had teachers who were unwilling to acknowledge my difference or, worse, lowered expectations for me, I lost confidence in my own ability to succeed and struggled with the subject. When I had teachers who accommodated my difficulties and promoted my strengths, I felt confident in my abilities as a student and was able to succeed. This support extended beyond academic accommodations to emotional support which helped me develop self-awareness about my disability and embrace that aspect of my identity.

—Excerpt from my personal statement for
admission to the Harvard doctoral program

IN WRITING my personal statement to get into the doctoral program at Harvard, I chose to openly discuss my learning disability. Over the course of my schooling, and in fact my life, my experience with dyslexia has shaped me in both obvious and subtle ways. Obviously, it caused me to have difficulties with reading and spelling, but subtly (as with other students in the book), it prompted me to develop strategies and metacognitive skills that I may not have gained otherwise. It also pushed me to embrace being different as a part of myself.

When I was four years old, I was fairly successful at reading three-letter words—*pat, hat, rat,* and so forth. Unfortunately, words got longer, and I could no longer read them. So I pretended. I would either look at pictures and make up stories from them, or I would memorize my favorite books and read aloud from memory.

My parents did not fall for my tricks and recognized that I was not reading as well as my sisters. About ten years ago, I emailed my parents asking them about their recollections of my difficulties. My dad noted, "I assumed it [my difficulty in reading] was because (a) you weren't as smart as your sisters, (b) you weren't trying as hard, or (c) we weren't spending enough time trying to teach you." Similar to Jennifer and Justin, I was fortunate to have parents who recognized something wasn't right and acted on their instincts.

When I was six, I was enrolled in a Montessori school, and my parents tried to transfer me to the feeder school of the school my sisters attended—a highly competitive school. After I was rejected from that school, one of the admissions people recommended that I be evaluated for a learning disability, and I was diagnosed with dyslexia at seven. Upon receiving this diagnosis, my parents were told by a school placement counselor that I would never get into the school my sisters attended and that they should not expect much from me academically. My mom recalled:

> When you were diagnosed my first thought was that I felt very strongly that I did not want you to feel less intelligent than your siblings. Both your father and I came from large families where one child seemed not to be as smart as the others and I had witnessed the emotional toll that took. I never doubted that you were as intelligent as Rachel and Danni because I knew you and saw you work on puzzles and play games and develop stories that were as sophisticated as your sisters, but I wanted to make certain that you felt that you were as smart as your sisters.

In retrospect, I feel fortunate to have remained in my Montessori school through third grade. In my Montessori classroom, students who would traditionally be in first through third grade were all in the same classroom. I knew I was different. I knew I wasn't reading as well as the other students in the class. I recall other students snickering when I read aloud. I remember feeling upset that I read books that were at the same level as the younger kids in the classroom rather than my friends. But being at a Montessori school, I was able to shine in math. Even though I was reading easier books, I was doing more in math. I remember working on long division when I was eight years old. The school had these massive rolls of graph paper, and I would do long division problems on the paper that were taller than the teachers. The largest one, we were able to hang from the ceiling to the floor. Because of this, I was able to maintain some confidence in myself as a student as well as an interest in learning.

After being diagnosed, I started working with a tutor, Sally. She changed my life. I remember she always welcomed me in her home with a cup of tea and an oatmeal raisin cookie (my favorite). She taught me to read mostly by playing games. She recognized that I had a very good memory, and worked with me to memorize words. After several years, I had memorized many words up through an eighth-grade vocabulary. She taught me to try and to take risks, and showed me that I could succeed. She also knew how to engage me. While reading books was very challenging for me, she saw that I enjoyed poetry. So we read children's poets, like Shel Silverstein, but also adult poets, like Maya Angelou. She liked that I was reading. It didn't matter that the format was different from traditional books, she just wanted to foster my interest in poetry and keep me reading. Like many other students featured in this book, including Alex and Daniel, I was fortunate to work with a service provider who connected with me, supported me, and challenged me.

Again, similar to many students in this book, at home my parents and my sisters went above and beyond to support me. My mother would work on my reading but also expose me to different methods for learning. She would show me videos or take me on field trips. She recalled, "I have noticed that many parents who learn that their child has problems reading try to solve the problem by making the child read tons of books. I always felt it was important for you to learn alternate solutions—visiting Monticello, [watching] video tapes, etc." In particular, I loved our visit to Monticello. It was an opportunity to spend time with my mother without my sisters, and I got to learn more about a subject I loved—the presidents. I still recall on that trip learning that Thomas Jefferson was the first American to ever eat a tomato. That summer we also visited the homes of James Madison and James Monroe. After each visit, I decided to write mini-reports on their lives for my mother to read. I then decided to write reports on other presidents as well.

My parents would also get my sisters to read aloud and tape-record books for me so I would continue to get access to books. I remember my sister Danni, in particular, spent hours recording books for me. While my friends would be proud for reading a one-hundred-page book, I was proud when I finished a twelve-tape-long book.

In third grade, I applied to the school my sisters attended, a private all-girls fourth- through twelfth-grade school known for having high standards and being a competitive environment. I was accepted, but I was on the cusp; it had helped that I had two sisters there. My family had agreed with the school that they would periodically check in on my progress to ensure I was meeting the school's high academic standards.

The school was arranged so that grades four through six were lower school, grades seven and eight were middle school, and grades nine through twelve were high school. My sisters were in middle and high school when I started. Even though they were in separate buildings, it was comforting having them there. It also helped that my family already knew many of the teachers and school leaders.

In lower school, the school did not have any official accommodations policy, but I was fortunate to have a librarian and a teacher who were willing to create informal accommodations for me. My librarian would help me find books that were appropriate for my reading level but did not appear from the outside to be that different than the books the other kids were reading. Mostly they were big books with a large font. Having these books made me feel like I wasn't so different from the other girls, who seemed to be reading hundreds of chapter books in a day.

My fifth-grade teacher noticed that my writing was essentially non-existent. In fact, when I was little I had a journal. Typically each entry consisted of two sentences—something like, "I went to the park today. It was fun." Or, "I played with Mary Kate today. It was fun." According to the journal, I had a lot of fun as a child, but I didn't offer any detail on *how* it was fun. My fifth-grade teacher noticed the same lack of detail in my classroom writing, and sat me down. She told me that she didn't care about my spelling, my handwriting, or my grammar—she just wanted to hear what I had to say. Without having to worry about making these basic mistakes, I had the opportunity to express myself. By the end of fifth grade, my stories had gone from a couple of sentences long to a couple of pages long.

Some teachers frequently relied on the "read aloud" technique for classes while I was in lower school. I'm sure many of you have experienced this as well; each student in the class reads a paragraph of the text. When teachers used this technique, I would panic. My anxiety was terrible. I would begin sweating before the first person started. I did develop a strategy to deal with the situation. I would count the number of students in front of me, count the number of paragraphs, figure out what paragraph I was supposed to read, and read it over and over again to myself. Sometimes this strategy worked, and I would read the correct paragraph. But other times, being completely oblivious to what anyone else had read, I would read the wrong paragraph—perhaps because I miscounted or because another student read two paragraphs. Of course, in these moments, I would be embarrassed for reading the wrong paragraph, but I'd be even more embarrassed when I would stumble over the paragraph that I was actually supposed to read.

■ ■ ■

Similar to Lisa's family, who all learned to sign to show acceptance of her disability, my mother decided early on that she did not want me to be ashamed of my learning disability. She frequently discussed it with me, and she even discussed it with other people. I recall her once introducing my sisters and me to another adult, and turning to me, saying, "This is Laura; she is severely dyslexic." I was mortified—why did she have to tell this person that I was different, that I was not as capable as my sisters? In retrospect, I think she was doing it to show me that she was accepting of my disability to try to help me accept it, but I was completely embarrassed at the time.

For a long time, I hid my disability from my friends. Because of my processing difficulties, I would often say things that would be off—sometimes mixing up the conversation a bit, or reading a word as a completely different word largely because I was relying on my memory to read it quickly. In those times, I remember preferring that my friends think I was a "dumb blond" rather than admit to them that I was dyslexic. In middle school, in particular, I did not want to be different. Being in middle school is hard enough, but being in middle school and being different can be even harder. Being ditsy felt okay; being disabled did not. As described in chapter 5, in middle school in particular, Eric developed the strategy of being a "badass" to control how others perceived him. To control how people perceived me, I associated with being ditzy.

In seventh grade, I had a teacher who just did not understand. For assessing our performance, she relied heavily on pop quizzes from the reading. She was unwilling to provide any accommodations for me, and I was not doing well. One day after our middle school assembly when all the students were in the hallway, she came up to me in front of my friends and said, "Laura, you are failing my class." I was completely humiliated. I went to the bathroom and burst into tears. I knew I was smart. I knew that I understood things, but at that moment I felt stupid. I had never been the best student in the class, but I had also never failed a class before. At that point, though, the failure didn't matter to me. What mattered to me was that my teacher had said that *in front of my friends.* Would they see me as stupid too? Would they see me as a failure? From then on, I was not engaged. I didn't want to do the work. I didn't pay attention in the class. I hated the class, and I hated my teacher for doing that to me.

A few months later, I was giving a tour to some sixth graders to welcome them to seventh grade, and one student asked me what I thought about this particular teacher. I often speak without thinking and I said, "Oh, she's terrible. She's a liar." That's what I thought of her. Someone in the hallway overheard and reported me to the head of the middle school. My mother and I got called in to meet with him. The head decided I needed to write and *read aloud* an apology letter to this teacher as a punishment. While what I said was wrong and inappropriate, he never considered why I might have said it. This teacher had humiliated me, and now I was even more humiliated having to read *her* an apology—not just write her one, but face her and read it aloud. She had shattered my self-esteem when she told me I was failing in front of my friends. Now, having to read this to her, I was even more vulnerable. In response to her shattering my self-esteem, I retreated and rejected everything she said. To protect myself I tried to make other people not believe her also. Ultimately, though, I was punished, and she faced no consequences.

■ ■ ■

After ninth grade, I started to learn more about dyslexia (in large part because my mother pushed me to), and to recognize my own strengths and weaknesses. One area in particular where I struggled was Spanish. I had done well in middle school Spanish because it was primarily conversational. When I reached high school that shifted, and our Spanish classes became more about reading. I would spend several hours on my Spanish homework every night. I would need to translate every word to English, write it out, and then try to read it. I had to sacrifice my other work to get my Spanish assignments finished. My mother noticed this as well, and thought it was not beneficial for my learning. She went to the school and spoke with the administrators about what she was seeing at home. They agreed to change the language requirement for me, and instead of taking two years of Spanish I was allowed to do a cultural study of Spain. In retrospect, while I know this change was necessary because I could not have kept up with my other work, I regret the fact that I never learned Spanish. I wish there could have been a way for me to continue with the language conversationally rather than tying it so closely to reading.

Similar to Amy, whose mother advocated to get her access to advanced classes, I also faced challenges in high school with school policies. Given my interest in American history, in eleventh grade I applied to take AP U.S. History. I was not accepted in the advanced class. The school administrators told my mother they were concerned I would not be able to complete the work. I did take advanced math and science classes, but I think they were concerned with the amount of reading that was required in AP U.S. History. Fortunately, I still had the AP teacher as my teacher for the regular U.S. history class, and he challenged our class. He also appreciated my interest in American history. I decided to take the AP examination anyway, and I was able to get a 4 out of 5 on the exam. Even though I was rejected for the AP class, the history department awarded me with the History Award at graduation because I had proven myself capable.

I was lucky in high school to have several supportive teachers. These teachers, like the other effective teachers described in chapter 2, provided me with access to the curriculum, challenged me, engaged my strengths, and supported my weaknesses. The aforementioned history teacher and an English teacher were both willing to meet with me before class to discuss the readings and answer questions that I had. While in some classes I would not do the assigned readings because I would not get anything from them, these meetings pushed me to do them and the conversations helped me actually learn from them.

My chemistry teacher saw my strengths in chemistry and my ability to explain complex material in different ways. She allowed me to share my own explanations of confusing topics with other students who were having difficulty. I noticed that my perspective helped those students understand chemistry, and that I enjoyed teaching them.

In high school, I developed metacognitive skills similar to the students featured in chapter 5: I learned how I learned. I learned that I really did not get much from textbooks at all. I learned that, like Eric, I could skim the readings, discuss them with my friends, and then make big-picture connections. I learned I had to attend class and pay attention. I became an efficient learner. And, as a result, I was not as stressed out as many of my friends.

By tenth grade, I had also learned to self-advocate. In my geography class, I was getting a C. I was struggling. I decided to meet with the teacher. I spoke with her about how I was having difficulty in her class, how I thought I could do better, and how she might be able to help me. Rather than blowing me off, assuming that I was just a bad or lazy student, she was fully willing to help me. She met with me frequently, and I became invested in wanting to do well in the class not just for myself but also for my teacher who had spent the time working with me.

That was when I learned that a key to my success in school was talking with my teachers. I learned that teachers appreciated that I could explain to them my own strengths and weaknesses. They also were much more willing to provide accommodations for me when I could tell them what accommodations I needed.

In eleventh grade, two of my teachers recognized my ability to address my own challenges by writing in my report card:

> Earlier in the semester when she was having difficulty with a particular course she listened to my suggestions and tried everything possible herself to work things out. She does not expect a quick fix from an adult but only seeks direction so that she can handle the issue herself.
>
> —[Advisor]

> From the first week of class, she worked consistently and energetically, and, most impressively, when her results fell short of her hopes, she resisted any temptation to whine or abandon her efforts and instead targeted her weaknesses.
>
> —[History teacher]

■ ■ ■

As mentioned earlier, my mother was always pushing me to accept my disability, and in tenth grade, she pushed me to start a club for students with learning disabilities. I didn't want to, but after a lot of nudging I agreed. We had an assembly in high school where everyone stood up and gave a brief introduction about their club. In the fall of my tenth-grade year, I still hadn't really gotten my footing yet in high school. At the assembly, I was nervous. I spoke very briefly about starting this club to help spread awareness about learning disabilities, and I gave the time for the first meeting at my house.

The day of the meeting arrived. I had plenty of food all set out on our coffee table. I had made a list and had printed pictures of famous people with learning disabilities and had them scattered throughout the room. I waited anxiously for people to come. First, ten minutes went by, then twenty, then an hour. No one showed up. I couldn't believe I had put myself out there, and had gotten this response. I remember yelling at my mother— how could she have made me do this? I felt so alone and so vulnerable, exposed to everyone at my high school for being different. I remember my mom trying to calm me down, saying, "It's okay, Tom Cruise has a learning disability." At that point, I couldn't have cared less that Tom Cruise had a learning disability. He wouldn't be there with me at school the next day.

Luckily, one of my friends, who was recently diagnosed, and a popular senior both reached out to me that night and said they were interested in joining. So in our club's first year, we had three student members, and the dean of our high school, who also had a learning disability, agreed to sponsor the club.

In that first year, we planned an assembly for the high school, and our dean spoke about her experience with a learning disability. In the second year, when I was in eleventh grade, the club had expanded and had about a dozen members. We had also decided to make the club coed with the all-boys school. For the assembly that year, I actually decided to speak to the whole high school about my own experience with dyslexia. I had written my speech and practiced repeatedly. I was terrified. I was nervous about how people would perceive me after hearing my story. I was undoubtedly shaking during the entire thing. Fortunately, over the few days after the assembly I received notes from several of the teachers and students about how they appreciated my willingness to speak.

As we described in chapter 4, many of the students featured in this book engaged in and valued extracurricular activities. I did as well, playing sports throughout my schooling. In my twelfth-grade year, our lacrosse team was doing well, and the *Washington Post* wanted to profile a member of our team. My coaches put forward my name. The article focused not just on me as an athlete, but also as a student with a learning disability.[1] At one point the article mentioned my speech:

> Until her junior year, only Schifter's close friends knew she had dyslexia. Then Schifter told the entire school about it at an assembly. Schifter felt it was important to make clear that people who have learning disabilities can learn. They just do so in a different way. "I was so terrified [before the speech]. I had it written out in big print on 50 index cards and I had it memorized," Schifter said. The speech "really took a burden off. When I was a freshman, I was really humiliated about it. In my sophomore year, I started caring less about what other people thought."

So by the time I graduated high school I was, as Tom says, an "out" dyslexic. I was out not only to my high school, but to the greater Washington, DC, area too. I felt comfortable with myself as a dyslexic. I had also become a confident self-advocate.

———■-■-■———

When I entered Amherst College, I decided to rely again on my system of talking with my teachers about the accommodations I needed. Early on in college, I had a professor who, I could tell, did not appreciate our conversation. This professor was notorious for always giving students an A–. I think after I told him I was dyslexic, he then assumed I could not do well in the class. He was not interested in providing additional supports, and for every assignment, regardless of the amount of effort I put into it, he gave me a B or a B–. Don't get me wrong, those can be very good grades, but in this class I saw my other friends, again regardless of effort, consistently get an A–.

Whether the professor did actually tie my grades to assumptions about my disability, I perceived it that way. For the rest of my college experience, I did not volunteer to have conversations with my professors about my disability. I went back "in the closet." Only at one other point did I come out. I had one class later on in which my professor requested that we write index cards to introduce ourselves to her. She then explicitly said, "Please write on the index card if you have any disabilities and need accommodations." I remember when she said that I felt such a huge sense of relief. It made me feel accepted, and it made me feel like I could express what I needed without being judged. In all my other courses, I kept the information to myself and relied on my personal strategies to help me get through. I didn't even tell my advisor, who taught two of my classes and whom I worked with extensively on my thesis. During my graduation, my mother mentioned it to him, and he was surprised I hadn't told him. He told my mother he wished he had known so he could have better supported me along the way. But I had been too afraid after my prior experience with my earlier professor.

———■-■-■———

After graduating, I started teaching first grade, and then second grade, at a private school in San Francisco. During the reading lessons, I recall feeling anxious about my ability to teach reading when I had struggled so much learning how to read. I observed the head classroom teacher intently during the reading lessons, trying to pick up every detail of what she was doing. I also learned new things about reading that I had never known before—particularly in phonics. The "Kiss the Cat" rule to describe when to use a *K* and when to use a *C* was an epiphany for me at twenty-two years old.

One of my second-grade students was diagnosed with dyslexia while I was her teacher. I remember talking with her about what it means to be dyslexic. I felt for her. I could tell that she was somewhat reassured by receiving a diagnosis and gaining an understanding of why she was having difficulties where other students were not. I was hopeful because she had supportive parents, but I was also worried about the struggles she might face embracing this aspect of herself.

As the assistant teacher, I felt much more confident in my abilities to teach math because of my own struggles with the fundamentals with reading, and as a result took on more of a leadership role with the math curriculum. In particular, I worked closely with the students who struggled in math. I knew how they felt when they were confused, but I also felt I had a solid understanding of the content and could successfully break things down for them. In my third year in San Francisco, I decided to focus solely on being a math specialist and worked exclusively with students experiencing difficulty in math.

In my second year of teaching, after seeing students struggle— some of whom were diagnosed with learning disabilities—I again decided to talk about my own experience. Working with the learning specialists at the school, I gave a presentation to parents and teachers about my experiences with dyslexia and research-based successful supports for children with learning disabilities. Several parents spoke with me afterward about having so many fears and worries about their children, but they felt reassured hearing from an adult who had "made it." My mother came up to me afterward and jokingly pointed out that I had the word *strengths* spelled incorrectly—and not only that, but spelled incorrectly three different ways—in the presentation. Spelling has never been a strength for me, but fortunately, spell check has gotten much better!

■ ■ ■

After three years, I decided to apply to the Harvard Graduate School of Education for the Mind, Brain, and Education master's program. I wanted to learn more about how students learn to be able to better support those who struggled. In order to get into the program, I needed to take the GRE. Now, if my friends wanted to take the GRE, they could sign up and take it the next week. This was not an option for me. I began my process for taking the GRE about five months before actually taking it. I, of course, needed to devote considerable time to studying for the verbal sections, but I also needed to get access to accommodations. I needed more recent documentation to prove I needed the accommodations. After finding someone to conduct the evaluation, I scheduled it for her first available weekend—about a month later. I had to spend $1,400 for the evaluation, and waited about six weeks for the write-up. Then I had to submit the documentation and wait another six weeks to confirm my eligibility. I had to do this all before actually signing up for the test. Eventually, everything was confirmed and I was able to take the assessment with accommodations. I knew I needed the accommodations, but I also worried about the stigma tied to them. Would Harvard let me in if there were an asterisk next to my score indicating that I needed accommodations? In his interviews, Eric spoke of similar concerns related to the "asterisks" and actually opted to take the standardized test without the accommodations. Even with my accommodations, my verbal score was lower than the average of students accepted at Harvard, but somehow I was accepted.

Before starting school, I was incredibly nervous. I was starting over in a new place and going back to school. How could I have gotten into Harvard? My grades at Amherst had been average. My GRE scores were high in math, but low in verbal. Who let me in? It had to be a mistake. How would I ever do well at Harvard? I had envisioned all the other students belonging at Harvard, but I wasn't so sure how I would ever be successful. I was excited to voluntarily be in school for the first time of my life, but I wasn't sure it was going to work out.

I figured since the program was geared toward diversity in learning, I was in an okay position to "come out" as dyslexic. During orientation, I set up a meeting with one of the professors from my program. The professor was one of the more prestigious ones at the school, and I remember my hands sweating before I entered his office. Having meetings with and opportunities to learn from professors like him is a primary reason why you go to Harvard. I was thinking, "Maybe if I can get him to understand, then it will be a sign that I can do well at Harvard." I was prepared with my little speech about being dyslexic, and the accommodations I usually use in class. After hearing my speech, he looked at me and said, "Okay, well, the most important thing is that you need to make sure your work is your own." I was taken aback—how could he think I wouldn't do my own work? Did he think that just because I was dyslexic I didn't produce my own work? Maybe it was a complete mistake that someone let me in. I stumbled over my response, assuring him that of course my work would be my own. I don't remember anything else we said during the conversation because my mind was racing about his assumption. Once I got out of the building after the meeting, I burst into tears, more afraid than ever that I would not be able to hack it at Harvard. I remember thinking that this was confirmation that I would not be able to do well here.

Throughout the year, I ended up developing a positive relationship with this professor, and he appreciated my interest in the material and my work ethic. I also found out (I had not known this previously) that there had been concerns prior to my coming here that students were being oversupported and their work was not entirely independent. In the moment, though, I did not know where he was coming from with his comment, and it made me fear my decision to be "out" at Harvard. Fortunately, during that year, I also met professors, like Tom Hehir, who made it very clear that I was appreciated and accepted as a dyslexic student.

■ ■ ■

Like the students featured in chapter 6, I couldn't have gotten through all my readings without the text-to-speech technology. When I got to Harvard, I learned quickly about how much technology had advanced since the days when my sister recorded books for me. I looked up "screen reader" online and was so relieved to learn that there was one built into my Mac laptop. I used, and still use, the screen reader for most readings. I also rely on it heavily when I write papers (and even emails) to catch my typos. I introduced this feature to several classmates, both with and without disabilities, and many of them continue to use it for proofreading their own work.

During the course of the year, another student asked me if I was going to apply to the doctoral program. I was surprised, and immediately said, "No, I wouldn't get into the doctoral program; I'm not that type of student." She responded by saying she was surprised because she had thought of me as being exactly that type of student. I went home and thought how incredible it would be to go from being told I couldn't get into the same school as my sisters to getting a doctorate from Harvard. I had been successful throughout the course of the year, particularly in statistics, and I actually was honored with the Intellectual Contribution/Faculty Tribute award for my program after being nominated by my classmates and voted for by the faculty. So I thought, "Why not apply?"

■ ■ ■

In taking Tom's class, I developed an interest in education policy. Having missed the deadline to apply the following year, I moved down to DC to work for Senator Dodd on the Senate Health, Education, Labor and Pensions Committee. While working, I found myself drawn to policy related to students with disabilities. With my personal experience, I felt engaged and committed to the issues.

After I finished my coursework for the doctoral program, I returned to DC to work on education and disability issues. I ended up working for Representative George Miller as an Education and Disability Advisor on the Education and Labor Committee. In my interviews, I was not concerned about coming out as being dyslexic—after all, a major component of my job was disability advocacy. However, when I started, I didn't feel comfortable asking for accommodations, specifically a screen reader. I felt I had to prove myself in the office, and I was worried that asking for a screen reader would make me vulnerable. Although I was working for George Miller, an original cosponsor of the first Individuals with Disabilities Education Act and a major disability advocate, I was still intimidated. I was anxious, feeling like I was "asking" for something. When you are starting a new job, you don't want to ask for anything from your employer. You want to show that you can handle the work—that you can make the employer's life easier, not harder. I ended up downloading a free screen reader from the Internet, but I would have likely been able to get something more efficient if I had just asked.

While working, I realized how much my dyslexia affected my lens on policy. It gave me a foundational understanding of issues for students with disabilities that was instinctual. I understood what disability groups were talking about when they were advocating for different issues. For instance, when Representative Miller requested a Government Accountability Office study on access to accommodations for students with disabilities on standardized testing for postsecondary admissions, I could relate because of my own experiences getting access to accommodations on the GRE.

I felt empowered working in DC and advocating for students with disabilities. I had a community. I had people who were in my corner. I recall feeling especially appreciative while attending the celebration of the twentieth anniversary of the passage of the Americans with Disabilities Act at the White House. I looked around and I was surrounded by people with and without disabilities who had fought to end discrimination. I was still in the beginning of my career, but other people at the celebration had been fighting for people like me for decades. It was equally humbling and comforting.

—■■■—

I feel like my story is a successful story; I had the right people in my life—my parents, many teachers, and my tutor—to support me and push me along the way. I developed strategies to support my learning. I participated in extracurriculars and stayed engaged in school. These factors are present not just in my own story, but also in the stories of the other students in this book.

Despite having this solid foundation, though, I have struggled with my identity. Dyslexia has always been a key part of my identity, but my own willingness to embrace it as such has been dependent upon how I imagine others will perceive it. On the whole, now, I feel comfortable sharing my dyslexia with people, but even with a doctorate from Harvard, I find myself nervous about saying things in certain situations for fear that people will assume things about what I can and cannot do.

I recognize that my dyslexia has shaped me, and I like the fact that I am dyslexic. One thing it has certainly taught me is that you can never truly understand what it is like to be anything other than yourself. Even though many dyslexics do, I'll never know what it is like to love the process of reading. I'll never know what it is like to be a fast reader. But I do know what it is like to see the big picture. I do know what it is like to understand the concept.

UNDERSTANDING DISABILITY AND IDENTITY

In thinking about the other students featured in this book, I don't know what it is like to be blind. I don't know what it is like to be deaf. I don't know what it is like to have cerebral palsy. What surprised me in writing this book, though, is how much the experiences of the other students we interviewed resonated with me. Regardless of the type of disability, I saw my own experiences and feelings reflected in their stories, particularly in how the students have dealt with being different. Each of the students has in some way addressed and considered how disability or being different impacted his or her identity.

Before each semester, Eric also spoke with his professors about his learning disability, and similarly felt concerned about needing to prove himself despite it. He remarked, "I feel like I've been here long enough now and done enough good work that I feel pretty comfortable as a doctoral student here at Harvard. Most of the people that I interact with now—they either know me or know somebody I've worked with. So I feel less like I have to prove myself all the time. My first and second years, when I was still meeting new people, I didn't."

Eric only recently felt comfortable identifying himself as having a disability and admitted it is still challenging. "That's been really difficult for me. I struggle with identifying as that." As with my own experience, Eric struggled with admitting to a previous employer his need for accommodations. When asked if he identified himself, he noted, "No, I don't. Luckily, most professional work around here tends to be electronic anyway."

As we discussed in chapter 6, Eric did ask an office manager for software on his computer, but he chose not to mention it to his superiors. When he was given something that was not electronic, he said, "I just had to take care of it myself. I'd scan it. I make it readable."

Jennifer sees her learning disability as being "intertwined" with and a positive aspect of her identity. She commented, "I've learned that the things you bring to the table if you do have a learning disability are different, and that can make for a much more dynamic team than when everybody learns the same way. I see things differently literally and figuratively. I solve problems differently." In fact, she thinks a learning disability "enhances what you can do."

Jennifer decided to enter special education initially to better understand herself. "At the beginning it was self-discovery. It was understanding why I was the way I was. It was taking those neuro-development classes and understanding why I learned the way I did and what does that really mean. You know, they [the teachers] would say things like, 'Learning disabilities have nothing to do with your intellectual capability,' and we finally were hearing it on an academic level."

Yet, despite the positive aspects of understanding her disability, Jennifer still struggles with how to disclose information about her disability to prospective employers.

> But I've also really struggled with, when I interview for a job, how much do you disclose? I mean, I don't ever want somebody to hire me and then have these expectations of stuff that I can't do because that doesn't seem fair, either. But at the same time, without people understanding what it means, I mean, how much do you disclose? So, I do always struggle with that. I try to figure out as I'm looking for jobs and they say "strong writing component." What does that mean? Does that mean that there could be an accommodation? Does that mean I have to learn how to? Does that mean I have to write something one time and immediately send it out? Do I have time to get things edited? I mean, how much do you say in

an interview? Do you disclose? Do you say how much? So, it's all kind of a balancing act.

In thinking about how his dyslexia affects his identity, Justin noted that he goes "back and forth a little bit." He continued, "Are people going to view you any differently if they know? . . . I mean, I definitely think it's a part of me, of who I am, and it definitely affects the way I think about how I need to structure things for myself. So, knowing that I have dyslexia it's not like I identify myself as the key characteristic, but [it] really prompts me to make certain decisions and to follow things in a certain way, that I might not otherwise do." He also noted, "the ones [people with disabilities] that have been successful that I've noticed are the ones that have really been able to internalize that having a disability is not a commentary on who they are as a person or what they are capable of, and really embracing that and going in a direction that allows one to use that disability to their advantage." As we mentioned in chapter 5, though, at the point of the interview, Justin still had not come out publicly as dyslexic at work.

Justin, Jennifer, Eric, and I have no visible attributes to our disability. We can choose to disclose or not disclose to people. And what is cross-cutting in our stories is that each of us sees it as a choice and deliberates about when to disclose or not. We each know that disclosing our disability can come with stigma and can lead people to make assumptions about our capabilities. Even as adults who have all attended Harvard and come to appreciate that our disability is a part of us, we have had anxiety about disclosing in professional settings.

— ■ ■ ■ —

Facing concerns over societal perceptions, Erin chose to keep one disability hidden until she was an adult.

I didn't deny being deaf, but it wasn't always obvious to people who were outside of my class who didn't know me. There were eight hundred students in these different levels of school and not all eight hundred other students knew that I couldn't hear, but those that had classes with me, they did know. Actually, I never told anyone about my vision impairment until I was twenty-five.

So one disability was closeted, simply because I didn't feel that society would understand. I was afraid that they would just claim that it would be more—it's hard to explain. I'm sorry, I'm deafblind . . . so I felt that I had to protect myself from extreme ignorance. And I didn't want my disabilities to be what people saw and met. I wanted them to see my ability first, and I didn't mind them knowing about the disability second to ability.

Erin described the additional pressure she felt to keep her vision impairment hidden when looking for work. "I was actually trying to find a job myself, but nobody would hire somebody who could not hear. I knew how much discrimination I faced as a deaf person, so, again, I wasn't ashamed that I couldn't see, it was just I already had so much. This combination of someone who couldn't hear—I can't imagine how much more discrimination I would have faced if I had told them of both disabilities."

Erin saw coming to Harvard as a way to combat people's stigma about her abilities. "I don't want to try to capitalize on the reputation of Harvard, but I figured that having a degree from Harvard University meant that people were going to have to see past the disability and realize that I was very, very capable. And so having a Harvard degree has helped me in a professional capacity." In fact, she has also chosen to pursue a career related to disability, and works with people with disabilities in developing countries.

Erin's personal experience with her disability has pushed her to want to advocate for people who are deafblind.

I see so much about how people who are deafblind are marginalized . . . I see a lot of nondisabled people doing the work for their disabilities, for the deafblind. I see organizations for the deafblind as they're run by people who do not have deafblindness, and it's making me realize that there's so much more that I could do as a role model. I don't know if that's the best words that I want to use here, but I'm deafblind. I'm the same as them, and I can show them what they're technically capable of if they have their rights organized, if they have the rights to an education, to healthcare, to being part of society.

Similarly, when Monica was younger, she did not want anyone to know she was different. "Well, I would never let anybody know . . . I just so badly did not want it to be an issue." Daniel, on the other hand, did not have a choice as to whether or not disclose his disability. He remarked, "I will always have to deal with it in one way or another, but if you're asking whether it alone has defined who I am, absolutely not." At the same time, Daniel noted, "I have found a voice and an area of passion because of my cerebral palsy."

Amy wishes she had the opportunity for people to see her and notice her before her disability. She commented on the visibility of her disability:

I use a dog guide. I often wear sunglasses, 'cause glare is difficult. So in many ways I have a very, very visually, you know, detectable disability. And some people do it because they want everybody to know. For me it's a practical thing, but it does also mean that everybody knows, and everybody knows it before they've ever met me, and that does change dynamics. If I had my way, that would not be the case, but I'm sorry, sun and, you know, light hurts my eyes, and the dog is the fastest way to get from point A to point B and do all the things I want to do. So, you deal. So it's this, kind of, tension between what I need and what I'm not going to let try-ing to fit in take away from me, but also trying to have people meet me and not the disability first.

She added:

People who know me a little probably know me as the Irish music fanatic, the aikido fanatic, the girl who knows way too much about whiskey and Guinness . . . the girl who speaks Japanese, the girl who speaks Irish. And I would say, you know, definitely that's more of my life. That's what I would want my life to be about. And that is what my life is about, but unfortunately because of how society and the environment is arranged, a lot more of my energy than I would like is devoted to blindness and getting people to under-stand it. You're expected to be a full-time advocate and full-time teacher/educator about your disabilities. Sometimes you just want to be a person [and] not have to do this education thing.

Michael also noted the perceptions that come along with his limp:

It's all internal; it's not external. The experiences—you see me, you see I have a limp. That limp is a signifier; it carries certain weight. But I can go anywhere I want with it. I can think about why I walk. I can think about how I walk. I can try to change the way I walk. And if I do that, then I've really changed the perception of someone and all the weight that it might carry. And because this leg has been—the condition of it has been—fluid, there have been times in my life where everything was way more pronounced. I wasn't quite hunchback, but it was worse. And I think you get a harsher experience in life the more pronounced the limp is. And that is kind of sobering. I don't know what you make of that, but I think the more pronounced the physical difference is, the more fear it will engender. Then it's . . . it takes all the more strength to realize that it's not you.

With his disability being visible, Michael does not have the choice of whether to disclose it, and in fact, struggled with how to approach the issue when online dating.

My feeling was that with online dating it was . . . such a slight thing and I consider it incidental to my being. So, I was choosing for many of those years not to disclose it. Then, one day I had dinner with a good friend of mine from [name] College, and he happened to be president of the LGBTQ whatever. I was telling him that I'm doing online dating, blah, blah, blah, and he was aghast that I did not disclose even slight CP up front and, to his mind, explain—you have to do that because it's deceptive. You must. And I would ask different people, and different friends of mine would have very different opinions on it. And then what I found when I ran back to my online profile and put something sort of delicately in there—not saying CP, but sort of saying I have a slight limp, delicately describing it—that a lot was off my chest and the dating was much easier for me because I didn't have anything looming over me. And there wasn't the possibility that a woman would think that I was intentionally deceiving her. For example, if we are eating dinner and the dinner goes well, and then I get up to walk away and she sees a limp and she would think, "Oh, what's that?" That's a total surprise. But you have to understand, in my skin, I'm not limping. I don't even think about it.

R.J. sees his disability as a "part of" himself, but not as "central" to who he is. Despite this, R.J.'s disability did influence his decision to pursue education. "I think part of that comes from my own disability as feeling like, you know, everyone should deserve an equal opportunity for education—whether you have a disability or not, whether you were born in south Orange County or South L.A. . . . I think that growing up with a disability and realizing what I've been given—the fact that I was born with a disability, but I wasn't discriminated against in the sense that I was put into special ed programs that I didn't need. So, yeah, definitely, I think it influenced that."

Lisa remarked about deafness: "I don't consider it a disability. It *is* a disability, socially speaking. But I do not think of it as a disability." She sees her deafness as being central to who she is, and in identifying with her disability she can be a part of the larger Deaf community. She is proud to call herself "a Deaf woman." Saying "Deaf" first helps her connect to Deaf culture: "If I said it in another way, I would alienate myself. If I said I am a person who is Deaf, that is more alienating because I want to be part of that group." She added, "I feel like being Deaf is primary. So the other things would be just adding on and not really—they don't really explain who I am."

From stating that disability is primary to considering it a trait, these students, myself included, have considered how disability relates to who they are. In conducting the interviews, I was surprised to hear how other students have negotiated this relationship. For many, including myself, we did not want to be perceived as different. For Lisa, however, identifying as Deaf was not being different, but rather being a part of a community.

As we indicated in previous chapters, the students reflected in this book, including me, developed self-awareness and strategies to address our weaknesses—what are commonly called *self-determination skills*. Even though we developed these mechanisms and many of us came to appreciate our disabilities, we still fear how *others* will view the disability and how they will view our abilities in light of it. These concerns seem especially true in professional situations. It is a fear of others' ableist assumptions.

On a positive note, for many of us our experiences, both positive and negative, with disability have helped shape our professional trajectory. To learn more about her own learning, Jennifer pursued a special education major. Erin now works with people with disabilities, and Daniel said CP helped him find an "area of passion." R.J.'s positive schooling experiences made him want to ensure that all students can have them. My own experiences with teachers' appreciation for my disability or lack thereof pushed me to pursue education.

In writing this book and hearing other students' stories, I have had the opportunity to reflect on my own experiences in relation to their experiences. While it has not changed my perception of my own identity, it has helped me appreciate the shared experience and community of disability. I hope that other individuals with disabilities can connect with the stories in this book as well and recognize a connection to the larger disability community. There is considerable variability in the manifestation of disability, but I now have a greater appreciation for the commonalities across the disability experience—the shared stories, shared fears, and shared goals.

CHAPTER 8

"I Thought I Knew Something About Disability"

Thomas Hehir

M<small>Y INITIAL REFLECTIONS</small> after interviewing these students and analyzing the data were to look for evidence that corresponded with my work as a researcher, consultant, and writer. I found plenty in these interviews that fit nicely into my previous work. However, as is often the case in qualitative work, the picture that emerged was more nuanced than I had anticipated.

INCLUSION?

There is much in these interviews that supports the thrust of the inclusion movement, with which I have been associated for most of my career. For most of these students, inclusion in general education classrooms was central to their success. Most explicitly acknowledged this in their interviews.

However, Justin, Nicole, Lisa, and Alex spoke mostly positively about their experience in special schools. Though for each of these students special schools served a different role, they found in these environments the acceptance and expertise that they needed at crucial times in their education career. All defended the importance of having such schools.

Martha Minow writes in *Making All the Difference* about the tension inherent in the inclusion of students with disabilities in typical schools.[1] Do we create environments where the difference of disability is the norm, such as a school for the deaf, or do we try to accommodate difference in a mainstream environment?

Writing of the Supreme Court case concerning the appropriate education of a deaf girl named Amy Rowley, Minow posits, "The choice between segregated and integrated education for a deaf child presents the dilemma of difference in stark form. In separate schooling the child may feel less different in the classroom but more different in society, while in the mainstream classroom the hearing impaired child may be treated as different from other children even while sharing education experience."[2]

Minow goes on describe the lawful choices considered by the court given IDEA's requirements for Free Appropriate Public Education (FAPE) in the least restricted environment (LRE). She asserts that the parents who wanted full-time interpreters for Amy, thereby giving her full access to communication, and the school district that offered significantly less, were arguing about what the "same treatment" meant for Amy. Minow finds this unsatisfactory because "both approaches, in different ways, single her out and assign the difference to Amy."

A "difference stance," according to Minow, would question the "existence of classroom instructional mode to be natural and necessary. Some alternatives to the status quo in the very processes of communication in the classroom would need consideration." To Minow there is no simple answer to this question, and thus she characterizes it as a dilemma.

Indeed, the dilemma of difference plays out in virtually every one of these interviews. With only a couple of exceptions, the mainstream was, at times, a difficult environment for these students. Yet it is doubtful that they would have ultimately been as successful as they are without access to high-level curricula that appears to be difficult to replicate in separate schools. For instance, though Alex and Lisa support the importance of having schools for the deaf, both described these schools as suffering from low expectations. Lisa credited her high level of writing ability to her partial integration into a Jesuit high school while she attended a school for the deaf.

So how have these students influenced my advocacy for inclusive education? On the one hand they definitely have reinforced my belief in the importance of inclusion. Yet they also reinforced my experience that changing the mainstream to better accommodate students with disabilities is difficult work. Further, these narratives support my increasing belief that it is important that alternatives are available to students and families when the mainstream fails to meet their needs. However, separate schools were never a permanent placement for any of the students profiled here. All needed access to demanding educational environments not typically found in separate schools.

The critical question that arises from these narratives is where one locates the problem of disability, in the child or in the environment—the dilemma of difference. Though there are exceptions, such as Jennifer's and Lisa's high school experiences, the "problems" arising out of these students' disabilities were in my view disproportionately centered on them. Daniel's struggles to get scribes and his early experience of not being able to color in the lines in elementary school, the early struggles of all of the dyslexic students to learn to read, the lack of communication access for the deaf students, and the lack of access to materials for the blind students are examples of inappropriately locating the "problem" of disability on the child while insufficiently addressing the need for changes in school and classroom practices. In most of these cases, at various times in their educational careers, the students had to bear the "burden" of disability more heavily than the schools. Institutional school norms were not sufficiently questioned.

ABLEISM

The inadequate responses of schools to the dilemma of difference are closely connected to ableism. As I discussed in my introduction, I have done considerable work examining ableism in education. After conducting these interviews from this obviously select sample, I was taken aback by the degree to which ableism was evident in the experience of these students. Frankly, given their intellectual gifts, I did not expect to find the level of struggle so many of these students had to endure, and I believe that ableism is at the core of many of the difficulties they experienced.

First, particularly for those with dyslexia, their inability to learn to read, write, and spell seemed to trump their overall intellectual ability in the eyes of too many educators. The initial negative judgment by teachers and administrators of the capabilities of Eric, Justin, Laura, and Jennifer was so severe that it is unlikely these students would have succeeded without their parents' intervention. (Though, as we hopefully have demonstrated in this book, their success was due to a number of other factors as well.) Brian was the only student with a learning disability in this group whose gifts were recognized early by teachers. Daniel also experienced constant questioning of his ability due to his significant physical disabilities. Amy's desire to take higher-level courses in high school was challenged by her guidance counselor even though she was a straight-A student. Erin was counseled out of a career in medicine. These examples, among many others, reinforce the view held by many of my colleagues with disabilities that the most pernicious ableist assumption is low expectations.

As I discussed in chapter 1, most of the parental behavior described in this book conforms to Asch's construct of minimizing disability impact and maximizing opportunity to participate. Most of the accounts from the students presented here indicate that their parents "got" this concept instinctively. As I wrote in *New Directions in Special Education*, this construct is a useful one to inform the important decisions that are made in IEP meetings or in constructing 504 plans, and the advocacy it promotes was clearly reinforced by these narratives.[3]

However, what is also evident in many of these narratives is that the schools' approach to disability forced these students, and at times their parents, to "deny" disability (through denial of accommodations) or overemphasize it (through the way in which schools delivered special education). Thus, my advocacy for Universal Design for Learning (UDL) was reinforced, though negatively.

UNIVERSAL DESIGN FOR LEARNING

First applied to architecture, the principle of universal design calls for designing buildings with the assumption that people with disabilities will be using them. With the legal backing of the Americans with Disabilities Act, these principles are applied increasingly to new construction and renovation of public buildings. Ramps, automatic door-opening devices, accessible toilets, and fire alarm systems with lights activated for the deaf are examples of universal design features incorporated into contemporary buildings. Other examples extend to technologies. Captioning devices are required features on all televisions, and digital text can be read from computers with screen readers. Universal design allows for access without extraordinary means and is based on the assumption that disabled people are numerous and should be able to lead regular lives.[4]

Universal design applied to the school context seeks to develop curriculum, strategies, and school administrative practices that assume that children with disabilities will be participating in all aspects of schooling. For instance, we should universally design our reading programs assuming that children with dyslexia will be in virtually every school and classroom. Given that dyslexia directly impacts learning to read, different approaches and interventions are needed to design reading and literacy programs that will be effective for these children.[5] Researchers have demonstrated that schools that design reading programs with these students in mind can have more effective reading programs for all students while preventing unnecessary referrals to special education.[6] The current efforts in schools to implement Response to Intervention (RTI) reading approaches in the primary grades is an example of universal design.

UDL is based on neuroscience that demonstrates how recognition networks, strategic networks, and affective networks influence learning. UDL has been greatly enhanced by new technologies, particularly digital text.[7] Combining these technologies with neuroscience, Rose and Meyer have developed UDL based on the following principles:

- "To support recognition learning, provide multiple, flexible, methods of presentation.
- To support strategic learning, provide flexible methods of expression and apprenticeship.
- To support affective learning, provide multiple, flexible options for engagement."[8]

The narratives of these students demonstrate the importance of these concepts in education. Most attended school before these new approaches were available, and several could have benefited from them. However, not all UDL is high tech, and there are examples in their stories where what we now regard as UDL principles were evident.

The issue of access and accommodation was a theme in several of these interviews. Amy and Monica struggled to obtain accessible materials. Erin struggled with issues of communication access. Jennifer struggled with taped books designed for the blind but not the dyslexic. The universal design principle of multiple means of presentation as well as new technologies would have helped enormously here.

Others struggled with demonstrating what they knew and were able to do. Daniel's struggle over access to competent scribes speaks to this point. Had his parents not provided this support, it is doubtful he would have been as successful. All of the dyslexics in this group panicked over being required to read out loud. Eric would act out in class rather than read out loud. Jennifer valued her placement in a special class as a buffer from that requirement in general education classes, even though she felt she was not challenged intellectually in that environment. Requirements that students be competent spellers were an issue for Justin, Brian, Jennifer, Laura, and Eric. The principle of having multiple available means of demonstrating what students know and are able to do was clearly supported here.

Considering the principle of engagement, all of these students found ways to ultimately become engaged. As we discussed in chapter 3, their engagement may have been greatly enhanced by their own intellectual drive. In some students' cases, their participation in extracurricular activities, discussed in chapter 4, gave them the extra edge they needed to keep them engaged in school. Even though most endured struggles getting the accommodations and supports they needed, ultimately engagement through multiple means benefited these students.

SPECIAL EDUCATION

A variation of the dilemma of difference has been the longstanding debate in disability literature between the social construction of disability and the medical model. As previously discussed, the question of where you situate the "problem" of disability has been argued for years. Some seek to emphasize the social construction of disability. This view posits that disability is "created" by the demands of the environment in which diverse people must perform. The work of Nora Croce concerning deaf residents in Martha's Vineyard during the 1800s is used as an example of how social constructs can impact disability. Her research focused on the fact that a relatively large number of deaf residents on the island resulted in many hearing people learning sign language. Thus, deafness was not a "disability" on the island.[9]

The social construction critique of special education is longstanding and continues. Noteworthy among writers in this vein are Alan Gartner, Dorothy Lipsky, and Thomas Skrtic.[10] Not only is the impact of disability lessened in more accommodating environments, these authors also allege that special education and disability identification is often used as a vehicle by which schools avoid accountability for effectively educating all children. The historic significant overplacement of minorities in special education is used as evidence to support this contention. This view receives further support in a study I recently conducted in Massachusetts in which I determined that the odds ratio for being placed in special education is approximately 2 for students on free and reduced lunch compared to those who are more affluent.[11] This finding was independent of race, with low-income white students being placed in special education at comparable rates to nonwhite students. Further, lack of English language proficiency seems to be a significant factor in special education placement for Spanish speakers in San Diego, Houston, and Massachusetts.[12] These researchers question whether disability identification is masking other problems in education and is thus a social construct.

The other perspective in this debate, often framed as the "medical model," views disability as residing in the child. This model frequently advocates for the need for special education interventions and programs to ameliorate disability "conditions." Inclusion activists see this as promoting segregation and often decry this model.

I feel the debate over social construction versus the medical model is ultimately unproductive. There are important perspectives and approaches, as well as limitations, in each model.

The social construction critique has done much to promote inclusion, universal design, and the unconditional acceptance of people with disabilities. Clearly students in this study have benefited enormously when they were in accommodating environments. Digitized text capable of using screen readers, interpreters, extra time on exams, spell check, text-to-speech technology, and power wheelchairs are all examples of innovations that situated the "problem" of disability in the environment, thus enabling these students to access education and lead more productive and satisfying lives.

However, the nature of most of these students' disabilities required that they receive interventions and services not generally provided to other students. They had differences within them that mattered. Merely situating the issues arising from their disabilities in the environment (social construction) would have been insufficient. Most, but not all, needed special education interventions to provide them with the skills and confidence they needed to perform in the mainstream.

The way in which schools met these needs for these students was decidedly mixed. Some students received excellent specialized services from their school districts and thrived. Others did not, and for still others the picture was mixed.

Eric's and Nicole's parents' rejection of the special class options for their children forced them into a Hobson's choice that imperiled their children's education. The special class option offered to them seemed worse than doing nothing at all. Both Eric and Nicole suffered from a lack of appropriate special education options. They needed an option that took into account their learning differences due to dyslexia but did not overaccentuate that difference through inordinate segregation.

Justin's experience with dyslexia was very different. After early struggles in the primary grades, his placement in a special school for a couple of years not only taught him to read but also gave him valuable strategies to deal with his dyslexia, including a positive attitude toward learning. Lisa's movement between special schools and the mainstream had a similar impact. Brian's special education teachers not only helped him learn to read but also gave him the self-confidence to go on to graduate in the top 10 percent of his class. Jennifer's high school special education teacher had the wisdom to recognize that Jennifer no longer needed special education interventions but could do well receiving appropriate accommodations in the mainstream that the teacher ensured were provided. Jennifer also achieved valedictory status.

I believe the stories of these students' education do not resolve ideological debates around models of disability or even inclusion, but rather call for thoughtful individual decision making in which both interventions and school accommodations are central. I have previously written that IEP meetings should focus on two overriding questions. *What, if any, interventions are needed to minimize the negative impact of this child's disability? What accommodations, modifications, and strategies are needed to ensure that this child will be able to access the curriculum?* The stories here reinforce that view. Those students whose education seemed to embody these principles have done the best here.

In addition to the students interviewed, I have more recently encountered some students whose stories reinforce this point as well. Nick, from chapter 5, is a blind student who lost his vision in the primary grades due to brain cancer. After his vision loss he was put in a special program for blind children in a mainstream school that taught him braille and orientation and mobility. He was subsequently fully included—with continuing orientation and mobility training, and the provision of braille and recorded text, among other accommodations. He has since been a successful teacher in Japan.

I asked Nick recently if he would mind demonstrating to my class how he used his technology. He demonstrated how he uses a software program called JAWS specifically designed to give blind people access to technology and to help them organize material. He also demonstrated how he used apps on his iPhone to access email and GPS for mobility. I asked him about his use of braille. He responded that braille was too slow for him to keep up with the volume of reading at Harvard, whereas his screen reader's pace is quite rapid. However, he said he uses braille for pleasure reading. "Reading braille is real reading for me! I'm not listening to another's voice but creating the words and images for myself." The joy that was evident in his voice as he described reading for pleasure through braille rivaled my own joy in reading.

Another student I recently met, a Harvard Law School graduate mentioned in chapter 6, is deaf and blind. I had no difficulty having a conversation with her as she handed me a keyboard in which I typed while her device read my words back to her with a braille relief on her computer. Contrast Nick's and this student's experience with those of Erin and Monica. The latter two vision-impaired students didn't learn braille, and I believe they should have. Monica's statement that she never read a book for pleasure due to her struggles seeing print struck me as profoundly sad.

Shouldn't all children learn the great pleasure that can be derived from reading, whether they are blind, deaf, or dyslexic? Nicole's love of reading, though she is dyslexic, came through in her interview, and I frequently ask Eric, an avid reader through text-to-voice technology, for book recommendations. Lisa is an English teacher. The point is that disability should not be an impediment to reading. However, some children with a disability will have to learn to read in a manner that might be different from their nondisabled peers, and they may need specialized interventions to do so.

Special education played an important and mostly positive role in the education of most of these students. At its best, special education provided students with targeted instruction that gave them skills and strategies to minimize the negative impact of their disability. However, none of these students attributes his or her success solely to special education. All had access to education in the mainstream as well. These stories thus reinforce the need to recognize that disability does not reside solely in the environment or within the individual. Yes, dyslexia, blindness, deafness, and physical and other disabilities are differences within people that matter and often require specialized interventions. However, it is also true that the success of these students was greatly enhanced in environments in which disability accommodations and universal design vastly decreased or eliminated the negative impact of their disability.

THE IMPORTANCE OF EARLY IDENTIFICATION AND INTERVENTION

Another insight that I derived from these narratives was the importance of early identification. Some of these students' disabilities were obvious in the first years of life. All of these students appeared to have benefited from early intervention services. Erin, Alex, and Lisa clearly benefited from the early language development afforded them because their parents learned to sign. Alex and Lisa also benefited from preschool programs designed for deaf children that emphasized the development of manual language. Daniel talks of how beneficial preschool was for him and how his teacher recognized his intellectual gifts before he could speak. Clearly, Daniel also benefited from intensive, early, and ongoing speech therapy. Monica benefited from a Montessori program accommodated for visually impaired students, and her mother's early recognition of her eye cancer may have saved her life. As a veteran special educator I left these interviews with a greater appreciation for the emphasis my field has had on developing systems of early intervention and preschool options for children with disabilities. It is heartening to see how early education is becoming a major policy issue for other children as well.

However, for the students with less obvious disabilities, particularly the students with dyslexia, their early experiences in school were largely negative. Justin, Nicole, Eric, Brian, Jennifer, and Laura all had negative experiences in early elementary school over their struggles to learn to read. I am generally struck by how poorly schools dealt with this common disability. Jennifer, Laura, and Nicole all had their intellectual ability called into question. Eric acted out when asked to read out loud and was labeled a discipline problem. Even Justin, whose mother, as a school psychologist, recognized his dyslexia before kindergarten and sent him to private schools, was kept back as he failed to learn to read in the primary grades.

Though it is clear that some of the students with obvious disabilities identifiable early in life benefited from early intervention and preschool, the question arises whether students with less obvious disabilities such as dyslexia would benefit from earlier intervention. Traditional approaches have often involved waiting to see if the child truly has a disability after he has received instruction in the primary grades. Advocates of this approach cite the difficulty in identifying some disabilities early in life without seeing how a child responds to instruction. The issue of disability stigma is often cited as a reason not to identify children early.

Increasingly, educators and researchers have recognized that not intervening early when children experience difficulty with reading or behavior may exacerbate the impact of children's disabilities.[13] However, identifying children as disabled based on soft signs of reading and/or behavioral difficulties may lead to overidentification.

The dyslexic students profiled here provide an interesting window through which to view this issue. All experienced significant early reading difficulty in school that could have easily prevented them from ever being successful students. As Laura's, Jennifer's, Nicole's, Eric's, and Justin's stories demonstrate, failure to learn to read can be educationally catastrophic if not handled well. As we have recounted already, the ultimate success of these students was due to a number of countervailing forces, such as parental involvement, extracurricular activities, and their own intellectualism. Some eventually got what they needed from the school system or their parents purchased services for them. What is striking, however, is how difficult their first years of schooling were and how tenuous their ultimate success in school appears to have been.

Would earlier identification and intervention have changed these stories? Possibly. Laura, Justin, and Jennifer were identified early. However, in Laura's and Jennifer's cases, the identification of disability resulted in markedly lower expectations for school and life. Had their parents not countered that expectation, it is doubtful Laura and Jennifer would have been successful. Even Justin, identified by his mom prior to first grade, experienced a good deal of failure before his needs were met.

Brian, Eric, and Nicole experienced early failure in school. All had negative behavioral and/or emotional reactions to their failure to perform in school in the early grades. For all of the dyslexics interviewed for this book, the emotional toll of early failure in school seemed fresh, provoking expressions of anger and even tears.

Should we seek to identify these students with less obvious disabilities earlier and intervene? Of course, the narratives of these students should not totally inform the answer to this question. Much research has been done on this issue, and in general this research leads me to conclude that ignoring early reading and behavioral difficulties in young children is not a good practice.[14] However, identifying these children as disabled without the benefit of intervention may also be a questionable practice. These stories support Response to Intervention (RTI) approaches for addressing the needs of young children experiencing early learning and behavioral difficulties. Basically, these approaches call for interventions and accommodations in general education when these problems are evident, and disability identification occurs only when these efforts have been unsuccessful. The narratives presented here broadly support that approach.

However, though these newer approaches may be promising and in retrospect may have alleviated some of the problems these students experienced as young children, what is striking about these students' stories is how much context matters. Unfortunately, identifying a child as having a disability is not a neutral act. As these narratives show, disability almost always carries with it some negative connotations that at times limit rather than expand opportunities. And, as Laura's reflections on disability and identity demonstrate, the struggle concerning others' perceptions if these students disclose their disability is a delicate dance.

On the other hand, one of the factors central to the success of these students was developing a metacognitive understanding of their disability—that is, having a deep grasp of their disability and the strategies they needed to succeed.

These narratives thus support the importance of children and families having an understanding of the children's disabilities as early as possible. However, the identification process should lead to greater opportunity for the children and actively counter the negative assumptions so often associated with disabilities. The success of the students profiled here provides a basis for that counternarrative.

As to the question of intervention, these stories are mixed as well. There were clearly interventions some of these students experienced that minimized the negative impact of their disability, such as Alex's speech therapy or Nick's braille instruction. However, Nicole's and Eric's parents' resistance to special class placement in retrospect may have been wise. Again, context matters. Thus, disability identification should ideally be coupled with interventions that are designed to minimize the negative impact of disability and increase access to high-quality instruction. However, the label of disability still carries with it the risk of negative assumptions and discrimination.

THE POLICY PROBLEM

My background as a policy maker, as well as my experience conducting these interviews and teaching these and other students with disabilities over the past thirteen years, has provided me with a reality check on both the power and limits of policy. As the former director of the Office of Special Education Programs (OSEP)—the position with statutory responsibility over IDEA—I am well aware of the federal policy environment supporting special education.

For decades advocates have looked to the federal government to provide access to effective education for students with disabilities. In response to widespread exclusion of students with disabilities from school and spurred by exposés of state institutions, Congress passed Section 504 and PL-94-142 (now IDEA) in the mid-1970s. These laws sought to provide access to those previously excluded, and to provide appropriate education to those already enrolled whose needs were not being met. Broadly speaking, Congress relied on two policy mechanisms to achieve this result: regulatory requirements ensuring FAPE in the LRE backed by strong parental rights, and funding discretionary programs in research, technical assistance, technology development, and parent education. IDEA has also funded early intervention and preschool programs for over two decades.

From my perspective this strategy has been partially successful. Educational exclusion based on disability is virtually nonexistent, and successful approaches for educating many students with disabilities have been developed through the discretionary programs. Studies show increasing educational attainment levels for most students with disabilities. Yet many students with disabilities still do not finish high school, and large numbers face unemployment upon leaving school.[15] Further, special education continues to enroll disproportionately large numbers of African Americans and English language learners, and those students are more apt to be educated in segregated settings.[16]

How does this study inform my views of policy? First, given the complex stories behind these students' success and the degree to which that success is dependent on a myriad of forces from personal drive to parental intervention, it might be tempting to interpret these stories as supporting the view that regulations are not important. I do not.

Though in most cases it is difficult or even impossible to infer causation concerning policy—that is, that policies such as special education regulations cause a result—I came away from these stories with an appreciation for the importance of having strong federal policies that safeguard the rights of children with disabilities. Two of the students, Jennifer and Lisa, spoke specifically about how their parents used due process protections in IDEA to secure better treatment for them. It is doubtful that Daniel's parents' insistence on inclusion for their multiply disabled son would have been as effective without the standing these protections provided them with their large urban school district. And, as a student at Harvard, Daniel used a 504 complaint to leverage appropriate accommodations, having learned important lessons from his parents. It is doubtful that Brian's impoverished inner-city schools would have hired the special education teachers that he needed without the force of law, or that Nicole's district would have voluntarily funded the expensive residential placement so central to her success. In these stories I see the direct impact of the law.

Even for the five students in this sample who were not on an IEP for a good deal of their education, there is evidence that IDEA, Section 504, and possibly the ADA had an influence on their education. Though the impact of laws on culture is a source of much scholarly debate and not the subject of this book, the existence of laws seeking the inclusion of people with disabilities in all aspects of American life may have had an indirect influence on their parents, their service providers, and their schools. The public narrative about disability during these students' lifetime is significantly different from that of previous generations. The culture that gave rise to institutionalization and shame associated with disability has been replaced by one in which the accomplishments of people with disabilities are celebrated regularly in the media. I believe strong disability laws support that change and, in this area, policy has led practice. Long before we knew how to include students with significant disabilities in the mainstream, special education law encouraged it through its LRE provisions. From my perspective, this dynamic tension between law, culture, and practice provided an important foundation on which many of these students' successes depended.

The discretionary programs funded under IDEA and other disability programs may have had an indirect influence on their success. Our current understanding of dyslexia—that this disability is not associated with overall intelligence—has been greatly enhanced by federal research. Further, many of the accommodations these students have used, such as voice-to-text technology or speech-to-text, have been supported by federal research.

It appears that for all of these students federal policy has been influential, either directly (such as parents using due process mechanisms) or indirectly (such as students having access to technology). So has my experience interviewing and getting to know these students reinforced the status quo of disability policy? Not entirely. First, it would be entirely inappropriate to let the experience of this highly select group of students have inordinate sway over anyone's policy beliefs. However, if one believes as I do—that far too few students with disabilities reach high levels of academic performance—these stories, along with other more quantifiable evidence, clearly have policy value.

First, as previously mentioned, strong civil rights protections embedded in disability law were used by some of these parents to secure access and services for their children. Therefore, in my view, those protections should not be weakened. However, it is important to note that this sample was overwhelmingly from the middle and upper classes. The use of parental advocacy mechanisms was evident in most of these interviews, with three families choosing to purchase their child's education through private schooling. The three students in the sample who came from lower-middle-class to poor families appeared to have no such leverage.

I have done other work that informs my view on parental advocacy.[17] This work shows markedly different treatment patterns for students with disabilities from low-income backgrounds compared to those for higher-income groups. Low-income students are much more apt to be in segregated classrooms, and these placements are associated with much lower academic performance than inclusive settings, even when controlled for a myriad of factors including race and poverty. Low-income students have less access to the kinds of out-of-district special schools that appeared to have a positive impact for three of the students in this group.

One of the things that impressed me about most of these interviews was how difficult it was for many of these students to secure appropriate education even with their parents' significant social capital. Though I hope things have changed since most of these students entered school twenty or so years ago, I was struck by how rigid and nonaccommodating many of the schools these children attended were. Indeed, there are schools and districts where great progress has occurred.[18] However, there are many places where children and parents struggle to get what the children need. These students' success, as we have pointed out, was so often dependent upon exceptional parental advocacy, superb individual teachers and service providers, and the extraordinary innate gifts these students possessed. In short, most of these students' success was fragile and could have easily been thwarted. The "system" by and large did not nurture these students' gifts. The need, therefore, for a countervailing force in the form of legal protection and effective advocacy was critical in many of these cases, and these mechanisms should be available to all parents. I have advocated for parents of low-income children to have free legal representation as a strategy to overcome this inequity. These narratives reinforce and strengthen that view.[19]

One area that I think needs increased attention in law has to do with technology and accommodations. As we have noted, many of these students have greatly benefited from the technology revolution. Technology has become a critical means by which many of these students access education, particularly the large amount of academic work they have to do at a school like Harvard. It is central to all aspects of their lives.

Yet I am concerned that the education system is often stuck in a predigital world, particularly as it involves testing. For instance, all but one of the dyslexics and blind students in this sample, as well as Daniel, who has significant cerebral palsy, rely on text-to-voice technology to complete the large volume of reading required of them. All of these students can read print; it's just not an efficient means for them to interact with text. However, most states prohibit or severely restrict the use of this modality in statewide tests. This needs to change. Prohibiting the use of these technologies for these and similar students will not only artificially depress their scores but will also have a chilling effect on the use of these technologies in instruction. Ironically, the goal of standards-based reform—improving academic performance for all students—will be thwarted. The federal government should intervene here by establishing national accessibility standards for testing.

Finally, these narratives reinforce my belief in the discretionary programs funded under IDEA and other federal disability programs. As one who has been involved with special education for forty years, I am heartened to see how much more we know about how to effectively educate students with disabilities than we did when I was a young teacher. The fact that students with significant disabilities are enrolling at Harvard and other colleges and universities is testimony to this progress. For many of these students, technologies and approaches facilitated through federal research indirectly have supported them. However, these programs have been underfunded for years.

The amount of federal resources devoted to these activities has actually decreased in real dollars from the time I left OSEP in 1999. Though Congress has increased its funding for state grants to support special education, discretionary programs have not been a priority. I think this is shortsighted. Simply funding special education, without seeking to innovate practice, runs the risk of reinforcing a status quo that is not working for large numbers of students. Wouldn't it be wiser to take some of this money to help replicate the successful practices most of these students experienced?

TEACHER, TEACH THYSELF

One unexpected outcome of conducting these interviews was the impact it had on me as a teacher. As I stated earlier, I had all these students in class and I advised several as well. I thought I knew them well. I did not. The experience of interviewing these students had a profound impact on me as a teacher. Hearing about their struggles, triumphs, insights, and dreams gave me a deeper appreciation for these students, who largely excelled in my classes, which range from forty to a hundred students. More than that, they helped me improve my practice. Reflecting my Catholic background I tend to be hard on myself, always questioning,

"What I have done or failed to do?" These interviews fed right into that proclivity.

One issue that came up in several interviews was the anxiety that several of the students experienced. In retrospect, this is something that should be expected, given how many felt their success was tenuous. As a general rule, teachers should avoid situations that might provoke intense anxiety in their students. Anxiety activates the amygdala—the part of the brain associated with the "flight or fight" response—and learning does not take place when it is active. These interviews sensitized me to the high level of anxiety some of these students experienced and of which I was largely unaware until after I had them in class. One student spoke about how each of my writing assignments was an occasion of significant anxiety to her, which was greatly alleviated by support from her husband. Another talked about the elaborate strategies she employed to control her anxiety while writing her dissertation. After these interviews I thought how I wished I had known that when I had them as students. I could have alleviated that unnecessary stress through mutually agreed-upon strategies. However, anxiety is often stigmatized and the students felt reluctant to bring it up.

One of the blind students reminded me of how inaccessible Power-Point slides can be: "You know, Tom, like most instructors you occasionally point to a slide. What good is that for me?" A conversation with Erin, who is deaf and was losing vision when I had her in class, was particularly informative. We had a meeting in my office without the benefit of an interpreter. I tried using my limited signing ability to communicate with her. Though she is a very competent lip reader, this was becoming more difficult due to her vision loss. She suggested we try Dragon speech-to-text on my computer, as she could enlarge text. We conducted the rest of the meeting in this manner to her satisfaction, and we began to use that accommodation in class with some success.

The important lesson that Erin taught me was to have in-depth discussions with students about their disabilities and how they most efficiently learn *before* you have them in class. Typically, professors get notified by disability services about accommodations students may need. These usually involve checklists that verify the need for various standard accommodations, like extra time or note takers. These only go so far and don't account for subtle issues that have an impact on success. Using Erin's lesson, I now ask students who need accommodations to meet with me early in the semester. These meetings have been very beneficial.

This past year I had a deaf student in class who was an excellent lip reader and used the CART (Communication Access Real-Time Translation) service on her laptop. She does not know ASL, and therefore interpreters would be of no use. In my conversation with her, she told me that class was going well for her except for one problem. My classes are very interactive and she was having trouble locating responding students so she could read their lips. This is a function interpreters usually provide for deaf students—pointing to responders in class. I told her I could do that easily. This also became an opportunity for me to demonstrate inclusive practice to my students, as I had to explain to them why I was pointing at them as I called out their name. In a similar vein, I now read every PowerPoint slide verbatim and describe visual elements to my students to provide access to blind students. Again, this might seem a bit unnatural to sighted students, so I am clear to all that this is a disability accommodation that hopefully they, too, will employ when they teach. As both of these examples illustrate, it is important to be explicit about some accommodations. I am trying to establish an atmosphere where disability is natural.

Other accommodations that I have employed are private in nature. One student, a stutterer, met with me about how she would like to participate in class. She asked that I never cold-call, as she wanted to be able to anticipate her responses. We agreed that we would have a brief conversation before class about her participation based on her weekly online posts. Another student confided in me that she was undergoing severe anxiety that had resulted in a total writing block. She was a brilliant student who made outstanding contributions in class. We developed a weekly strategy where she would meet with me or one of my teaching assistants as we moved from outlines to taped papers and eventually to typed papers that were of the highest quality.

Finally, these interviews and my subsequent meetings with students with disabilities have affirmed my commitment to UDL. It is impossible for any teacher to keep the needs of all his students in mind. By employing multiple means of presentation, engagement, and expression, I think

I am better able to meet the needs of my very diverse students. Thankfully, several acknowledged that in their interviews.

I am sure there are many ways in which my teaching can be improved further. I think that is the nature of teaching. Still, having these individual meetings with students with disabilities, I believe, has enhanced my teaching and at a minimum assuaged my Catholic guilt.

ATTITUDES TRUMP ALL

IEP meetings frequently start out with the question, "What is wrong with this student?" As we have emphasized, societal attitudes about disability are largely negative and at times discriminatory and oppressive. Ableism is pervasive and evident in these narratives. Virtually none of these students escaped its impact.

Clearly the students profiled here have a good deal right about them. Several discuss their disabilities in positive terms and attribute some of their success to their disabilities. However, as Laura relates in chapter 7, no matter how they have experienced their disability, it is part of who they are but does not fully define them.

For too many of these students, however, disability defined them in the eyes of others in ways that were pernicious and limiting. Fortunately, the counternarrative is also evident here, in which parents "got" their children's disability and some teachers and service providers saw their potential. It is so clear how important attitudes are.

Discussions among educators here in the United States concerning students with disabilities often center on the high cost of special education. Sometimes special education is expensive, and certainly some of the students in this sample had expensive services. However, the relative availability of special education services was a minor theme in these narratives; attitudes others had about their disabilities dominated most of the interviews. Simple accommodations and access issues were frequent themes in these interviews. The fact that students struggled to get relatively low- or no-cost services speaks to the broader issue of how others viewed them and their right to equitable treatment. However, the struggle to allow Amy to take advanced courses, or Daniel to color outside the lines, or Erin to have interpreters rather than go to a residential school, or Jennifer to not have to read out loud in class are examples of practices that were more influenced by attitudes than cost.

I am convinced that we have enough resources in the special education system for students as well. However, those resources are often used to separate students rather than provide them with access. We still segregate large numbers of students in this country. Though some students may need these types of placements at times, the number of students served outside the mainstream is far greater than it should be. Further, we engage in other expensive practices that separate students from their peers, such as providing large numbers of students one-on-one paraprofessionals. In too many places, schools and school systems seem more than willing to spend resources to segregate kids rather than fundamentally change.

In a recent study I conducted for Massachusetts on out-of-district placements, we found that 6 percent of students with disabilities were placed out of their districts in mostly segregated out-of-district placements.[20] Part of this study involved qualitative interviews with parents and providers. Several parents told us that although they wanted their sons and daughters included in their local schools, they were told that their school did not serve students with their child's disability and that their child would have to be placed out-of-district. One had a kindergartener with Down syndrome and another a preschooler with cerebral palsy. Both described their child as well behaved and making great strides developmentally. In looking at individual communities in the state, we found great variability in student placement, with some communities sending out large numbers of students and others being very inclusive. The parents we interviewed for this study, like the students interviewed for this book, focused on battles around attitudes.

So what can be done about attitudes? Most research demonstrates that attitudes change slowly, and though many of these students struggled, the fact that they made it to Harvard speaks to a change in attitudes. Indeed, narratives of the few students with disabilities who attended Harvard a generation before them indicate much progress in recent years. Michael Stein, a current law professor at Harvard, attended the law school as a student in the 1980s and has written about his struggles getting into selective higher education schools as a person with physical disabilities. Virtually all schools rejected him after his high school guidance counselor deemed him inappropriate for college simply because of his physical disability. He eventually went to college and attended Harvard Law. Yet even though Section 504 should have required accommodations, he struggled with simple architectural access. Contrast this with Daniel's experience at the Harvard Graduate School of Education, where Dean McCartney constructed a new crossing and improved ramp and asked Daniel to do the ribbon cutting. These narratives, though frequently focusing on struggles, also demonstrate that attitudes are changing.

More can be done at Harvard and within society to change attitudes. As I have also stated, enforcing existing laws and giving parents and people with disabilities more leverage to change institutional practices could go a long way. However, as other struggles concerning civil rights have demonstrated, this can only go so far.

Ensuring that all children have opportunities to learn and play together will promote a more fundamental change in attitudes. This is yet another reason that inclusion is important. However, simply educating students together will not be sufficient to change attitudes and eliminate ableism. Students with disabilities need to have opportunities to demonstrate their capabilities to their peers as well as opportunities to interact outside of schools in natural ways. Daniel spoke of a class trip to Disney World as a highlight in his life. His friends provided him with the supports he needed to fully participate in this event. This trip, taken for granted by his nondisabled classmates, represented a major milestone of acceptance and inclusion in Daniel's life and served as a basis for enduring friendship. I am sure the other students who participated with Daniel were changed by the event as well. These opportunities are the basis for a fundamental attitude change that needs to be more ubiquitous.

Finally, we have written this book in the hope that it will also serve to change attitudes. The extraordinary stories of these students' educational odysseys need to be ordinary. It is to that end that we dedicate this book.

"How Can More of You Get Here?"

Wendy S. Harbour

THE STUDENTS IN THIS BOOK have shared how they pursued their intellectual interests despite the disability-related barriers they and their families faced, using strategies they picked up or developed along the way while working with allies and advocates wherever they could be found. I identified with much of what these students had to share, given that I also have disabilities, and I took Tom Hehir's courses while completing my doctorate at Harvard. I am currently a professor at Syracuse University, where I direct the Taishoff Center for Inclusive Higher Education. Since I work on disability issues with college students, faculty, and administrators every day, Tom and Laura asked me to write the concluding chapter of this book, connecting these students' stories to broader trends and concerns in higher education across the country. My essential question is not "How did you get here?" but rather "How can we get more of you here?" But first, I want to set the context for my reflections and comments by sharing some of my own story about how I ended up at Harvard.

MY HARVARD STORY

I start my story in eighth grade, when I was diagnosed with a mild-to-moderate hearing loss in both ears. My family and doctors suspect that I may have started having difficulties as early as first grade, but it wasn't until middle school that it became obvious in school hearing tests. At first, I was accused of faking my hearing loss to get attention, and my doctor justified this by saying that my good grades proved I was faking, because "hearing-impaired children can't be good at math and English." After I continued to fail every hearing test they could imagine, it was my audiologist who explained that many hard-of-hearing students learn coping strategies, just like children with other disabilities. For example, I tended to sit at the front of the classroom, watch the teacher closely, and do all of my homework. While these behaviors match up with expectations of what "good students" do, they are also strategies that help someone who is learning how to lip-read and frequently missing things in class. I was motivated to work hard—I just didn't realize how much work I was actually doing.

My work ethic came from my Minnesota born-and-raised parents, who always believed hard work was its own reward, and education was the ticket to a better life. My parents always expected me to go to college. My mother had never gone to college and she regretted it, wondering frequently where she would be if she had pursued her interest in science. My father received a certificate from the University of Minnesota, and also regretted not going forward with a bachelor's degree to become a math teacher. I was often confused about what "going to college" entailed and had difficulty getting basic information (like what different degrees meant, how financial aid worked, etc.), but the basic message was clear: I was going to college somehow. Thanks to guidance from my eighth-grade teacher, I got a scholarship to attend high school at a wealthy college preparatory school in St. Paul where 100 percent of the graduates went to college. I felt very lucky to be there. I met students and teachers who talked with me about things I had never imagined for myself, like learning foreign languages, writing books, and traveling to other countries.

Unlike many of the students profiled in this book, my family and teachers were not necessarily working for me as tireless advocates. Nor were they oppressive, standing in my way. My parents never really discussed my hearing loss with me, and I never wanted to tell them about any problems I was having because I knew how much they were sacrificing for me to be at the private school. And honestly, for most of my high school experience, issues of class were a bigger problem than my hearing loss; surrounded by wealthy peers who were better educated than I was, it seemed like I could never have the right clique of friends, the right interests, the right clothes, or even the right family vacations. So, unlike many of the students interviewed in this book, attending a private school actually saved me from many disability-related dilemmas, because I was never offered special education services, and my parents had no idea we could receive them.

In fact, I remember only two "pep talks" about my hearing. I had just been diagnosed with a progressive hearing loss and my mother found me crying in my room, worrying about what it all meant. She told me I could do whatever I wanted to do, and must not let anything (including hearing aids) stand in my way. And after I had to quit a summer job as a receptionist because I couldn't hear well on the phone, my principal told me that there was an anonymous quote carved into a stone wall at our school that read, "She who will fly must first lift up her wings." These are the only two discussions about my hearing I remember, even though I was surrounded by a loving family, warm supportive teachers, and an audiologist who seemed to really care about me. Looking back, I think we all believed that as long as I was getting decent grades, everything was probably fine.

The constant message I internalized, however, was that it was up to me to shape my future and overcome my disability. Like Eric, Sarah, Erin, and other students in this book, I self-accommodated. I clearly remember the first time I realized my problems might not all be my fault, and hard work or being as "normal" as possible might not be enough to overcome what I was facing. All of us were required to do senior speeches on any topic of our choice, and I talked to the student body about being hard of hearing. After the speech, I remember the college counselors telling me that it was okay for me to defer college, because it might be too difficult with my hearing loss. I was appalled at the thought of being one of the rare students at my school to not attend college—I was the same person I had been for four years. Why did my hearing loss suddenly take away the possibility of college? I didn't have words for these experiences yet, didn't think of myself as "disabled," and lacked the vocabulary and consciousness to label negative experiences like this as "ableism," even though it was.

At the same time, around the end of my junior year and during my senior year, my hearing loss began to change dramatically, becoming much worse. My major interest was music, and I was offered full scholarships to colleges based on my ability as a pianist. Yet I found myself unable to consistently distinguish between songs in music classes, and I had trouble hearing others well enough to accompany them in concerts. People tried to help me feel better by reminding me that Beethoven was deaf, but I knew I was not my generation's Beethoven! Adding to my stress, I could see my parents sacrificing even more. In addition to all the medical testing to figure out why my hearing kept deteriorating, every six months my parents were buying new hearing aids for me, which were not covered by insurance. After selling various possessions and Mom taking extra work, we had to turn to the Lion's Club for help, and I still owe them a great deal for making it possible to get the equipment I needed. With my parents' support, I turned down the full music scholarships and accepted a partial general scholarship to a small liberal arts college in Indiana. I decided a four-year college would be the perfect place to get used to my new hearing aids and equipment, while also trying out different majors to see what career options might replace my plans to study music full-time.

In my junior year of college, my hearing suddenly decreased again, and this time my hearing aids and FM system were not helping me. Class discussions became impossible to follow, and I couldn't participate in conversations with friends in the cafeteria or at restaurants. When my parents called, I didn't understand them on the phone. Friends noticed a lisp developing in my speech, and slurring when I was tired. I frequently overslept or relied on my roommate to wake me up, because I couldn't hear my alarm clock anymore. Once again, everyone around me was as supportive as possible, but this time I became very depressed. My hearing loss had always been a problem, but I could work through whatever came my way. Now it seemed that no amount of hard work was going to help me. I couldn't imagine how or where I would work. I assumed the state would take away my driver's license. Visions of ever having children faded as I imagined them crying alone or trying to talk to a mom who couldn't hear them. My parents and I began to have conversations about me dropping out of school.

Then I took a course called "The Psychology of Handicapping Conditions," taught by my advisor. She set up a field trip to see the National Theater of the Deaf perform in Indianapolis, and it was the first time I'd ever met culturally Deaf people (indicated by the capital *D*) whose primary language was American Sign Language. I was stunned. They were coming from work, driving cars full of kids, and looking pretty happy. They were using ASL, and it wasn't just gestures and mime like I had assumed. I was medically deaf (with a lowercase *d*), struggling to lip-read people next to me. Yet the Deaf people in Indianapolis could communicate across the entire theater to one another, clearly telling stories or jokes, and communicating with ease and fluency. I realized everything that would be possible if I could just learn the amazing language of ASL. I still remember telling my college roommate that it felt like every door closing to me was suddenly being opened again.

I announced my plans to the disability services office at my college, which was staffed by one full-time professional who had no experience with hard-of-hearing or deaf students. After checking with the dean, my disability services provider informed me that although the Americans with Disabilities Act had passed, it did not yet apply to private schools, so legally they were not obligated to provide me with interpreters unless I paid an additional $15,000–20,000 per year. Knowing my parents were already building up debt and scraping by to afford tuition, I admitted defeat. Unwilling to fight, I moved back home to Minnesota.

But my imagination was still burning with possibilities that all seemed reasonable if I could learn ASL. My parents were thrilled to see something break through my depression, so they helped me enroll in courses at the local community college and I began a self-imposed immersion experience in ASL. I made copies of signs from books and posted them all over the house, labeling everything from ketchup to hammers with little papers showing ASL signs. I went to bars where Deaf people were hanging out, I attended community events with interpreters and Deaf people, and I even hired a tutor to spend an hour each week teaching me signs that weren't being taught in classes (like signs for my degree in psychology, religious signs, swear words, signs about sex, and even signs for food items at the grocery store).

In the process, I realized this "problem" of mine was not such a negative thing. I learned about Deaf culture rooted in ASL, which has a long tradition and history, a vibrant community, a literary tradition, humor, and much more. The people I met were proud to be Deaf and shunned any suggestion that they were disabled or unable to do things hearing people could do. They also embraced me as a new member of the group, introducing me to more Deaf people, encouraging me, and teaching me how to use equipment to do simple things like make phone calls, watch TV, or wake up in the morning. I blossomed with this new perspective on my deafness and loved becoming bilingual.

I enrolled in the University of Minnesota to finish my degree, but I had a growing sense of dread, remembering how my previous college had balked at setting up interpreters. Much to my delight, the university had a disability specialist who knew sign language and he was pleased I was learning ASL. He had no problem with me learning while I also worked with interpreters in the classroom, and was open to me experimenting with whatever might work best for me. The director of the disability services office used a wheelchair and crutches, and was a very public activist and advocate for "disability rights" and "disability pride and culture." She had supported students in setting up the first Disabled Student Cultural Center (DSCC) in the world, where students with all kinds of disabilities could build pride and community on campus. I was stunned to see Deaf and Deafblind people at the DSCC—I had thought Deafness was a culture, not a disability. And "disability" was a negative thing, so why were they trying to rally around it?

During my two and a half years at the University of Minnesota finishing my degree, I met people who had depression, who were blind, who used wheelchairs and walkers, or who identified as having dyslexia or ADHD. The disabilities were more diverse than I could have imagined. They were galvanized around the idea of building a disability community and culture on campus. I started to join them in their activism, protesting Jerry Lewis telethons that pitied us as poster children, hosting ASL and signing nights on campus, and bringing in comedians, writers, and artists with disabilities to share their stories with the entire campus.

My view of "disability" as something to overcome evolved into a more positive orientation, and I began to think of disability as part of my identity. I now had academic information and theories to explain many of the barriers I encountered, and sociopolitical models of disability taught me how much of my negative disability experiences were rooted in others' attitudes and society. I grew comfortable with the paradoxes of being a Deaf person who also identified as disabled, realizing disability is not an inherently negative thing. I started to want to work more on improving things for students with disabilities.

After graduating and working in an elementary school integrating children with multiple disabilities into regular general education classrooms, I then worked for a while back at disability services at the University of Minnesota. In both jobs I was "on the other side of the desk," providing services and accommodations to students. I applied and was accepted to graduate school at Harvard after I realized I still had many questions about disability, and I wanted to teach and do research about those questions.

Harvard was a shock. I had heard good things about the campus services from undergraduate Deaf students, but had not realized that the disability services were completely decentralized. This meant that the staff providing disability services was different for undergraduates, law students, the business school, or the School of Education. I had no current documentation proving I was Deaf, so I arranged for audiological testing to happen as soon as I arrived in Boston, assuming my fifteen-plus years of using ASL would be enough temporary "proof" of having a disability. Harvard's disability services office instead refused to provide interpreters, noting that I had excellent speech and seemed able to lip-read well. They asked me if I had some kind of psychological or attention-related disability that made me want to have interpreters accompany me around campus when I clearly didn't need them. The lack of documentation bolstered their assumption I was faking and trying to abuse services in place for students who needed them. My own experiences as a Deaf person using ASL and as a disability specialist at the University of Minnesota were completely discounted. I had also just acquired a service dog to help me respond to sounds around me and in my apartment, and she also helped me feel safe on my frequent early-morning or late-night walks to and from campus. While just showing her ID as a service dog should have been enough, Harvard told me that unless I provided detailed lists of every way I needed her and these were approved by their offices, she was not allowed anywhere on campus (including my on-campus housing). I missed all of my Harvard orientation and most of the first two weeks of courses because I had no interpreters. My partner, a sign language interpreter, ended up interpreting at one dinner my advisor told me was required; faculty and peers told me that if I missed it, my reputation at Harvard would be irreparably damaged. Because she was working all night, Tracy never got to meet other partners, spouses, and significant others. And having her work with me pro bono was awkward for both of us.

Even after I got documentation, the problems continued. Interpreters were not qualified, and my preferences were not honored. Every meeting, lecture, committee, and work assignment was examined to determine if I was misusing my services; many interpreters stopped working with me because every invoice was questioned, and it took months for them to be paid. In protest and with advice from the Massachusetts Commission for the Deaf & Hard of Hearing, I brought my hearing/service dog everywhere with me, but I wondered if the disability services office would call the police. I started tape-recording meetings with disability services and saving e-mails from them, realizing I would probably need evidence if I ever wanted things to change.

But it wasn't all negative, and there are some valuable lessons to be learned here. The first is that, like the other students in this book, I thrive on learning itself. Going to courses and being in a stimulating intellectual environment soothed my mind and spirit and helped me get through. Even though I wasn't doing my best in my courses, they offered me respite from personal problems and allowed me to focus instead on academic things.

The faculty were also terrific. While many administrators and peers lost patience with me, the faculty seemed to be genuinely concerned for my well-being and interested in how to make things better—not just for me, but for any other student experiencing disability-related problems. Like other students in this book, I found refuge in Tom Hehir's courses, as well as in a course on universal design taught by David Rose. I eventually became a teaching fellow (i.e., teaching assistant) for both of them, and I started to realize how students with disabilities were gravitating toward these courses, even if they weren't interested in a career related to disability. Clearly, Tom and David were viewed as allies and their courses were safe havens where it was okay to have a disability, chronic illness, or other "difference."

I also had a core group of interpreters, two of which worked with me every day. As I built trust and working relationships with them, we also started to become friends. They knew everything I was experiencing, positive and negative, and they wanted me to succeed almost as much as I did!

At the same time I was dealing with disability-related issues, I began to experience severe asthmatic episodes related to a bout with whooping cough the year before I moved to Massachusetts. These asthma attacks were probably exacerbated by all the stress I was under, but they involved multiple hospitalizations, missed courses, and difficulty concentrating and paying attention due to the high doses of steroids, trouble breathing, and problems sleeping. Sometimes in class I was doing brilliantly, and then the next day I would be unable to follow even the simplest train of thought, or I would be so tired I would misread the syllabus and do the wrong assignments.

Unlike my previous experiences there with my deafness, Harvard was excellent at handling a disability involving a chronic illness and hospitalizations. With policies in place for medical leaves, incompletes, and waivers of degree requirements, it seemed to have solutions for nearly every issue that came up. I struggled to adjust to a disability that didn't invoke the pride, identity, and community I associated with my other disability, and I needed to learn how to "come out" about an invisible disability like Laura describes in this book. I had to learn ways to ask for what I needed, have better balance in my life, and get accommodations when necessary. But I also wondered how a single university could do so well with one of my disabilities and be so terrible with the other.

After two years, Harvard and I came to some resolution about what was happening, and I was happy with the result. Through mediation with the federal Office of Civil Rights, we agreed I would take over all of my interpreter scheduling, so I could control the interpreter requests and follow my hiring preferences. I continued to do that for my remaining four years at Harvard.

I had walked away from a bad situation once as an undergrad, but in grad school I didn't give up. And it was worth it. By 2007, the year before I left, Harvard hired a single person to oversee interpreter services for the entire campus, instead of asking each college to fend for itself. I have watched as culturally Deaf and Deafblind students arrived one by one after I left, and I have seen them all thrive. I feel like a proud godmother of sorts, seeing the next generations of Deaf and DeafBlind students get their degrees and become active members of the Harvard community without any major problems. Harvard is now a different place for Deaf students.

Now I run the Taishoff Center at Syracuse University. The Taishoff Center works with college students across the country, and we have a "virtual" online disability cultural center called DREAM (Disability Rights, Education, Activism, and Mentoring), where I am trying to help students gain new perspectives and experiences like the ones I had in Minnesota. We also run several programs and services for students with intellectual disabilities (like Down syndrome) who want to audit standard university or college courses; they want to pursue an education after high school just like many of their peers, and we help make that possible. We're also trying to look at ways for campuses to move beyond disability services as the only means by which people understand disability; we encourage faculty to include disability perspectives in courses, to use Universal Design for Learning strategies, and to think about disability as part of the valued diversity on campus. We also frequently connect students with disabilities to staff and faculty with disabilities—seeing administrators and instructors "like them" is as important for students with disabilities as it is for other traditionally marginalized groups of students on campus.

But stories like mine are still quite common. I recently worked with a student who has cerebral palsy, and people in his dorm nicknamed him "The Retard." One dyslexic student at a Big 10 university admitted she has never met another person with a disability and feels completely isolated. A student with a traumatic brain injury just learned he can never fulfill his dream of being a kindergarten teacher because he can't take a full course load each semester to keep up with teacher education requirements. An autistic student attained a master's degree, but was haunted by traumatic experiences in special education and a high school IEP that had goals like "coloring in the lines of a drawing." A young woman with Down syndrome fought to leave low-level segregated high school classes teaching independent skills (like counting change and riding buses); she wanted to take regular courses in math and English so she could some-day go to Syracuse University with her nondisabled brother.

Like Tom and Laura sifting through these narratives, I have noticed many themes among the experiences of college students with disabilities. The stories in this book are about people who ended up studying at Harvard, but in many ways their stories could be about students attending rural community colleges, large public state universities, small liberal arts campuses, online for-profit universities, or any campus in the United States. On the other hand, each of our stories is unique, with its own twists and turns. As a lesbian, I have a "coming out" story that unites me with every other person who has ever come out. And as Laura describes in chapter 7, as a disabled woman, I have a second "coming out" story that unites me with other people with disabilities as well.

We need to hear these stories, because research and narratives about disability and higher education are scarce. In the courses I teach about disability and higher education, I struggle to find any readings about students with disabilities—especially stories where authors identify as having a "disability" of any kind. Research and narratives about faculty and staff with disabilities are even rarer. Some first-person accounts feature experiences in higher education by people with illnesses or mental, emotional, and physical disabilities, but the authors never use the word *disability*.

It may be tempting for some readers to suggest that narratives about Harvard students with disabilities are too far out of the norm. After all, this is Harvard—a place that advertises itself as being unique and of a higher caliber than any other school in the country. The average person in the United States might assume that students with disabilities at Harvard come from exceptional families that allowed them to do exceptional things. They might believe the students' intelligence somehow eclipses any negative aspects of their disability or helps them overcome it. I have had many people assume I got into Harvard only because people took pity on me, or because the admissions office was trying to do an overly generous disability twist on affirmative action. And some people might assume an Ivy League education would be accompanied by Ivy League disability services, giving students with disabilities an extra edge that might not be available at a typical public university or community college.

But as these narratives show, all of these assumptions are wrong. Our families sometimes did have higher-than-average wealth or cultural capital that helped them "work the system," but not always. Our intelligence may have helped us along the way, but many of us had to first fight others' beliefs that disabled people are unable to learn and not likely to be intelligent. We arrived at Harvard and used a mix of strategies to make things work: not all of us used disability services; many of us didn't realize our "difficulty" or "difference" was actually a "disability"; we struggled with others' attitudes; professors questioned our academic integrity; and nearly all of us had to self-accommodate or work out individual accommodations to supplement whatever the university provided. In other words, even though we went to Harvard, we experienced what many of us with disabilities experience in our fight to learn. We are intelligent and have privileges associated with our admission to Harvard, and that's exactly why readers should be troubled. If it's hard for us, imagine how difficult it would be for others who lack the same resources and privileges.

I recently planned to present to a group of parents and college-bound high school students with disabilities at a transition conference in upstate New York. The most distressing questions the group asked took various forms and were never asked outright, but essentially were "Can students with *any* disability go to college? Can *my* child go to college?" While some disabilities might make college difficult, and some students don't want or need to go to college in the first place, disability itself should not preclude someone from considering higher education.

The questions of "How did you get here?" or "How can I go there?" are the same ones Tom, Laura, and those parents are asking. The question may take many forms, but I find it disheartening. Why should our society and our educational system be so ableist that we are still wondering how students with disabilities manage to actually make it into colleges and universities and succeed? Regardless of our intentions, college students with disabilities are often held up as "supercrips" just for doing something that many of their peers are doing as a matter of course. In my case, one of my elderly aunts was stunned to learn I was attending Harvard. "I didn't know they had a special education program!" she said in wonder. Since I was studying special education and disability in higher education, Tom and I enjoyed the inside joke—Harvard did indeed have a "special education program" of sorts, but it wasn't the segregated classrooms, cubbies, and dumbed-down curriculum my aunt most likely imagined.

Yet even though I am concerned by the questions of "How did we get here?" or "How can more of us get here?" we must start asking these questions more often. If we had more narratives and first-person accounts readily available, we would have a fuller picture of what is happening with students who have disabilities, and we would understand how disability is constructed on campuses. We would know what can make things better for students, staff, and faculty with disabilities. The qualitative research and narratives could also guide quantitative researchers using statistical methods. For example, it's difficult to find large-scale or longitudinal studies of students, standardized tests, financial aid, or college attendance that have demographic questions about disability status. We can follow students by their gender, race, religion, ethnicity, socioeconomic status, and even their political leanings. But we can't track what's happening with students who have disabilities, or learn how disability interacts with other characteristics to positively or negatively affect college success.

The timing couldn't be more critical. As this book goes to press, higher education lobbyists are trying to block TEACH legislation that would make college textbooks and other course materials more accessible to students who have difficulty reading print (e.g., students with dyslexia and visual impairments). Congress debated and passed in December 2014 the ABLE act that allows parents to save flexible funds for their children with disabilities to use as needed when they become adults (funds that could be used for college, as well as for disability-related needs). And the Higher Education Opportunity Act (HEOA) is coming up for revision in Congress.

In 2008 the HEOA made a landmark move by including several provisions related to disability and students with disabilities, such as a national task force on assistive technology in higher education, support for research and programming related to students with intellectual disabilities accessing higher education, mandatory teacher education about Universal Design for Learning, and a national technical assistance center for students with disabilities. All of these initiatives are currently in jeopardy, and the technical assistance center mandated in 2008 still remains unfunded in 2014. Research conservatively estimates that 6 to 11 percent of undergraduates may have disabilities, meaning there are currently somewhere between 1.2 and 2.3 million students with disabilities in the United States (based on statistics at http://nces.ed.gov/programs/digest/d13/tables/dt13_303.10.asp). We have no idea how many graduate students, faculty, and staff have disabilities since there is no large-scale research in this area. Even the undergraduate number may be off, with up to 90 percent of students with disabilities not registering with disability services offices (and therefore not being counted).[1] As President Obama calls for the United States to be the "first in the world," educating our population through colleges and universities, it is critical that 6 to 11 percent of future doctors, lawyers, mechanics, business professionals, engineers, small-business owners, computer programmers, teachers, scientists, and other professionals with disabilities be supported in their journeys of getting to college and entering the work force. This is one more way we can also change the culture of this country for all people with disabilities.

In the next pages of this chapter, I combine my personal and professional experiences with those of the students profiled in this book, considering implications for policy and practice. While Tom and Laura suggest several recommendations for K–12 educators and special education, I connect them to the work in higher education as well.

"TRANSITION PLANNING" IS WHATEVER PARENTS AND STUDENTS CAN CREATE

As someone who has studied disability in both K–12 and higher education, I immediately noticed that not one student involved in this book mentioned transition planning. Significantly (and perhaps following the lead of their research participants), Tom and Laura also make no mention of transition services. While IDEA and Section 504 may be helping students with disabilities in schools, the policies designed to help students with disabilities successfully graduate and move out of schools are clearly not working.

Special education law (IDEA) mandates that beginning at age sixteen, all students with IEPs receive assistance planning for the transition out of high school into community living, work, the military, higher education, or whatever they wish to do. However, the large-scale National Longitudinal Transition Study (NLTS-2) has found evidence that families are getting information too late for it to be useful.[2] Even though transition planning and college attendance rates are improving, information and advice about college planning is often contradictory or difficult to understand.[3] When it does happen, transition planning may set up two parallel processes within the system: the process of choosing a college (with school counselors), and the process of choosing a college as a disabled student (with special education professionals). Expectations may also be inherently ableist, or more focused on vocational planning. For example, nondisabled students are expected to "find themselves," have fun, and figure out goals during college, while students with disabilities are typically expected to work out their goals and aspirations during transition planning, before they get to campus. Once they are there, students are expected to follow goals and work toward employment—with very little attention to the social and developmental aspects of college.[4]

We also know very little about transition or college planning for the multitude of students receiving Section 504 plans for their disabilities (an option for students who have disabilities or chronic illnesses that may not impact their education enough to qualify for a full IEP). We do know parents of children on 504 plans may not receive the same level of due process rights, and that students with 504 plans may not get adequate transition planning or disability documentation for college.[5] We also know that many college and university disability services offices see 504 plans as evidence that the student doesn't have a significant disability, even though the Association for Higher Education And Disability (AHEAD), the national organization of disability services providers, has issued guidelines urging higher education to take 504 plans seriously when considering student eligibility for services.[6]

The students in this book offer a counternarrative that redefines how educators and policy makers define *transition*. Instead of saying how much transition planning meant to them, these students started "transition" planning to college as early as preschool. Parents, teachers, and students believed college was a possibility. Most of the students took intellectually challenging classes (or challenged themselves intellectually), they learned explicit strategies to "self-accommodate" when courses were not universally designed, they practiced self-determination to decide how services would be provided, and they got information about their disability and possible services for whatever was coming next, whether the transition was for middle school, high school, or college. Even when they were in segregated classes or schools for kids with disabilities, the push was ultimately toward a college degree (see, for example, the discussion in chapter 3).

Many school districts set up transition specialists to handle all the post–high school transition planning for high school students in the district. The students in this book suggest that preschool, elementary, and middle school teachers also need to think about their students as future college students. None of the students in this book started preparing for college at age sixteen. If the students or their parents had waited that long, I doubt any of them would have ended up at Harvard, and some of them probably wouldn't have attended college at all.

For most of the students in this book, they devised their own path to Harvard, or parents played key roles in navigating the transitions between high school, college, and graduate school. For example, Jennifer's parents helped her look at disability services offices on every campus she visited (see chapter 1). A classic article by Mark A. Mlawer discussed the "advocacy expectation" schools have for parents of students with disabilities; schools automatically assume parents will be their childrens' best advocates.[7] As the students in this book can attest, it clearly seems to still be the case. But as Tom Hehir states in chapter 1, "Expecting parents to become service providers and experts in disability is clearly not appropriate."

Instead of relying on an ineffective high school transition process, parents, or students' savvy, it seems clear that higher education needs to do better outreach. Since it is impossible to know who has a disability, and many students with disabilities do not identify as "disabled," the best approach may be to think about campuswide strategies for reaching all students when they start their undergraduate or graduate school training. For example, there is a brief one or two weeks where every new undergraduate student has mandatory orientation sessions. Think of what questions students may have. *Where are disability, medical, and counseling resources and who can use them? Can disability services help people who don't think of themselves as disabled? Are people with disabilities welcome as part of campus diversity? Are there courses about disability, student groups, or other ways to connect to disabled students and allies on campus? What does this campus mean by the term "disability," and could my "difference" actually be a "disability"? If I have a disability, isn't that a bad thing?* Providing this information to all students may be one way to offer early support to students with disabilities or chronic emotional, mental, or physical conditions. It would reduce the isolation that students like Eric or Brian felt when they arrived on campus but couldn't yet identify as "disabled." Another campuswide option is to encourage faculty and teaching assistants to utilize Universal Design for Learning, discussed by Tom in chapter 8. UDL asks instructors to think about the full diversity of students in the courses (including students with disabilities), and to design a flexible curriculum that can help everyone meet high expectations for learning and academic success.[8]

DISABLED INTELLECTUALS AND UNIVERSAL DESIGN FOR LEARNING

A major part of my current work is experimenting with ways to provide access to higher education for students with intellectual and developmental disabilities, like Down syndrome or Fragile X. These students have traditionally been excluded from higher education altogether. Even though most campuses have some kind of open enrollment component (like community education or extension courses) or options for auditing classes, higher education has presumed that people with intellectual disabilities would not be taking advantage of these opportunities. That is starting to change.

When I first heard of "inclusive higher education" for this group of students, I couldn't imagine how it would work. Then I started to learn more about it, and I started meeting students with so-called "intellectual disabilities" who were actually quite intellectual. At Syracuse University, we have students labeled with "severe" disabilities or "third-grade IQs" who are mastering content in courses on critical theory, physics, child psychology, and political science. Their IQ or reading skills may be on a third-grade level, but their homework is the same work and reading given to matriculated peers. They do field placements, labs, theater productions, and study groups alongside full-time, traditionally enrolled undergraduates. Most of the students with intellectual disabilities are auditing courses instead of taking them for credit, but in a few cases professors have recommended that students enroll for course credit and consider degree programs. We all have a good laugh when professors occasionally call to ask which student is "the disabled one." I constantly watch students from segregated high school courses thriving in a higher education environment, mainly because we have incredibly high expectations, we accept individualized personal support in classrooms, and we provide the proper accommodations and technology for academics and social interactions. Despite many of the students with intellectual disabilities spending years in life skills classes in high school, they no longer need these courses because they are learning life skills with peers in the student center, the gym, the cafeteria, and campus landmarks like Varsity Pizza.

These students have also had discussions with me about what it means to be an intellectual, and how higher education claims to want diversity, but that never means neurodiversity. Many of the students with intellectual disabilities identify with students who have other cognitive disabilities, like dyslexia, ADHD, or traumatic brain injuries. They see how their struggles to relate socially seem similar to students who are autistic. Many students with intellectual disabilities also have depression, anxiety, or other mental and emotional conditions like so many of their peers. They see themselves as part of the student body, but are learning to also see themselves as part of the community of people with disabilities. This is especially poignant given that well-intentioned "inclusion" efforts in K–12 usually contribute to academic success, but isolate students with disabilities from one another and from opportunities to learn about disability and Deaf communities and history.

Most professors judge intellectualism by one's ability to read printed text, to understand and use spoken conversation, and to do exams and essays under pressure and timelines. Intellectuals never miss class. They do not have flashbacks or depressive episodes requiring hospitalization. They don't need to leave class in order to use the bathroom every thirty minutes, check their blood sugar, or feed a service dog. They do not talk off-topic or speak out of turn. They follow unspoken and untaught rules. They overcome problems, look as nondisabled as possible, and don't bother professors or peers. There is an implicit belief that intellectuals and academics are nondisabled.[9]

When I talked to Tom and Laura about this chapter, all three of us wondered how to discuss intellectualism without being elitist. But the students in this book clearly show that our traditional definitions of intellectualism and our assumptions about intellectuals need to change. To look at a student with a disability and presume a lack of creativity, intellectual ability, or mental agility is a serious mistake. As students at Syracuse University and other campuses are proving, even students with "intellectual disabilities" can be intellectuals, just as students with "learning disabilities" can still learn, students with "communication disabilities" still have something to say, students with hearing loss are still capable of receiving information and "listening," and students with visual impairments can still read and have "insight" because having "clarity" and "a vision" have nothing to do with the act of seeing. The authors and the students in this book are not talking about an elitist traditional version of an intellectual. We are talking about a neurologically, emotionally, and physiologically diverse set of intellectuals. We are talking about people who love to learn and value an education. Some people with disabilities may not be cut out for higher education and may not constantly strive to learn more, but we should not cut off educational opportunities and resources for anyone who wants them.

This is not easy for many faculty to accept. Like Tom's, most of my courses seem messy compared to typical ones. I've got students using so many accommodations that the School of Education now automatically overestimates my actual enrollments so the registrar will give me enough physical room for interpreters, assistants, wheelchairs, dogs, or whatever else might be showing up in class. I have students coming out about their disabilities all the time, privately or in the middle of lectures and discussions. When I have a Deaf student in class, I automatically stop speaking and switch to American Sign Language, so all my hearing students become the language minority. I have students coming and going during class time when they need to do so, and the students and I all need to support one another to make it through the semester. We're in this together. I love it and wouldn't have it any other way. My students and I are still learning and being challenged, but I am open to the many ways we will learn together. I assume I will have students with a variety of disabilities, students learning English, students from different religions who will be gone when they have religious holidays, and students with difficult personal situations who may need support.

Tom and I both try to use Universal Design for Learning as a guiding philosophy. Neither of us is getting it right, and we readily admit that we're both still learning. That's part of the process and the delightful, complicated, messy nature of UDL. We presume all of our students have registered for class because they are intellectuals who are capable of doing well as long as they have the right supports or services—whether that's being able to stay home when a child is sick, or being able to have digitized textbooks read by a computer. UDL principles encourage us to seek different ways to teach and honor the different ways students learn. We use a variety of teaching strategies to keep them engaged. We assume our courses will change a bit each time we teach them, and we figure out how to do them better. We have high expectations and do not offer easy grading or assignments to students just because they have a disability.

Yet even as UDL is becoming more common in higher education, research about it is still scarce. We know very little about how to actually design a flexible higher education course for all students with disabilities. The students in this book offer a few clues for researchers to explore. Like Daniel using screen readers (chapter 6), students need technology of all kinds in order to succeed, and when professors use technology, they should consider any limitations of that technology and work around them. Attitudinal access is critical, as Laura realized when her professor asked students to feel open to discussing their disabilities with her (chapter 7).

But universal design won't work unless we start to expand our definition of intellectuals, and unless professors can imagine disabled intellectuals joining their courses and contributing to diversity in a positive way. Disability services professionals should openly discuss self-accommodation strategies and the daily negotiations students are having with professors, in order to complement and supplement those efforts. And conversations about disability need to move out of disability services and into admissions offices, advising processes, and student affairs. Students have barriers across campus, so disability activism, universal design, and policies reducing ableism should be across campus as well. Disability services cannot be the only place on campus that is interested in disability.

BEYOND SERVICES: DISABILITY STUDIES

Throughout the book, but most notably in Laura Schifter's chapter 7, students discuss their own perceptions of their illnesses, disabilities, and differences in mental, emotional, and physical ways that fall under the broad label of disability. As mentioned in that chapter, many of these students struggled with whether or not to stay "in the closet." They tried to reconcile relief at having a diagnosis and a better understanding of their disabilities with the stigma and anxiety about disclosing them to others. Some, like Amy, became outspoken self-advocates who also tired of perpetually educating others. One possible way to help these students while reducing attitudinal barriers is to integrate a disability studies sensibility into K–12 and higher education.

Chapter 8 includes information about models of disability, which is a part of disability studies. Disability studies, like women's studies, gender studies, or various ethnic studies, is an interdisciplinary field that not only applies to education, but also to the humanities, sociology, medicine, law, design, and practically every field that can be studied in higher education. Disability studies scholars are interested in how our society creates concepts of "disability" and how that definition changes over time and in different contexts. Sociopolitical models of disability fight back against pathological medicalized views of disability, where being disabled is inherently negative and professionals are always needed to help normalize or cure the disability. Social models of disability instead presume that disability itself is neutral, and is usually problematic only when systems are oppressive, or policy, architectural, and attitudinal barriers exist. Disability studies also promotes a "nothing about us without us" philosophy that encourages people with disabilities to advocate for themselves and what they want, while being involved in any decisions affecting their lives.[10]

In K–12 and higher education, the average person is likely to experience disability in a limited number of ways. He or she may participate in some kind of disability awareness event or activity; may have interactions with people who have disabilities, impairments, or illnesses; and may learn basic information about disability from special education or disability services providers. If students arrive at college and major in any of the health or service-oriented professions (e.g., social work, psychology, nursing, special education), they are likely to study different types of disabilities and diagnostic labels, with appropriate remedial and rehabilitation strategies for professionals working with these populations.

What is less likely is for students to experience disability as part of the diversity of people covered in the curriculum. When discussing World War II, they probably will not learn about the Nazis perfecting killing techniques on disabled people. When these students read poetry of contemporary authors, those authors will not be disabled. If authors do have disabilities, it may not be discussed in class even when gender, race, sexuality, or class is up for debate; or it may be utilized only as a metaphor for negative things like evil or death. In political science, marketing, and design courses, people with disabilities may not be considered as a group that votes, purchases things, and uses everyday objects. Multicultural centers and diversity training are unlikely to teach anything about disability beyond complying with any accommodation requests or bizarre "disability etiquette" trainings that seem to presume interactions with disabled people require a finishing school course.

I have written elsewhere about how disability studies may influence Deaf education and can help bridge K–12 and higher education.[11] As I read through this book, I noticed again and again how students self-accommodated, debated how to talk about their disabilities, wavered between shunning the label of "disability" or embracing it, and generally tried to negotiate what meanings their disabilities had in their lives. Whether or not they consider themselves disabled, it's clear that the label was being applied to their experiences by others.

In my own journey with disability and being Deaf, it was learning about disability studies that finally helped me articulate what was happening to me, while also figuring out possible options. My natural inclination to be an intellectual meant that intellectual information about disability was reassuring and helpful in pragmatic ways. It also helped me be more effective at what I was already doing with self-accommodations and using disability services. Taking courses by Tom Hehir or David Rose was not just educational, it was also personal.

In fact, several students in this book, like Brian and Eric, didn't realize they had a disability until they took Tom's course (see chapter 6). Because Tom was using universal design, the course was also accessible to these students. The information about disability reframed their experiences and helped them reconsider whether they had to do everything on their own. Those who were most comfortable with their disability at Harvard were those who had already learned progressive models of disability, like people who used ASL and interacted with the Deaf community. Others, like Amy, had connected with savvy adults who had the same type of disability, making it easier to identify technology, accommodations, and resources that could work for them. Some students, like R.J., even learned about disability identity from their parents (see chapter 1).

If campuses are not interested in setting up an entire disability studies degree program, it is still possible for them to offer disability studies courses, or to consider ways disability could be infused into coursework and degree requirements so it becomes part of the diverse world students are studying.[12] Student affairs professionals can think about disability-related programming on campus, and whether it's *awareness*, *cultural*, or *diversity* programming. They may also look at intersections and connections between disability and other communities, bringing in an African American blind speaker or a gay performer with ADHD and dyslexia. Provosts and academic deans can look at whether multicultural liberal arts requirements include any course offerings about disability, or whether ASL counts toward foreign language requirements. Administrators can follow the lead of the Harvard School of Education's ribbon-cutting ceremony (chapter 8), celebrating each time accessibility improves on campus. Then other students may not need to take a course with professors like Tom Hehir before they realize their "success" story is still limited by their own internalized ableism and that of others.

IN SUMMARY

My own story shows how unique stories of disability can be, and how stories of people with disabilities can also intersect through shared experiences. As I reflect on the implications of this book for higher education, I consider how often parents and students must become the experts on disability and navigate the transition to higher education on their own. I believe colleges and universities can make these students feel welcome, can help them better understand who they are, and can even benefit from having students with disabilities. Part of our task in higher education is to broaden our definition of what it means to be an intellectual, using universal design to embrace the diverse learners in college classrooms, including students with disabilities. Using UDL and disability studies as guiding philosophies (as imperfect as they may be) can help us ensure that the next generation of students moving through college will not have the same challenges as the students profiled in this book, and that the question of "How did you get here?" will become the statement of "Welcome! Of course you're here."

Notes

INTRODUCTION

1. Sara Lawrence-Lightfoot, *The Third Chapter: Passion, Risk, and Adventure in the 25 Years After 50* (New York: Farrar, Straus, and Giroux, 2010).
2. Lynn Newman et al., *Comparisons Across Time of the Outcomes of Youth with Disabilities up to 4 Years After High School: A Report of Findings from the National Longitudinal Transition Study-2 (NLTS2)* (Menlo Park, CA: SRI International, 2010), www.nlts2.org/reports/2010_09/nlts2_report_2010_09_complete.pdf; Thomas Hehir, *New Directions in Special Education: Eliminating Ableism in Policy and Practice* (Cambridge, MA: Harvard Education Press, 2005).
3. Hehir, *New Directions.*
4. Newman et al., *Comparisons.*
5. Joseph P. Shapiro, *No Pity: People with Disabilities Forging a New Civil Rights Movement* (New York: Times Books, 1993).
6. Ibid.

CHAPTER 1

1. Thomas Hehir, *New Directions in Special Education: Eliminating Ableism in Policy and Practice* (Cambridge, MA: Harvard Education Press, 2005).
2. Thomas Hehir, *Effective Inclusive Schools: Designing Successful Schoolwide Programs* (San Francisco: Jossey-Bass, 2012); Thomas Hehir, *Special Education at the Century's End: Evolution of Theory and Practice Since 1970* (Cambridge, MA: Harvard Educational Review, 1992).
3. Adrienne Asch, "Has the Law Made a Difference? What Some Disabled Students Have to Say," in *Beyond Separate Education: Quality Education for All*, ed. Dorothy Kerzner Lipsky and Alan Gartner (Baltimore: Paul Brookes Publishers, 1989), 181–205.
4. Philip M. Ferguson and Adrienne Asch, "Lessons from Life: Personal and Parental Perspectives on School, Childhood, and Disability," in *Eighty-Eighth Yearbook of the National Society for the Study of Education Part II: Schooling and Disability*, ed. Douglas P. Biklen, Dianne L. Ferguson, and Alison Ford (Chicago: University of Chicago Press, 1989), 108–140.
5. Harilyn Russo, "Fostering Healthy Self Esteem: Part One," *Exceptional Parent* 14, no. 8 (1984): 9–14.

6. Bill Henderson, *The Blind Advantage: How Going Blind Made Me a Stronger Principal and How Including Children with Disabilities Made Our School Better for Everyone* (Cambridge, MA: Harvard Educational Press, 2011).

7. Section 504 of the Rehabilitation Act of 1975, as amended, 29 U.S.C. § 794; IDEA (Individuals with Disabilities Education Act, P.L. 101-476, 1990; Amended Individuals with Disabilities Education Improvement Act of 2004, P.L. 108-446); ADA (Americans with Disabilities Act, 1990).

8. Sara Lawrence-Lightfoot, *The Essential Conversation: What Parents and Teachers Can Learn from Each Other* (New York: Random House Publishing Group, 2004).

CHAPTER 2

1. William L. Sanders and June C. Rivers, *Cumulative and Residual Effects of Teachers on Future Student Academic Achievement* (Knoxville: University of Tennessee Value-Added and Research Assessment Center, 1996); Barbara Nye, Spyros Konstantopoulos, and Larry V. Hedges, "How Large Are Teacher Effects?" *Educational Evaluation and Policy Analysis* 26 no. 3 (2004): 237–257; Johan E. Rockoff, "The Impact of Individual Teachers on Student Achievement: Evidence from Panel Data" *American Economic Review* 94, no. 2 (2004): 247–252; Steven G. Rivkin, Eric A. Hanushek, and John F. Kain, "Teachers, Schools, and Academic Achievement" *Econometrica* 73 no. 2 (2005): 417–458.

2. Frederick M. Hess, *Common Sense School Reform* (New York: Palgrave Macmillan, 2004), 102–103.

3. Dan Goldhaber, "The Mystery of Good Teaching," *Education Next* 2, no. 1 (2002): 50–55; Elizabeth Green, "Building a Better Teacher," *New York Times Magazine*, March 2, 2010, http://www.nytimes.com/2010/03/07/magazine/07Teachers-t .html?pagewanted=all; Gary D. Fenstermacher and Virginia Richardson, "On Making Determinations of Quality in Teaching," *Teachers College Record* 107, no. 1 (2005): 186–213.

4. Anne Meyer and David H. Rose, ed., *A Practical Reader in Universal Design for Learning* (Cambridge, MA: Harvard Education Press, 2006); Anne Meyer, David H. Rose, and David Gordon, *Universal Design for Learning: Theory and Practice* (Wakefield, MA: CAST, 2013), http://udltheorypractice.cast.org/home?5.

CHAPTER 3

1. Sharon Field and Alan Hoffman, "Development of a Model for Self-Determination," *Career Development for Exceptional Individuals* 17, no. 2 (1994): 164.

CHAPTER 4

1. Anne Meyer, David H. Rose, and David Gordon, *Universal Design for Learning: Theory and Practice* (Wakefield, MA: CAST, 2013), http://udltheorypractice.cast .org/home?5; David H. Rose and Anne Meyer, *Teaching Every Student in the Digital*

Age: Universal Design for Learning (Alexandria, VA: ASCD, 2002), http://www
.cast.org/teachingeverystudent/ideas/tes/.

2. Mary Wagner et al., *The Other 80% of Their Time: The Experiences of Elementary and Middle School Students with Disabilities in their Nonschool Hours* (Menlo Park, CA: SRI International, 2002), http://www.seels.net/designdocs/Wave_1_components _1-7.pdf.

3. Michael Benz and Lauren Lindstrom, "Improving Graduation and Employment Outcomes of Students with Disabilities: Predictive Factors and Student Perspectives," *Exceptional Children* 66, no. 4 (2000): 509–529; Bob Algozzine et al., "Effects of Interventions to Promote Self-Determination for Individuals with Disabilities," *Review of Educational Research* 71, no. 2 (2001): 219–277.

4. U.S. Government Accountability Office, *Students with Disabilities: More Information and Guidance Could Improve Opportunities in Physical Education and Athletics* (Washington, DC: U.S. Government Accountability Office, 2010), http://www .gao.gov/assets/310/305770.pdf.

5. Ibid., 19–22.

6. Ibid., 21.

CHAPTER 5

1. Anne Meyer, David H. Rose, and David Gordon, *Universal Design for Learning: Theory and Practice* (Wakefield, MA: CAST, 2013), http://udltheorypractice.cast .org/home?5; David H. Rose and Anne Meyer, *Teaching Every Student in the Digital Age: Universal Design for Learning* (Alexandria, VA: ASCD, 2002); Alison Gopnik, Andrew N. Meltzoff, and Patricia K. Kulh, *The Scientist in the Crib: What Early Learning Tells Us About the Mind* (New York: Harper Perennial, 1999).

2. Steven E. Petersen et al., "The Effects of Practice on the Functional Anatomy of Task Performance," *Proceedings of the National Academy of Sciences* 95 (1998): 853–860, http://www.pnas.org/content/95/3/853.full.pdf; National Research Council; *How People Learn: Brain, Mind, Experience, and School* (Washington, DC: National Academies Press, 2000); Manfred Spitzer, *The Mind Within the Net: Models of Learning, Thinking, and Acting* (Cambridge, MA: MIT Press, 1999); Denis Mareschal et al., *Neuroconstructivism: How the Brain Constructs Cognition* (Oxford, UK: Oxford University Press, 2007).

3. Meyer, Rose, and Gordon, *Universal Design*; National Research Council, *How People Learn*.

4. Meyer, Rose, and Gordon, *Universal Design*.

5. At this point and to my knowledge, Kindle is fully accessible only when used as an app on iDevices; the Kindle devices themselves are still not accessible in menus or user navigation. Blio is an e-reader developed by K-NFB, a partnership between Kurzweil Technologies and the National Federation of the Blind.

6. Besides being told not to leave my home unaccompanied, I was also denied a stove for fear I would burn down my apartment. This went on for several months until

the director of my local school board used my story as a symbol of "overcoming diversity" at a prefectural conference on English teaching. At that point, I offered an ultimatum that I would be given my rights as a human or I would leave the country.

CHAPTER 6

1. Sally Shaywitz, *Overcoming Dyslexia: A New and Complete Science-Based Program for Reading Problems at Any Level* (New York: Alfred A. Knopf, 2003).

CHAPTER 7

1. Tara Finnegan, "Stick-to-itiveness Drives Lax Star Schifter," *Washington Post*, May 9, 1999.

CHAPTER 8

1. Martha Minow, *Making All the Difference: Inclusion, Exclusion, and American Law* (Ithaca, NY: Cornell University Press, 1990).
2. Ibid., 83.
3. Thomas Hehir, *New Directions in Special Education: Eliminating Ableism in Policy and Practice* (Cambridge, MA: Harvard Education Press, 2005).
4. Thomas Hehir with Lauren Katzman, *Effective Inclusive Schools: Designing Successful Schoolwide Programs* (San Francisco: Jossey-Bass, 2012).
5. G. Reid Lyon et al., "Rethinking Learning Disabilities," in *Rethinking Special Education for a New Century*, ed. Chester E. Finn Jr. et al. (Washington, DC: Progressive Policy Institute, Thomas B. Fordham Foundation, 2001), 259–287; Sally Shaywitz, *Overcoming Dyslexia: A New and Complete Science-Based Program for Reading Problems at Any Level* (New York: Alfred A. Knopf, 2003); G. G. Sugai and R. Horner, "The Evolution of Discipline Practices: Schoolwide Positive Behavior Supports," in *Behavior Psychology in Schools* 24, ed. James K. Luirelli and Charles Diament (Binghamton, NY: Haworth Press, 2002): 23–50.
6. Catherine Snow, ed., *Preventing Reading Difficulties in Young Children* (Washington, DC: National Research Council, 1988).
7. David H. Rose and Jenna W. Gravel, "University Design for Learning," in *International Encyclopedia of Education, 3rd Edition*, ed. Eva Baker, Penelope Peterson, and Barry McGaw (Oxford, UK: Elsevier, 2010).
8. David H. Rose and Anne Meyer, *A Practical Reader in Universal Design for Learning* (Cambridge, MA: Harvard Education Press, 2006).
9. Nora Ellen Groce, *Everyone Here Spoke Sign Language: Hereditary Deafness on Martha's Vineyard* (Cambridge, MA: Harvard University Press, 1985).
10. Alan Gartner and Dorothy K. Lipsky, "Beyond Special Education: Toward a Quality System for All Students," in *Special Education at the Century's End: Evolution of Theory and Practice Since 1970*, ed. Thomas Hehir and Thomas Latus (Cambridge, MA: Harvard Education Press, 1987), 123–157; Thomas M. Skrtic, "The Special

Education Paradox: Equity as the Way to Excellence," in *Special Education at the Century's End: Evolution of Theory and Practice Since 1970*, ed. Thomas Hehir and Thomas Latus (Cambridge, MA: Harvard Education Press, 1987), 203–272.

11. Thomas Hehir, Todd Grindal, and Hadas Eidelman, *Review of Special Education in the Commonwealth of Massachusetts: Report Commissioned by the Massachusetts Department of Elementary and Secondary Education* (Boston: Thomas Hehir & Associates, 2011), http://www.doe.mass.edu/sped/2012/0412sped.html.

12. Thomas Hehir and Nonie Lesaux, *San Diego Unified School District Special Education Recommendations Document: Improving Educational Outcomes for Students with Disabilities in San Diego* (Boston: Thomas Hehir & Associates, 2011), http://www.sandi.net/cms/lib/CA01001235/Centricity/Domain/11240/SDUSD%20Special%20Education%20Recommendations%20Document.pdf; Thomas Hehir and Eduardo Mosqueda, *San Diego Unified School District Special Education Document* (Boston: Thomas Hehir & Associates, 2006), http://www.sandi.net/cms/lib/CA01001235/Centricity/Domain/155/relatedfiles/HehirReport/hehir_issues.pdf; Thomas Hehir, Todd Grindal, and Elizabeth Marcell, *Review of Special Education in the Houston Independent School District* (Boston: Thomas Hehir & Associates, 2011), http://www.houstonisd.org/cms/lib2/TX01001591/Centricity/Domain/7946/HISD__Special_Education_Report_2011_Final.pdf.

13. Lyon et al., *Rethinking Learning Disabilities*; Shaywitz, *Overcoming Dyslexia*.

14. Lyon et al., *Rethinking Learning Disabilities*; Shaywitz, *Overcoming Dyslexia*; Sugai and Horner, "The Evolution of Discipline Practices"; Snow, *Preventing Reading Difficulties*.

15. Lynn Newman et al., *Comparisons Across Time of the Outcomes of Youth with Disabilities Up to 4 Years After High School: A Report of Findings from the National Longitudinal Transition Study-2 (NLTS2).* (Menlo Park, CA: SRI International, 2010), www.nlts2.org/reports/2010_09/nlts2_report_2010_09_complete.pdf.

16. Hehir and Mosqueda, *San Diego Unified School District Special Education Document*; Hehir, Grindal, Eidelman, *Review of Special Education*.

17. Ibid; Thomas Hehir, Shaun Dougherty, and Todd Grindal, *Students with Disabilities in Massachusetts Career and Technical Education Programs* (report commissioned by the Massachusetts Department of Elementary and Secondary Education), 2013, http://www.doe.mass.edu/sped/2012/0412sped.html; Thomas Hehir et al., *Use of Out-of-District Programs by Massachusetts Students with Disabilities* (report commissioned by the Massachusetts Department of Elementary and Secondary Education), 2013, http://www.doe.mass.edu/sped/2012/0412sped.html.

18. Hehir and Katzman, *Effective Inclusive Schools*.

19. Thomas Hehir, "Looking Forward: Toward a New Role in Promoting Educational Equity for Students with Disabilities from Low-Income Backgrounds," in *Handbook of Education Policy Research*, ed. Gary Sykes, Barbara Schneider, and David Plank (London: Routledge, 2009).

20. Hehir et al., *Use of Out-of-District Programs*.

CONCLUSION

1. Catherine S. Fichten et al., "College Students with Disabilities: Their Future and Success," as cited in Patricia L. Davies, Catherine L. Schelly, and Craig L. Spooner, "Measuring the Effectiveness of Universal Design for Learning Interventions in Postsecondary Education," *Journal of Postsecondary Education and Disability* 26, no. 3 (2013): 5–37, http://www.eric.ed.gov/ERICWebPortal/detail?accno=ED491585.

2. Renée Cameto, Phyllis Levine, and Mary Wagner, *Transition Planning for Students with Disabilities: A Special Topic Report of Findings from the National Longitudinal Transition Study-2 (NLTS2)*, 2004, http://nlts2.org/reports/2004_11/nlts2_report_2004_11_execsum.pdf.

3. Ibid; Jennifer M. Hogansen et al., "Transition Goals and Experiences of Females with Disabilities: Youth, Parents, and Professionals," *Exceptional Children* 74, no. 2 (2008): 215–234; Mary Wagner et al., *Changes Over Time in the Early Postschool Outcomes of Youth with Disabilities: A Report of Findings from the National Longitudinal Transition Study (NLTS) and the National Longitudinal Transition Study – 2 (NLTS2)*, 2005, www.nlts2.org/reports/2005_06/nlts2_report_2005_06_complete.pdf.

4. Sue Caton and Carolyn Kagan, "Comparing Transition Expectations of Young People with Moderate Learning Disabilities with Other Vulnerable Youth and with Their Non-Disabled Counterparts," *Disability and Society* 22, no. 5 (2007): 473–488; Beth Tarleton and Linda Ward, "Changes and Choices: Finding Out What Information Young People with Learning Disabilities, Their Parents, and Supporters Need at Transition," *British Journal of Learning Disabilities* 33, no. 2 (2005): 70–76.

5. Stan F. Shaw, Joseph W. Madaus, and Lyman L. Dukes, *Preparing Students with Disabilities for College Success: A Practical Guide to Transition Planning* (Baltimore: Paul H. Brookes Publishing Co., 2010).

6. Ibid; Association on Higher Education and Disability (AHEAD), "Supporting Accommodation Requests: Guidance on Documentation Practices," April 2012, https://www.ahead.org/uploads/docs/resources/Final_AHEAD_Supporting%20Accommodation%20Requests%20with%20Q&A%2009_12.pdf.

7. Mark A. Mlawer, "Who Should Fight? Parents and the Advocacy Expectation," *Journal of Disability Policy Studies* 4, no. 1 (1993): 105–116.

8. David H. Rose et al., "Universal Design for Learning in Postsecondary Education: Reflections on Principles and Their Applications," *Journal of Postsecondary Education and Disability* 19, no. 2 (2006): 135–151.

9. For further discussion, see also Robert McRuer, *Crip Theory: Cultural Signs of Queerness and Disability* (New York: New York University Press, 2006); Margaret Price, *Mad at School: Rhetorics of Mental Disability and Academic Life* (Ann Arbor: University of Michigan Press, 2011).

10. For more information on disability studies, see also Adrienne Asch, "Disability, Bioethics, and Human Rights," in *Handbook of Disability Studies*, ed. Gary L. Albrecht, Katherine D. Seelman, and Michael Bury (Thousand Oaks, CA: Sage

Publications, Inc., 2001), 297–326; Simi Linton, *Claiming Disability: Knowledge and Identity* (New York: New York University Press, 1998); Tobin Siebers, *Disability Theory* (Ann Arbor: University of Michigan Press, 2008).

11. Wendy S. Harbour, "Education Students Who Become Hard of Hearing or Deaf in School: Insights from Disability Studies," in *Ethical Considerations in Educating Children Who Are Deaf or Hard of Hearing*, ed. Kathee Mangan Christensen (Washington, DC: Gallaudet University Press, 2010), 87–100; Wendy S. Harbour, "Inclusion in K–12 and Higher Education," in *Righting Education Wrongs: Disability Studies in Law and Education*, ed. Arlene S. Kanter and Beth A. Ferri (Syracuse, NY: Syracuse University Press, 2013), 294–306.

12. For more information about disability studies, see Simi Linton, *Claiming Disability* (New York: New York University Press, 1998); Steven J. Taylor, "Disability Studies in Higher Education," in *New Directions for Higher Education* 154, ed. Wendy S. Harbour and Joseph W. Madaus (San Francisco: Jossey-Bass, 2011): 93–98.

Acknowledgments

There are so many people who helped us with this book. First, we would like to thank the students who opened up their lives to us. Their willingness to participate in this project will hopefully make the way easier for others who follow. We would also like to thank the parents who added further insights into this work either through informal interviews or by reviewing the details contained in their children's interviews for accuracy.

FROM TOM

I would like to particularly thank Judy Heumann, whose lifetime of advocacy and personal friendship has had a lasting influence on my perspectives on disability and the importance of including the voice of the community in all my work. I would also like to acknowledge the late Adrienne Asch. Her use of personal narratives to influence disability policy has had a lasting impact. Our lengthy dinners when she was teaching at Wellesley are sorely missed. Also, my colleague at Harvard, Sara Lawrence-Lightfoot, provided support and critical feedback on the project. Bill Henderson is another influential friend who provided insightful feedback to me. Finally, I would like to thank my many teaching fellows at Harvard who have supported me in my teaching and research, particularly: Monica Ng, Jenna Gravel, Matt Shaw, Chris Wilkens, Liz Marcell, Kevin Mintz, Todd Grindal, Lauren Katzman, Rebecca Lebowitz, Seth Packrone, and of course, Wendy Harbour and Laura Schifter.

FROM LAURA

I would like to thank my parents, Jennifer and Rick Schifter, and my sisters. Their encouragement and understanding of my disability are the reasons I have accomplished any success in my life. I would like to acknowledge my husband, Matt Scriven, and daughter, Eleanor, for bringing happiness to my life every day. I would also like to thank my tutor, Sally Halvorson, for teaching me to read, and the many teachers I had from elementary through graduate school who maintained high expectations for me. I would like to acknowledge my former colleagues from Washington who helped me fight to improve policies for students with disabilities. And finally, I would not be a part of this book without Tom Hehir. Tom introduced me to education policy. He has been an incredible mentor, advisor, and friend. We asked students in this book how they got here, but we did not ask them how they were able to graduate once they got in. Without a doubt, for me, the answer to this question is Tom Hehir.

FROM BOTH OF US

We both owe a debt of gratitude to Tom's assistant, Judy Wasserman, for her superb editing skills and critical feedback as a parent of a student with disabilities. The enthusiastic support for this book from our publisher, Doug Clayton, is deeply appreciated.

We would like to thank Wendy Harbour for the wonderful job she did in concluding this book and extending the message to all students with disabilities. Wendy was part of this project from the beginning and helped shaped it in so many ways.

Finally, we so appreciate David Rose for framing this book and teaching us what it means to universally design education for all.

About the Authors

Thomas Hehir, EdD, is the Silvana and Christopher Pascucci Professor of Practice in Learning Differences at the Harvard Graduate School of Education. As director of the U.S. Department of Education's Office of Special Education Programs from 1993 to 1999, Hehir was responsible for federal leadership in implementing the Individuals with Disabilities Education Act (IDEA) and played a leading role in developing the Clinton administration's proposal for the 1997 reauthorization of IDEA. In 1990, Hehir was associate superintendent for the Chicago Public Schools, where he implemented major changes in the special education service delivery system, enabling Chicago to reach significantly higher levels of compliance with IDEA and resulting in the eventual removal of oversight by the U.S. Department of Education's Office for Civil Rights. Hehir served in a variety of positions in the Boston Public Schools from 1978 to 1987, including that of director of special education from 1983 to 1987. An advocate for children with disabilities in the education system, he has written extensively on special education. His previous books include Effective Inclusive Schools: Designing Successful Schoolwide Programs (Jossey-Bass), New Directions in Special Education: Eliminating Ableism in Policy and Practice (Harvard Education Press), and Special Education at the Century's End: Evolution of Theory and Practice Since 1970 (Harvard Education Press).

Laura A. Schifter, EdD, is an adjunct lecturer at the Harvard Graduate School of Education and a research consultant working with states and advocacy organizations to analyze data on the identification, placement, and performance of students with disabilities. Schifter has been published in the journal *Exceptional Children* and served as a coeditor for *A Policy Reader in Universal Design for Learning* (Harvard Education

Press). She recently graduated with a doctorate from the Harvard Graduate School of Education, where she studied issues in special education, specifically patterns and policies related to high school graduation of students with disabilities. Schifter previously worked as a Senior Education and Disability Advisor for George Miller (D-CA) on the Committee on Education and Labor, and she has worked for the White House Domestic Policy Council and the Senate Health, Education, Labor and Pensions Committee. She also taught elementary school in San Francisco. Schifter earned an EdM in Mind, Brain, and Education from the Harvard Graduate School of Education and a BA in American Studies from Amherst College.

Wendy S. Harbour is the Lawrence B. Taishoff Professor of Inclusive Education at Syracuse University, where she teaches courses in disability studies, inclusive K–12 education, and disability in higher education. Her areas of expertise are disability studies in education, universal design for learning, and postsecondary disability services. She recently contributed to *Righting Education Wrongs: Disability Studies in Law and Education* (Syracuse University Press) and coedited *Disability Services and Campus Dynamics: New Directions for Higher Education* (Jossey-Bass). She has served on the editorial boards of the *Harvard Educational Review* and the *Journal on Postsecondary Education and Disability*, and has been an invited reviewer for *Disability Studies Quarterly* and *Inclusion*. Harbour is the executive director of the Taishoff Center for Inclusive Higher Education, a research center that also runs programming for Syracuse University students with intellectual and developmental disabilities. She completed her doctorate in education from Harvard University, where she is currently an adjunct lecturer in education. Her master's degrees in education are from Harvard University and the University of Minnesota.

Index

post-secondary education, 3
Power Point slides inaccessibility, 197–198
prejudice toward students with disabilities, 41
problems, attitudes trumping all, 199–201
professionals
  challenging students, 59
  highly effective, 67–68
  holding student to high expectations, 52
  impact on success in school, 52
  intervening on behalf of students, 58–59
  providing access, 59–63
  shaping classroom experience for students, 63
progressive models of disability, 225
psychiatrist, 56–57
"The Psychology of Handicapping Conditions"
  course, 207
public schools, 30

quadralingual, 12

reading
  disabilities not impairment to, 188
  dyslexic students, 183, 189
  failure to learn, 190
  intervention with difficulties, 189–190
  Response to Intervention (RTI) reading, 183
  round-robin reading, 152–153
  strategy for, 159
recognition networks, 183
recorded text, 139, 140, 142–143
Recording for the Blind & Dyslexic taped texts,
  144–145
Rehabilitation Act section 504, 101
resources and special education, 200
Response to Intervention (RTI), 183, 190–191
retinitis pigmentosa, 141
R.J.
  disability part of him, 177
  disability service office, 119
  encouraging independence, 61
  finding way to get things done, 118–119
  friendships, 99
  high school, 63
  identity and disability, 177
  leadership role among students, 26
  learning to ask for help, 63
  minimizing impact of disability, 99
  natural supports, 118–119
  neuromuscular disorder, 11, 26
  positive school experiences, 178

private Catholic school, 26–27
public school system, 26
self-accommodations, 122
sports, 99
strategies, 27–28
teachers, 62, 66–67
therapist, 61–62
Rose, David H., ix–xii, 121, 210–211
round-robin reading, 18, 152–153
Rowley, Amy, 180
Russo, Harilyn, reaction to physical therapy, 43

Sachs, Oliver, 24
scanners, 137, 146
Schifter, Laura, 5, 7, 10
  accommodations, 167
  alternate solutions for learning, 157–158
  being ditzy, 160
  club for students with learning disabilities,
    163–164
  college, 165
  difficulties writing, 158–159
  dyslexia, 156, 161, 170–171
  Education and Disability Advisor on the Edu-
    cation and Workforce Committee, 169–170
  education policy, 169
  evaluating for learning disability, 156
  extracurricular activities, 164–165, 170
  family support for, 157–158
  GRE, 167
  hiding disability from friends, 159–165
  high school policies, 161–162
  history, 161–162
  informal accommodations for, 158
  memorizing words, 157
  metacognitive skills, 162
  middle school, 160
  Mind, Brain, and Education master's program,
    167–168
  Montessori school, 156–157
  openly discussing dyslexia, 155–156, 159
  poetry, 157
  policy related to students with disabilities,
    169–170
  presentation about learning disabilities, 166–
    167
  private school acceptance, 158
  read-aloud technique and, 159
  reading, 156–157, 166
  recognizing strengths and weaknesses, 161
  screen reader, 169–170